Creative Economy

This book series covers research on creative economies based on humanity and spirituality to enhance the competitiveness, sustainability, peace, and fairness of international society. We define a creative economy as a socio-economic system that promotes those creative activities with a high market value and leads to the improvement of society's overall well-being.

As the global economy has developed, we have seen severe competition and polarization in income distribution. With this drastic change in the economic system, creativity with a high market value has come to be considered the main source of competiveness. But in addition to the improvement of competitiveness, we are required to work toward fairness in society.

In the process of developing a mature market, consumers come to understand that what they require most essentially is humanity and spirituality. This cannot be given or bought, but requires sharing with others across cultures and learning and developing further from their richness. Long-term sustainability of a company in this new age also requires building the same values of humanity and spirituality within its own internal organizational culture and practices.

Through this series, we intend to propose various policy recommendations that contribute to the prosperity of international society and improve the well-being of mankind by clarifying the concrete actions that are needed.

Kazuo Mino · Tadashi Yagi
Editors

The Cultural Basis
of Economic Growth in India

 Springer

Editors
Kazuo Mino
Institute of Economic Research
Kyoto University
Kyoto, Japan

Tadashi Yagi
Faculty of Economics
Doshisha University
Kyoto, Japan

ISSN 2364-9186 ISSN 2364-9445 (electronic)
Creative Economy
ISBN 978-981-15-9307-9 ISBN 978-981-15-9305-5 (eBook)
https://doi.org/10.1007/978-981-15-9305-5

This Springer imprint is published by the registered company Springer Nature Singapore Pte Ltd.
The registered company address is: 152 Beach Road, #21-01/04 Gateway East, Singapore 189721, Singapore

Preface

This book is based on a joint research project conducted by the authors from 2016 to 2018. Our research was financially supported by the Japan Society for the Promotion of Science (JSPS Grant-in Aid for Scientific Research, project number: 16KT0089). The central purpose of our project is to study economic growth in India from a broader perspective than that of conventional economics research. In particular, we focus on the cultural basis behind the recent remarkable growth of the Indian economy. The standard growth economics usually ignores cultural differences in economies to focus on the general mechanics of economic growth. We maintain that such an approach may be insufficient for exploring economic growth in India because the Indian economy has distinctive cultural features that are not observed in other Asian countries. The traditions related to value judgment on various life matters such as marriage, religion, gender, and so on affect consumers' behavior and working environment. They also affect the competitiveness of the economy and the well-being of people. Since our study needs an interdisciplinary investigation, the participants of the project are economics researchers in various fields such as public economics, fiscal policy, macroeconomics, industrial organization, and socio-economics, as well as an expert in anthropological and historical studies on South Asia in general and on India in particular.

In the Chap. 1, Akio Tanabe characterizes economic development in South Asia, with a particular focus on India from the post-World War II period to the present. The author emphasizes that India is a diverse society in which various individuals and groups from different social backgrounds interact with each other. Hence, unlike efficiency-oriented development in Western and East Asian counties, India and other South Asian countries have experienced diversity-driven development. Tanabe first discusses Indian history in the early modern era as a process of diversification. He argues that India, after experiencing colonial and postcolonial diversions, reconverged to this development path from the 1990s when democratization and continuing growth were simultaneously realized.

The Chap. 2, written by Kazuo Mino, studies the linkage between economic growth and industrial structural transformation in India. As in other developing economies, the income share of the agricultural sector in India continues to decrease as the economy grows. However, compared to other developing economies such as China, the employment share of the agricultural sector in India has not decreased much. Since the standard neoclassical growth models fail to explain such a phenomenon, Mino constructs a multisector growth model in which there are frictions in labor markets that may prevent a smooth sectoral shift of workers who possess heterogeneous abilities. It is shown that the model may capture the patterns of structural change in India. The author also considers cultural and institutional factors that may give rise to labor market frictions.

While the first two chapters discuss the baseline features of India's economic growth, the subsequent chapters use micro-level information to characterize the behavior of the Indian people. Specifically, those chapters reconsider the standard view that well-being mostly depends on the level of consumption, so that the per capita income and consumption are the most important criteria to evaluate the growth performance of an economy. In Chap. 3, Yoshio Itaba first presents an overview of the large-scale survey on well-being in India conducted by our project in 2017. This survey pays particular attention to the evaluation of external and environmental factors represented as social capital. Itaba empirically analyzes the key determinants of social capital and confirms that the level of social capital has statistically significant effects on the happiness and life satisfaction of the Indian people.

In Chap. 4, Tadashi Yagi studies the differences in the determinants of well-being between India and Japan. Based on the World Value Survey, Yagi first compares the values emphasized by people in major regions and examines the relevant determinants of well-being in India. Then, he utilizes the survey data of our project and his foregoing research on happiness in Japan to compare the determinants of happiness in India and Japan. His econometric study reveals that the major determinants of happiness for the Japanese people are income, wealth, and length of leisure time, whereas in India, social status and a high level of activity in the community are relevant determinants of happiness.

Chapter 5 by Kanako Takimoto and Akihiko Kawaura is a study of happiness of women in India. The authors first point out that the gender gap in India is still quite large compared to the world average, and it has recently widened further. They conduct an empirical analysis based on data provided by Asia Barometer as well as by our survey to explore the determinants of Indian women's well-being. The authors find that other than income level, marital status, employment status, and health condition greatly affect the level of happiness of Indian women.

In the final chapter, Sayaka Sakoda, Ryuichi Fukuhara, and Pramod Tiwari focus on a traditional folk dance drama performed by a tribe in Rajasthan, India. It has often been claimed that the poor in India tend to spend too much money and time on local religious events, which is one of the reasons why they are still trapped in poverty. Based on their survey data and field research, the authors cast doubt on such a conventional view. Their econometric analysis on the specific event suggests that spending money and time on performing the drama does not stem from the short-term economic incentive but from the long-term incentive to make an investment in social capital within their tribal community as well as in the local society that they belong to. The conclusion of this chapter is compatible with the outcomes of the studies on happiness in India presented in the previous chapters.

Economic growth is a complex phenomenon that can be explored from various viewpoints. Although our research has examined only a small portion of the diverse issues, we have made it clear that it is not appropriate to study the economic growth in India from the same perspective as when analyzing the growth in Western and East Asian countries.

This book could not have been completed without the financial support of the Grant-in-Aid for Scientific Research. We are grateful to Japan Society for the Promotion of Science. We also thank Juno Kawakami of Springer Nature Japan for her valuable editorial work.

Kyoto, Japan   Kazuo Mino
March 2022   Tadashi Yagi

Contents

Editors and Contributors

About the Editors

Kazuo Mino is a former professor at the Institute of Economics Research of Kyoto University (KIER) and a professor emeritus of Kyoto University. He currently works at KIER as an adjunct professor. Mino obtained a Ph.D. in economics from Brown University in 1984. He is the former president of the Japanese Economic Association and the former editor of the *Japanese Economic Review*. Previously, he worked at Hiroshima, Tohoku, Kobe, Osaka, and Doshisha Universities. Mino has published extensively in scholarly journals on various topics in macroeconomic theory including growth and business cycle models, monetary and fiscal policies, and open economy macroeconomics. He also published a research monograph, *Growth and Business Cycles with Equilibrium Indeterminacy,* Springer 2017.

Tadashi Yagi is a professor in the Faculty of Economics at Doshisha University. He holds a Ph.D. in economics, awarded by Nagoya University in 1996. His research areas are wide-ranging, including public economics, human resources management, income distribution, welfare economics, and cultural economics. He has written many papers in refereed academic journals and chapters in edited volumes. His important papers include "Economic Growth and the Riskiness of Investment in Firm-Specific Skills" (with Taichi Maki and Koichi Yotsuya) *European Economic Review* (2005), "Income Redistribution through the Tax System: A Simulation Analysis of Tax Reform" (with Toshiaki Tachibanaki) *Review of Income and Wealth* (1998), and "Public Investment and Interregional Output-Income Inequalities" (with Nobuhiro Okuno) *Regional Science and Urban Economics* (1990). His recent works include "Moral, Trust and Happiness: Why does Trust Improve Happiness?" *Journal of Organizational Psychology* (2017), and "Happiness and Self-Determination: An Empirical Study in Japan" (with Kazuo Nishimura) *Review of Behavioral Economics* (2019).

Contributors

Fukuhara Ryuichi Center for Southeast Asian Studies, Kyoto University, Kyoto, Japan

Itaba Yoshio Faculty of Economics, Doshisha University, Kyoto, Japan

Kawaura Akihiko Faulty of Policy Studies, Doshisha University, Kyoto, Japan

Mino Kazuo Institute of Economic Research, Kyoto University, Kyoto, Japan

Sakoda Sayaka Faculty of Economics, Doshisha University, Kyoto, Japan

Takimoto Kanako Faulty of Policy Studies, Doshisha University, Kyoto, Japan

Tanabe Akio Department of Cultural Anthropology, Graduate School of Arts and Sciences, University of Tokyo, Tokyo, Japan

Tiwari Pramod Institute for Financial Management and Research, Krea University, Alwarpet, Chennai, India

Yagi Tadashi Faulty of Economics, Doshisha University, Kyoto, Japan

Chapter 1
The South Asian Path of Development: A Historical and Anthropological Perspective

Akio Tanabe

Abstract This chapter explores the cultural basis of economic development in the long-term history of India. India has always been a meeting place of diversities, where the development path is "diversity-driven". It did not rely solely on enhancement of productivity, but more on diversification of knowledge leading to the multiplication of the kinds of products and services. Early-modern India developed a socio-economic system that adapted to seasonal and inter-annual variations in rainfall, managed risks through a system of shares, and accumulated the fruits of labor in the form of specialized skills in social groups. The colonial period saw a partial divergence from the development path when caste hierarchy was "traditionalized" and various social groups were "peasantized". Today, we see a reconvergence to the diversity-driven path where the post-peasant masses are diversifying sources of income to secure livelihood and increase life chances. Also, there is a new reassembling of diversities where varied skills and knowledge meet and give rise to innovations. The agenda for the Indian economy lies in mediating and enabling a smooth linking between various sectors and modes of production with a balance between the rural and the urban, agricultural and non-agricultural, informal and formal, and livelihood and profit.

1.1   Introduction

This chapter explores the cultural basis of economic development in the long-term history of the South Asian region, focusing on India for the period from 1947 onwards. Today in India, many previously marginalized peoples and post-peasants are becoming active agents in the market economy and democratic politics, and diverse individuals and social groups are engaging in dialogues and interactions in the expanded lifeworld and the public sphere (Neyazi et al., 2014; Tanabe, 2017). I suggest that this dynamism can be understood as a contemporary evolvement of

A. Tanabe (✉)
Department of Cultural Anthropology, Graduate School of Arts and Sciences, University of Tokyo, 3-8-1 Komaba, Meguro-ku, Tokyo 153-0041, Japan
e-mail: tanabe@anthro.c.u-tokyo.ac.jp

© Springer Nature Singapore Pte Ltd. 2022
K. Mino and T. Yagi (eds.), *The Cultural Basis of Economic Growth in India*,
Creative Economy, https://doi.org/10.1007/978-981-15-9305-5_1

the South Asian path of development (Sugihara, 2010; Tanabe, 2015). This chapter discusses the characteristics of the South Asian path of development and its historical unfolding, focusing on the entanglement of culture, nature, and economy.

Previous studies of Indian society tended to focus on discrimination and poverty, and to ask why democracy is dysfunctional and the economy underdeveloped in India. The answer given often pointed to the discriminatory social structure based on caste and Hinduism (cf. Dumont, 1970; Weber, 1958). Such an Orientalist view of India defined academic understanding of India until the 1980s. This view is based on the understanding of India as a caste society with a fixed hierarchy, which impedes the free movement of labor and capital and thus proper allocation of resources in the political economy.

Today, however, as India moves from the postcolonial to the global era, it can no longer be described as a closed caste society, plagued by poverty and discrimination. Rather, India is vibrant as an open and diverse society, displaying remarkable economic growth with decreasing poverty. Democracy is deepening as the diverse populace participate in political processes. India's influence in international politics is also growing significantly. It is important to note, however, that there is also a dark side to these changes. The gap between the rich and the poor is widening in the global economy, and discrimination and inequality based on religion, caste, and gender continue to pose grave problems. While democracy deepens and the economy grows, socio-economic disparities persist. Also, the grip of power by the majoritarian Hindu nationalists poses a serious threat to the pluralist democracy. For all that, we should not lose sight of the fact that a major driving force for these socio-politico-economic changes is the increasing participation of diverse post-peasant people in the market and democracy in search of improvement of life chances to overcome inequalities and to make their voices heard for the betterment of their positions.

In the face of major changes, a new paradigm is needed to rethink India's past and present. India is now economically developing without losing its cultural uniqueness. What is this cultural uniqueness, and how is it connected to the pattern of economic development in India? What are the issues that remain unresolved? In order to answer these questions, we should think of India not only as a hierarchical society, which divides and discriminates, but as a *diverse society*, which affirms people's differences (Tanabe, 2015, 2021a). If we look at India's history, we see that in this diverse society, various individuals and groups from different ecological and social backgrounds have interacted and exchanged dynamically through society, the market, and the state, and have developed different roles and entitlements based on their functions and positionalities. Today, the historical and cultural characteristics of India as a diverse society is taking a new form under the present democratic politics and market economy.

By seeing India as a diverse society, I try to overcome the Orientalist view of India that presupposes its essence as a hierarchical order in contrast to the supposedly egalitarian order of the West. I also attempt to understand the development path of India in a longer term and more comprehensive manner. "Path of development" here does not refer to a model for economic growth, but rather to the socio-cultural and politico-economic forms that have been created and evolved historically, based on the region's ecological environment and inter-regional exchanges, in order to enrich the lives of people in the region.

Previous studies on the paths of economic development by Kaoru Sugihara, Kenneth Pomeranz, and R. Bin Wong among others have fruitfully discussed the capital-intensive, efficiency-driven Western path and the labor-intensive, resource-saving East Asian path (Austin & Sugihara, 2013; Pomeranz, 2000; Sugihara, 2003, 2020; Wong, 1997). They have taken comparative perspectives in measuring and depicting economic development in terms of increase in productivity in the context of regionally specific factor endowments, especially land/labor ratios. There have been important undertakings, especially by Tirthankar Roy and Kaoru Sugihara, to include South Asia in such a comparative framework (Pomeranz, 2004; Roy, 2004, 2005; Sugihara, 2004, 2008; Wong, 2004), and particular attention has been paid to the availability of water besides capital, land, and labor as one of the key production factors.[1]

This chapter is an attempt to make a contribution in this endeavor of delineating the regional characteristics of the South Asian path of development.[2] I argue, as an extension of the comparative approach, which focuses on factor endowments and forms of productivity enhancement, that attention to the South Asian path of development opens up wider issues including the very definition and direction of development. The South Asian path of development is oriented towards livelihood security in an unstable environment and forms of life enrichment that include but are not limited to productive efficiency.

The characteristics of the South Asian environment cannot be grasped solely by factor endowments, such as land/labor ratios, as in the case of East Asia or the West. We must also take into account unpredictable and fluctuating precipitation, abrupt spread of infections, and natural disasters that affect not only production but also human life. The importance of the environment for understanding Indian economic history has been highlighted by Roy's research (2005). But his emphasis lies in "the environmental barrier to technical change", which impeded "improvements in living standards" (Roy, 2005: 6). I would like to argue, however, that there were particular ways in which the Indian social system adapted to such an environment and attempted to secure and enrich livelihoods. In other words, the natural environment provided *conditions* rather than barriers for a path of development in South Asia.

This consideration leads us to focus on another characteristic of South Asian society: i.e., the persistence of diverse social groups—castes and communities—with various lifeways. These groups have been a reservoir of distinct skills and knowledge for utilizing the different aspects of natural and cultural resources. Importantly, it was by multiplying social diversity, besides increasing productivity, that South Asia was enriched with multiplied products and services.

---

[1] Another important production factor recently paid attention to is energy (Kanda, 2015, 2017). Sugihara suggests five factors of production where water and energy are added besides capital, land, and labor (Sugihara, 2020). This is certainly a significant development in global economic history.

[2] This idea of the South Asian path of development is a result of ongoing discussions among Professors Kaoru Sugihara, Kohei Wakimura, myself, and others.

In this way, the key to understanding the South Asian path of development lies in focusing on how it has adapted to socio-ecological diversity and fluctuations, and managed to mitigate risk and secure livelihood amidst such an environment, and also on how it has evolved its unique form of enriching life (Sato & Sugihara, 2015; Sugihara, 2010; Tanabe, 2015). The South Asian path of development did not rely solely on enhancement of productivity, but more on diversification of skill and knowledge and consequently the multiplication of the kinds of products and services available for developing a richer society. Thus, the characteristics of the South Asian path of development may be summarized as "diversity-driven".[3] It is based on the affirmation, promotion, and combination of diversity in the pursuit of well-being.

In the following sections, I first suggest a shift in perspective on development in long-term history, followed by discussions on geographical, cultural, and historical characteristics of India, including socio-economic structure and change in early modern and colonial eras. Then I will go on to depict and argue how the contemporary economic development in India can be understood from the viewpoint of a diversity-driven path of development.

1.2 A Perspective on Development: From Productivity to Livelihood

In order to appreciate the significance of the South Asian path of development in world history, it is necessary to shift our focus *from productivity to livelihood* in understanding "development". Previous views have presumed that overall historical development takes place when there is an increase in productive efficiency. Teleological history based on the production-centered framework of modernization and globalization assumes that the combination of institutional development and market integration brings about productivity enhancement, which in turn leads to economic growth (Fig. 1.1). According to this perspective, economic growth results in creation of a middle class-based civil society leading the way to democratization, concomitant with improved education and decline in birthrate.

Fig. 1.1 Productivity approach to history

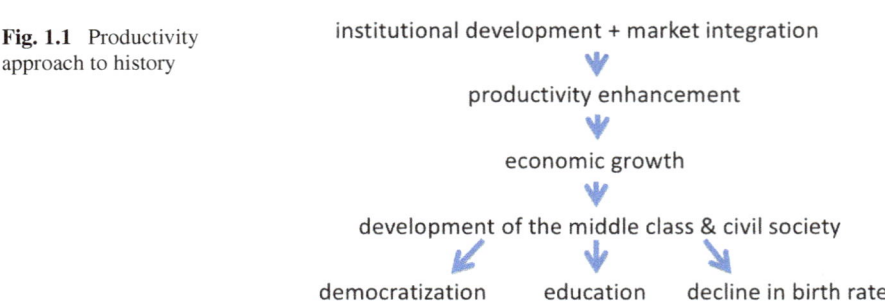

institutional development + market integration

productivity enhancement

economic growth

development of the middle class & civil society

democratization   education   decline in birth rate

---

[3] The term "diversity-driven" was first suggested by Prof. Kaoru Sugihara.

I suggest, however, that if we take a long-duration perspective, what is important in understanding the regional history of development is the expansion of livelihood security and human agency (Fig. 1.2). From this standpoint, development is the process of expanding the foundation of human life based on the interaction between nature and culture (Sugihara, 2012). Rather than productive efficiency, the first step in development is to secure the basic conditions for living by securing food, shelter, and sanitation and controlling infectious diseases. Then, after livelihood security, it is the development of human agency in the form of people's health and literacy as well as expansion of life chances that lead to economic development, democratization, and educational progress.[4] We can compare the two views of history in the figures.

Amartya Sen's capability approach stresses the importance of health and literacy for development (Sen, 1999). In addition to this universalist and human-centered approach, I suggest that we take into account the specific historical path of development that reflects the nature and culture of the region. Socio-ecological relations and cultural values particular to a region have a significant impact on economic structures and their course of development. In the following sections, I discuss the geographical, cultural, and historical background of India's economic development.

1.3 Geography and Culture of India: Meeting Place of Diversities

India is a major part of the subcontinent in the middle of the Eurasian continent, jutting out into the vast Indian Ocean, with towering Himalaya mountain ranges to the north. It connects the civilizations of the East and the West, not only though inland interactions and trade, but also through maritime networks. Diverse social groups,

Fig. 1.2 Livelihood approach to history

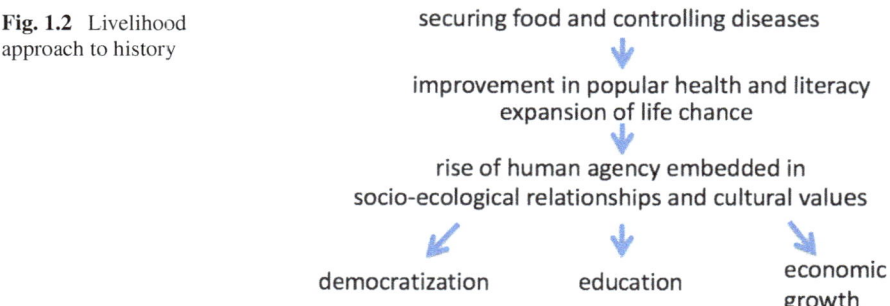

---

[4] Emmanuel Todd stresses the importance of mass literacy for people's political participation (Todd, 1987). Todd's view that the diverse political and economic systems of the modern world are the result of a combination of the rationality of literacy and the diversity of values is instructive. Figures 1.1 and 1.2 are also partly inspired by Todd (1987).

Fig. 1.3 India as the
meeting point of monsoon
Asia and the Afro-Eurasian
great arid zone

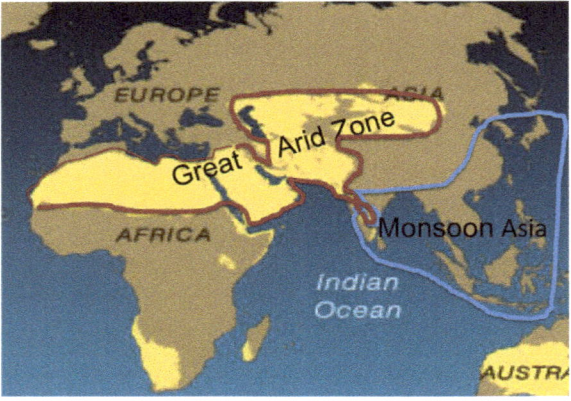

cultures, skills, and ideas met in the Indian subcontinent, as people, knowledge, and
goods moved incessantly. Its openness led to India's being a multicultural contact
zone.

Climatically, South Asia is located between monsoon Asia, the largest wet zone
in the Old World, and the great arid zone of Afro-Eurasia. It is the only region
in the world where these two zones are in direct contact, resulting in complex
and diverse ecological environments (Fig. 1.3). Diverse social groups—castes and
communities—with varied knowledge, skills, and culture came, settled, and flour-
ished in different ecological environments, and the unique dynamism of India was
born through close contact, cohabitation, and exchange among them. Different social
groups engaged in diverse productive activities, such as grain cultivation, slash-and-
burn agriculture, gathering, hunting, herding, and fishing, utilizing different dimensions of varied ecological environments. There were also merchants who engaged in
trade and commerce, as well as artisans such as potters, carpenters, barbers, blacksmiths, and goldsmiths. There were also professionals in learning, religion, astrology,
administration, and military affairs. In this way, diverse social groups with various
lifeways, cultures, knowledge, and skills interacted closely and exchanged frequently.

Diverse social groups interacted to produce a variety of goods and services under
India's pluralistic social structure that allowed different groups, each with its own
skills, knowledge, and lifestyles, to take advantage of various facets of the diverse
ecology. The various goods and services were consumed by a wide range of people
via market exchange and state redistribution.

In medieval and early modern India, exchange and distribution of goods took
place through political centers of kingship and royal capitals, religious centers of
temples and mosques, and economic centers of weekly bazaars and regular markets.
The royal capitals and temples upheld the so-called great traditions emulated by the
people as a refined model to integrate diverse local traditions. Villages, cities, and
regions were linked economically through markets and trade.

Rather than a single center defining the norms of civilization from above, as in the case of the Chinese and Roman empires, there were multiple centers in Indian civilization which were created through integration of diverse human and natural elements in the localities. The pluralistic and multi-layered Indian world was loosely held together by the polycentric networks built through bottom-up integration of diversities. This polycentric integration of diversities also involved discrimination and inequalities among the social groups. In sum, we can say that the South Asian development path is characterized by its openness, diversity, polycentricity, and hierarchy.[5]

1.4 Indian History as a Process of Diversification

The history of India can be seen as a process of gradual development of organic connections between diverse people and things, accompanied by increasingly complex organization of state and society. How did India maintain and increase socio-economic diversity? How is this diversity in Indian society related to the characteristics of its development path?

Max Weber famously claimed that Indian society, due to Hinduism and caste, cannot "out of its substance arrive at the 'spirit of capitalism'" (Weber, 1958: 325). There have been interesting debates on Weber's thesis about the relationship between Hinduism and economic development, and whether or not Indian society has a potential for modernization (e.g., Kantowsky, 1982; Singer, 1966). Nevertheless, instead of asking whether Indian can follow the Western path of modernization, what is more important is to ask what kind of actual development we see in Indian history and society.

What is remarkable about Weber's argument, as noted by Kotani (2014), is his point about the uniqueness of Indian social relations in the history of agricultural institutions. He pointed out that "peculiar Indian development occurred in the elaboration of a whole series of graduated rents based upon the tax duties of the peasants and payable out of the produce of the land. Above the peasant proper, the actual cultivator of the land, was one or, as a rule, a community of land renters who as proprietors of the land were held liable by the authorities for the tax levy. However, between these proprietors and the authorities there was usually a middleman—the Zamindar or Talukdar—who laid claim either to a share of the rent…or to seignorial rights" (Weber, 1958: 70). That is to say, above the actual cultivators of the land, there were several layers of land renters who had entitlements to a certain share of the land produce, and historical development in India meant the elaboration of these overlapping entitlements in terms of their segmentation and diversification. An inherent feature of Indian historical development was that as the productive forces and the social division of labor evolved, new entitlements entailing new roles were formed

---

[5] On how Indian philosophical and spiritual tradition is related to the affirmation of diversity based on ontological equality, see Tanabe (2018, 2021a).

on the same piece of land one after another (Kotani, 2014: 86). Such expansion of multilayeredness and diversity through the elaboration of entitlements to shares of economic produce was unique to the South Asian path of development.

Let me give an example from a local society, Garh Manitri, in Odisha (Orissa) where I have conducted historical and anthropological research for over three decades. Garh Manitri was annexed to the kingdom of Khurda around the late sixteenth century. This was a period when there was increasing interaction between the coast and the interior of Odisha as the Indian Ocean trade expanded. The forest-dwellers, called "tribals" since the colonial period, came to be on the move, searching for better positions in the "little kingdoms" that often emerged in forest and hilly areas (Berkemer & Frenz, 2003). People from the plains, including brāhmaṇas, artisans, and service castes, also came to settle in these newly opened villages in the little kingdoms. Such state-formation processes involved the Hinduization of many forest-dwellers, who turned themselves into warriors, peasants, and herdsmen. The tribalization of the kingdom's social formation accompanied this. The encounters of the different communities at the frontier and the subsequent dynamics led to the diversification of lifeways of the people who adopted various occupations and utilized different aspects of the natural resources. The management of diverse groups living together led to the stratified division of work and exchange of products and services, which I call "the system of entitlements".[6] This was a collective and careful management of the natural and social environment based on the affirmation of diversity and diversification.

1.5 Diversity-Driven Development and Commercial Expansion in Early Modern India

Let us look into how the South Asian, diversity-driven path of development manifested in early modern India. One must remember that there were "many and diverse paths along which the peoples of the eighteenth century had earned their livings" in India (Washbrook, 1988: 80). Furthermore, we need to understand the "diversification of the use of biological resources by endogamous groups" (Gadgil & Guha, 1992: 207), and how this enabled utilization of different aspects of resources.

The usage of natural resources and distribution of produce were managed under "the system of entitlements" in early modern India. The local community as a whole, consisting of a few to tens of villages, provided entitlements to a share of local products for households engaged in various roles in administration, military, agriculture, crafts, religious and secular services, and entertainment. When there was enough economic surplus, the community would further assign more families to roles required in the community. More administrators and soldiers were added or/and religious specialists, carpenter–artists or ironsmiths appointed depending on the needs

---

[6] See Tanabe (2021a) for the details of the system of entitlements and its subsequent transformation in Odisha.

of the community and/or the state. This was done by setting the entitlements to a share of local produce in the region. Various castes contributed to the continuity and growth of each of their specialized knowledge and skills while being supported by the community. Through this system, cultural plurality characteristic of Indian society was maintained and developed.

This was a system for socially accumulating the results of labor in the form of various knowledge and skills in different social groups. In South Asia, the natural environment is unstable and unpredictable as the overwhelming power of nature can be a great blessing or it can destroy in an instant all that has been built and stored. Hence, investment is made for human beings to acquire and accumulate diverse knowledge and skills (Nakamura, 1984; Wakimura, 2009).

This is in contrast to the development paths in the West and in East Asia. The West aimed to increase labor productivity by using capital intensive and resource/energy intensive technology, and accumulate the results of labor in the form of financial or material capital. East Asia aimed to increase land productivity by using labor intensive and resource/energy-saving technology, and accumulate the result in the form of improving the place of production, namely, land, factories, communities: e.g., constructing labor-intensive irrigated and terraced rice fields, refining production processes and layout of workplaces, and cultivating good human relations for cooperation through social gathering (Bray, 1986; Nakamura, 1984; Sugihara, 2003, 2004; Wakimura, 2009).

The South Asian path of development is diversity-driven and environment-adaptive. One important aspect of the system of entitlements in early modern India is that it incorporated a sociological mechanism to adapt to unpredictable rainfall in the area. There is extreme variation in the amount of rainfall between wet and dry regions and seasons in India. It is impossible to predict when and how much rain will fall, and when it does, it is necessary to act quickly. However, this does not mean that large numbers of agricultural laborers can be employed throughout the year because rainfall is seasonal due to the monsoon, and there are long periods in the year when agricultural labor is not needed. To deal with this, the system of entitlements in eighteenth century India created a large surplus of service castes (sweepers, barbers, laborers, etc.) and artisan castes (carpenters, potters, blacksmiths, etc.). These castes carried out their specialized work during the off-season and engaged in agriculture when the farming season came. This was a way for society to cope with fluctuations in weather by keeping surplus labor available for agriculture when needed (Wakimura, 2009). The agricultural surpluses created enabled the community to support a variety of social groups with diverse knowledge and skills (Nakamura, 1984).

Such diversity in the kinds of work, agricultural production, and seasonal activities functioned as mechanisms for reducing risk and absorbing labor. Based on these shifting diversities in production activities, the system of entitlements functioned to support the sharing of both the fruits of various activities and the agricultural risks in the local community.[7] It is true that under the system of entitlements, there was a large difference in the share of products depending on the occupation and work. So there certainly was an aspect of inequality. What is worth noting, however, is that even members of lower castes were assured of survival because of their entitlement to a share of the local community's total output. Crop yields varied from one year to the next depending on the level of precipitation and severity of damage due to natural disasters in any given year. Nevertheless, in contrast to a system that charges a fixed rent, the system of entitlements guaranteed each caste a certain share of the harvest, which enabled the local community as a whole to absorb the risks of fluctuating annual yields.[8]

Social adaptation to the environment in India can be better understood if we compare it to other places in the world. In his research in Thailand, Yoneo Ishii points out that in areas where water is abundant, it is possible to adapt naturally through "agronomic adaptation", such as selecting rice varieties that can cope with excess water (floating rice), while in areas where water is chronically scarce, "technological adaptation" is necessary, such as digging waterways, installing water-lifting devices, and constructing reservoirs. Ishii explains the differences in the community structure of rice-growing societies from this perspective (Ishii, 1978: 18). In comparison, many parts of India have unstable water conditions, with too much or too little water, for which manipulation of nature is not an option. As a result, India adapted to the environment not by agronomic action on the biosphere, nor by technological action on the geosphere, but by "sociological adaptation", that is, by managing the human society while adapting to the environmental changes.[9]

In areas of agronomic adaptation, each small peasant household was relatively autonomous, whereas technological adaptation on a large scale required the involvement of state power (cf. Wittfogel, 1957). Sociological adaptation, on the other hand, required a fine-tuning of the distribution of rights and duties between social groups and a high degree of order-forming capacity on the part of society. This is related to the fact that while India has historically had a high capacity for social order, the state has had a relatively weak capacity or need to intervene in society (Tanabe, 2006).

Thus, early modern India developed a unique socio-economic system that was adapted to seasonal and inter-annual variations in rainfall, ensured a surplus labor force that could cope with the changes in the form of service and artisan castes,

---

[7] See Tanabe (2021b) on the system of entitlements, which functioned as a mechanism to share risks in the early modern era, and how this system of risk management fragmented in the early nineteenth century, resulting in the loss of sustainability.

[8] Moreover, it should be noted that there was no scarcity of agricultural land in eighteenth-century India (Wakimura, 2009). Agricultural laborers were in demand when there was sufficient rainfall. The demand for labor increased still further because of an economic boom brought about by thriving trade across the Indian Ocean (Washbrook, 1993). It should also be pointed out, however, that the lowest level of agricultural laborers and entertainers were required to migrate to other areas if crops continued to fail. Thus, this was a form of social adaptation to the ecological environment that involved both sharing and discrimination.

[9] However, the role of the state, besides that of local society, was important in technological adaptation in the early modern period in Tamil areas where agricultural development was not possible without irrigation facilities (Mosse, 2003).

managed risks through a system of shares and social gradient, and accumulated the fruits of labor in the form of specialized knowledge and skills for each group in society. In the division of labor, each *jati* (caste group, unit of endogamy, associated with a particular occupation) was a site of human and cultural reproduction, accumulating inherited skills and knowledge.

The main logic of this system of entitlements was "participation and sharing" by a variety of social groups. The idea was for people to share a common space of interaction and exchange based on differences in the lifeways of various social groups and diversities of work they offered.

It was in the combination of the diversities that the Indian socio-economy displayed its ingenuity. It not only affirmed differences, but also devised ways of combining diversities. Indian cultural-economy was characterized by the "assemblage of diversities" in the successful combination of the diverse products of specialized knowledge and skills.

For example, Indian cloth, which has been highly appreciated in the market worldwide from the early modern period until today (Riello & Roy, 2009), is a result of the combination of various skills and labor, both highly specialized and basic. The raw cotton was first processed by the cotton-carders who carded and teased it into cotton wool, then by others (probably women of different castes) who spun it into thread, and then by handloom weavers who wove it into cloth. The cloth was also adorned with color and design through dying and/or printing by specialist dyers. It may have been decorated with some ornaments, each variety of which was also made by various specialized craftsmen. Finished cloth was thus a combination of diverse skills and knowledge.

It was such "assemblage of diversities" in early modern India that not only enriched life in the local community through the availability of diverse skill and knowledge but also enabled expansion of agricultural and manufacturing activities for the market, including the Indian Ocean trade of cotton textiles.[10] The eighteenth century was a time of commercial expansion for India (Bayly, 1983; Parthasarathi, 2001; Stein, 1989), with the establishment of trade centers and networks, accompanied by growth in the use of a variety of money (Perlin, 1984, 1987; Tanabe, 2022).

In this way, the South Asian path of development in early modern India was based on the affirmation of diversity and the ingenuity to combine diversities. The direction of development was not only towards increase in productivity but often towards diversification. It was the diversification that enriched the variety of products and services, and also enriched the culture and economy as a whole. This was an outcome of the combination of various products and services, each of which was the result of highly skilled specialized labor.

---

[10] The circulation of cowry shells was vital for such chains of transaction (Heimann, 1980; Perlin, 1987). In seventeenth-century and eighteenth-century Bengal, weavers were paid in advance in cowry (Perlin, 1986: 1045, 1987: 300, 320, Hossain, 1979: 340–341). This was probably also the case with Odisha in the same period, where cowry were widely used (De, 1952a, 1952b; Perlin, 1987: 241). See Tanabe (2022) for the varieties of money used in early modern Odisha and how they functioned to connect diversities through community, state, and market.

1.6   Colonial Divergence: Traditionalization, Peasantization and New Commercial Networks

After colonization, in the 1820s and 1830s, the system of entitlements at the local level was replaced by individual land proprietorship. The British government conducted systematic administrative measures over land. This was expected because the tax levied on land was the main source of revenue for the colonial government. The revenue administration of survey and settlement showed an almost paranoiac effort at systematic categorization and enumeration (Cohn, 1987; Appadurai, 1993). The new land settlement brought about profound changes in the economic system in India. The British colonial government sorted out the rights that had existed in multilayered ways on a certain piece of land, allocated a deed of right to one person, and thereby granted exclusive proprietary rights in addition to allocating the responsibility of paying taxes.

In this way, land was alienated, so to speak, from the socio-political relations it had formerly represented and supported. Consequently, the system of entitlements that had supported the collective sustainability and assemblage of diversity in the local community broke down. The land, instead of being a medium for organizing local community, became the object of individual ownership through which society came to be stratified. The British colonial policy created a "caste hierarchy", which "traditionalized" the privileged authority of the brāhmaṇas, the local elites, and the dominant caste, the hierarchy of which more or less matched the stratification in the landholdings. The colonial state, with its centralized bureaucracy and military, functioned to guide society into reproducing the newly traditionalized social structure and extracting the agrarian surplus.

Another phase of social transformation under colonialism came with the commercialization of agriculture in the latter half of the nineteenth century. The "traditionalized" structure of dominance established in the early nineteenth century went through a reshuffling as class differentiation developed. There arose the "new rich", on the one hand, who were successful in amassing wealth in the new economic opportunities. They were able to take risks under the colonial economy. On the other hand, there were poorer peasants, tyrannized by debt. Much of the "low-caste" population became landless bonded agricultural laborers. They were actually the ones who were forced to bear the costs of the new risks.

In this way, by the mid-nineteenth century, various castes that had been engaged in a wide range of occupations in the previous century, began to be concentrated in agriculture. This "peasantization" process is intimately related to the process by which India was transformed into a primary commodity-producing country under colonial rule. In step with the colonial commercialization of the agrarian economy, a larger number of rural residents began to engage in the production of cash crops, resulting in a significant narrowing of the diversity of occupations in the villages (Tanabe, 2021b). The peasantization, where labor was largely concentrated in agriculture in rural India, may be seen as a "colonial divergence" from the original diversity-driven path.

However, we should also not lose sight of the fact that there arose a new kind of commercial networks in colonial India, which led to reassembling of remaining and new diversities in the network that connected villages, towns, and cities. Indian socio-economy was quick to adapt to the new economic demand. Throughout the colonial period, India functioned as important production and trade sites, with nodes and networks for collection and distribution (Bayly, 1983), which extended wide into the Indian Ocean (Markovits, 2000; Oishi, 2015; Rudner, 2020). The expansion of Indian Ocean trade during the colonial period in turn stimulated the development of the domestic market, transportation, and communication (Kanda, 2017; Sugihara, 2015). India was not only a huge supplier of agricultural products but also manufactured commodities such as cotton textiles and jute (Riello and Ali, 2018; Riello & Parthasarathi, 2011; Roy, 2009). Villages, the site of agricultural production, were connected to small towns and cities, where commodities were manufactured, and then to the ports, from where the commodities were sent overseas (Gandhi et al., 2020). In this complex network of production, manufacturing, and trade, multifarious actors were involved, such as peasants, moneylenders, artisans, laborers, and merchants, reflecting the new combination of local knowledge and global demand.

1.7 Economic Development in Contemporary India

Now let us look at the economy in contemporary India. Immediately after independence, the primary sector accounted for 53%, the secondary sector 13%, and the tertiary sector 34% of India's gross domestic product. Although there was a certain amount of industrialization from the late 1920s, postcolonial India at its start was mainly an agricultural economy with a huge peasant population. The Nehruvian attempt at state-led industrialization staggered by the mid-1960s. Although the growth rate of the secondary sector between 1950–1951 and 1965–1966 was above 6.5%, it faltered to 4.3% in the period 1965–1966 to 1970–1971, and 3.8% between 1970–1971 and 1975–1976 (Economic Survey 2011–12).

Nevertheless, India's democratic commitment to development slowly bore fruit. People's access to food and education gradually improved after independence, and their political participation expanded from the mid-1960s. Corresponding to the popular demand, from the 1970s, subsidies to the rural society for poverty alleviation increased, and the people's participation in the consumer economy and party politics expanded. The Green Revolution, which began in the mid-1960s with wheat crops in a limited region such as Punjab, expanded to rice cultivation from the mid-1970s and to a wider region including south and east India (Fujita, 2002, 2015). Electricity for running tubewells and chemical fertilizers were heavily subsidized, and the government purchased the produce at a guaranteed minimum price. As a result of these policy efforts, food self-sufficiency was achieved by the late 1970s (Sarma, 1978). The spread of the Green Revolution from the mid-1960s to the 1980s provided an important basis for later economic development (Fujita, 2002, 2015; Roy, 2007).

The economic growth rate, which was staggering around 3.5% per year in the 1970s, rose to the mid-5% range in the 1980s. The political and economic vitalization of the 1980s was of great significance. Although frictions such as religious and caste conflicts arose as diverse populations participated in public life, these were also a part of the process of democratic politics and market economy expanding into rural society. It was a period of transition and churning of the lifeworld with the workings of the state and market. The economic policy of the 1980s, which included hefty subsidies, however, did not last long due to a heavy burden on the national finances. After an economic crisis caused by the accumulation of budget deficits and foreign debt, India took a major step toward economic liberalization in 1991.

What is remarkable about India since the 1990s is that there has been simultaneous democratic deepening and economic development. While political and public participation from below by the subalterns, such as people from low castes, tribal groups, religious minorities, and women grew consistently, India has also maintained a high economic growth rate averaging more than 6.4% between 1992 and 2019.[11] Although India's economy contracted by 7.3% in 2020 due to the COVID-19 pandemic, it is expected to grow by 9.5% in 2021 and 8.5% in 2022, according to IMF projections.[12] This is a situation worth noting. Historically speaking, in other parts of the world, democracy is only established after economic development has been achieved through industrialization. Besides India, no country has brought about industrial development after having established democracy (Varshney, 1995). How has this been possible?

The key to the answer lies, in my contention, in the contemporary unfolding of the South Asian path of development. In order to understand this, we must go beyond the conventional political economy viewpoint of the relationship between the state and the market, and broaden our perspective to include society. Society is where people make their living and where the workings of the market and the state are embedded.[13] As much as the Indian state has "depended on its ability to arbitrate between contending local groups, tribes, classes etc." and its strength has been a "reflection of the nature of society it was trying to govern",[14] the workings of the Indian market depend on its ability to connect between diverse groups, and its strength can only be a reflection of the diverse society for which it is trying to facilitate exchanges and transactions. In other words, the vitality of the Indian economy is largely embedded in the social relationships and cultural values of society (Gandhi et al., 2020).

---

[11] Data from the World Bank (https://data.worldbank.org/indicator/NY.GDP.MKTP.KD.ZG?locations=IN) accessed on 17 October 2021.

[12] Data from IMF (https://www.imf.org/en/Countries/IND) accessed on 17 October 2021.

[13] I agree with Raghuram Rajan about the importance of "the third pillar" of the community beside markets and the state. However, it is unfortunate that his emphasis on the local community tends to downplay the socio-economic importance of the people's dynamic movement and activities that connect the rural, urban, and abroad. It is in the "rurban" and "glocal", the social space in-between the rural/urban as well as local/global, that we note new dynamism in India (Mizushima, 2015; Tokita-Tanabe, 2021).

[14] Personal communication from C. Bayly to Kulke (1995: 47). See also Tanabe (2006).

From this viewpoint, the dynamism of contemporary India lies not solely on the liberalized working of the market but rather on the expansion of livelihood security with improved health and literacy, and politico-economic agency of people supported by the institutional provisions.[15] In this process, the hitherto rurally confined and traditionalized social relations and cultural values came to interact with the workings of democratic politics and market economy, bringing about a new dynamism.

Looking at livelihood security in India, the infant mortality rate (the number of deaths per 1,000 live births) has declined from 115‰ in 1986 to 47‰ in 2010, and the state-wise mortality rate, where there was a wide gap between a low of 52‰ (Kerala) and a high of 150‰ (Madhya Pradesh) in 1986, has converged between 13 and 60‰ in 2010 (IndiaStat.com, Economic Survey 2011–12). The crude death rate dropped steadily since the 1920s from around 47‰ in the 1910s to below 8‰ by 2011. The birth rate declined first slowly and then more rapidly, from nearing 50‰ in 1901–1911 to a little above 20‰ in 2010–2015. The total population will continue to grow for some time, but is expected to peak around the year 2060 and then decline (James, 2011).

The literacy rate has increased significantly in a short period of time from 18.33% in 1951 to 74.04% in 2011. Since 1991, the literacy rate in the backward states, such as Bihar and Uttar Pradesh, and backward social groups, such as those belonging to Scheduled Castes and Scheduled Tribes, has seen a significant increase. Comparing men and women, from 1999 to 2011, the male literacy rate increased by 18.01% from 64.13 to 82.14%, while the female literacy rate showed a larger increase by 26.17%, from 39.29 to 65.46% (IndiaStat.com, Economic Survey 2011–12). The disparities in literacy rates between regions, classes, and genders are converging, although the disparity in the quality of education remains an acute problem.

Since the 1990s, the disparities in economic performance between regions have been widening, and the disparities between classes have also been increasing (Fujita, 2015; Okahashi, 2015; Yanagisawa, 2015). This indeed poses a serious problem for the Indian economy. At the same time, it should also be noted that there has been a narrowing of disparities in livelihood and agency as represented by the decrease in infant mortality and the increase in literacy. Despite the economic disparity, this provides the basic opportunity for diverse people from different regions, classes, castes, and genders to become politically and economically active, supporting the vitality of democratic politics and market economy. What is important is to guarantee life chances to such people and to utilize their potential for the enhancement of public welfare.

---

[15] In addition to the reservation system and the panchayat (local self-government) reforms (1992), the Right to Information Act (2005), the Forest Right Act (2005), the National Rural Employment Guarantee Act (2006), the Right to Education Act (2009), and the National Food Security Act (2013) are important institutional supports.

1.8   The Agenda of a Post-peasant Society: Diversification of Sources of Income

As people's livelihood has been secured and politico–economic agency has expanded with the improvement in health and literacy, a new agenda has appeared. How is it possible for this gigantic mass of people, namely, post-peasants, to have a better living? Absolute poverty, in the sense of food shortage, has been almost overcome. Poverty headcount ratio at $1.90 purchasing power parity a day rapidly declined from 63.1% in 1977 to 47.6% in 1993, 39.9% in 2004, 22.5% in 2011, and 7.7% in 2019.[16] Most people, except for the 7.7% who require attention, have enough food at least in today's India. However, there is a persistence of relative poverty for the majority of the population. Importantly, this problem is structural.

The problem has shifted, in economic terms, from the "food problem" to the "farm problem" (Schultz, 1953) or "agricultural adjustment problem" (Hayami, 1988) in the mid-1990s in the case of India (Fujita, 2015). In the former, overcoming food shortage is the issue, whereas in the latter, when food prices and agricultural income decline as food production exceeds the demand, overcoming the problem of low-income of farmers becomes an important agenda. The large rural population, who used to depend mostly on agriculture, has diversified their source of income, although with difficulty.

This transition in rural India can be characterized as that *from a (post)colonially peasantized society to a post-peasant society*. Here, the term "post-peasant" is used to denote the huge population who used to engage in agricultural work as the main source of living but are now diversifying and combining different sources of income both agricultural and non-agricultural. Post-peasantry refers not simply to the ex-peasant masses but diverse people with different degrees of connection with the agrarian economy, who are struggling in the space of articulation between different modes of production, including corporate capitalism, non-corporate informal economy, and non-capitalist subsistence economy (Chatterjee, 2008a, 2008b; Tamanoi, 1983).[17] Most of the post-peasants, instead of abandoning villages completely to be proletariat laborers or white-collar workers, often maintain

---

[16] Data from the World Bank (https://data.worldbank.org/topic/poverty?locations=IN) and data from the Asian Development Bank (https://www.adb.org/countries/india/poverty) last accessed on 18th October 2021.

[17] Partha Chatterjee draws a comparison between formal and informal sectors by distinguishing between corporate and non-corporate capital. He argues that corporate capital pursues profit, whereas small-scale, non-corporate capital aims to ensure survival and secure livelihood (Chatterjee, 2008a, 2008b). Chatterjee's attention to the role of the non-corporate, informal sector for securing people's livelihood is important. But, he tends to overemphasize the contradiction between the two sectors which is only thinly connected with the redistribution of wealth by the state from the urban formal sector to the rural (post-)peasants. Instead of a dichotomous framework that clearly separates the formal and informal sectors, I suggest we should pay attention to the space of articulation between the two, and see not only how corporate capital exploits the informal sector but also how post-peasants strategically attempt to obtain both livelihood security and life chance expansion through diversifying sources of income and gradually upgrading their education and employment.

connections with their villages and agriculture while seeking new opportunities in the urban areas. They often utilize kin-caste-personal relationships to seek opportunities for education and work in the towns and cities while keeping, as long as the need remains, their connection with their home village and agricultural land as a safety net. These post-peasants, who are not completely farmers, laborers, entrepreneurs or white-collar workers but are often the combination of all these when we look at their seasonal changes in work and the collaborations in the family and kinship network, are the main population who are becoming both a potential and a problem for emerging economies such as India.

Let us take up the example of Garh Manitri again. Villagers say that until the 1960s, few people wanted to be office workers or live outside the village, which was predominantly agrarian. In those days, if they had any extra cash they used it to buy farmland, but today, they invest it in education or small businesses. Until the beginning of the 1990s, there was little chance for upward socio-economic mobility even if they left the village, so most villagers stayed in the village except for the educated few. Since the late 1990s, however, as employment opportunities increased, many people began to live outside the village to secure a steady income. By the mid-2000s, the number of people working outside the village had increased considerably.

According to a survey conducted by Tanabe and Fujita in 2016, there were 859 households and 5.24 members (2.56 males and 2.68 females) per household on average in Garh Manitri (Tanabe & Fujita, 2021). Out of these, there were 0.66 (25.7%) male members and 0.13 (5.0%) female members who stayed separately away from the village. Also, out of 1.85 members (1.56 males and 0.29 females) in the labor force, there were 0.60 (38.3%) male members and 0.03 (10.8%) female members on average who worked outside.

Members of the family working and living outside the village send remittances, and keep in touch with their families and relatives through telephone and SNS. They also support their families and relatives to get better education and employment opportunities in urban areas. Thus, the fact that these people work and live outside the village does not mean a collapse of family ties. Rather, it often implies the expansion of "intimate networks" that connect family members and kin across the village, the rurban, and the cities (Tokita-Tanabe, 2021). There are increasing communication and interaction between villages and cities today in terms of circular movement of people, money, commodities, and information. This has also led to spatial expansion of the lifeworld of villagers for education, work, and social and family life. Arguably, this dynamic movement of people, money, information, and commodities across the rural and the urban characterize the post-peasant society in India.

The non-farm income has increased in a major way in this process. In 2016, farm income constituted only 6.34% of household income, while non-farm income constituted 93.66%. Within non-farm income, labor wages constituted only 10.86% (agricultural wages 2.02% and non-agricultural wages 8.84%), and 89.14% of income came from salary, business, and pension sources (salary from the private sector was 39.20%, salary from the government 25.14%, business 17.86%, and pensions 6.94%). The average total household income per year was Rs. 217,720 (around US $3,266), out of which non-farm income was Rs. 203,918 (around US $3,059), and farm income only Rs. 13,802 (around US $207). This is a sea change from the situation in the early 1990s when farm income and agricultural wages still constituted the most important sources of income.

1.9 Growth Amidst Precarity: The Agenda of Labor Absorption

One of the biggest problems facing India and the world is how to provide jobs and livelihood to the huge population of post-peasants. Out of the 457.5 million employed persons in India (2004–2005), the "organized" sector (government, public corporations, and registered private enterprises) employs a mere 7.6%, and the vast majority of the 92.4% find employment in the so-called informal sector, or "unorganized" sector (Sengupta et al., 2008: Table 6). There is a process of casualization and informalization of the job market in India just as in other parts of the world. Also, there is no longer a stable socio-economy in the rural areas due to marketization of the lifeworld. People require sources of cash income, and cannot depend on agriculture, in order to pursue a better life. The "agricultural adjustment problem" for the post-peasantry society must be seen as a global problem of labor absorption on an unprecedented scale.

It has been pointed out that India is going through a "jobless growth" (Kannan & Raveendran, 2009). What is the mechanism behind this?

In the formal sector, there is a phenomenal expansion of the capital-intensive, high-productivity service industry, represented by IT. The IT service industry has exhibited a remarkable growth rate of 30% per year since 1991, and with software accounting for more than 26% (2010–2011) of total export values, has been the star performer in the Indian economy. While accounting for only 1.2% of GNP in 1997–1998, this industry's share in GNP rose to 7.5% in 2011–2012 (Economic Survey 2011–12). India indeed "stands out for its rapid expansion of high-productivity service sectors" (Tejani, 2016: 867). We should note, however, that unlike the manufacturing sector and informal sector, the IT service industry does not have a broad base, and that being an export-led industry (78.4% in 2010–2011) it is dominated by a section of the elite (Economic Survey 2011–12). This kind of high-tech formal sector lacks the "broad-based expansion of labour-intensive production that has been characteristic of fast-growing economies in East Asia" (Tejani, 2016: 867, cf. Sugihara, 2007, Austin & Sugihara, 2013).

If we look at the detailed components of the service sector in India, however, we find a different picture (Yanagisawa, 2014). A breakdown of the service industry as a whole (2010–2011) is as follows: trade, hotels and restaurants (16.3% of GNP), transport, storage and communication (7.8%), financing, insurance, real estate and business services (16.7%), community, social and personal services (14.4%), and construction (8.2%) (Economic Survey 2011–12). Although the IT industry is indeed leading growth, the business categories that are growing in step with the expansion of domestic demand are those providing the trade, retailing, and various kinds of services rather than the export-oriented sectors dominated by big capital and the elite. The importance of the construction industry should also not be overlooked. It is often the informal segments of the service sector that offer jobs to the huge chunk of less-skilled workers.[18]

If we look at the manufacturing sector, while it is once more the "(c)apital-intensive industries within the organized sector" that "accounted for much of the increase in output or value added by Indian manufacturing", most of the new jobs in manufacturing generated between 1999–2000 and 2004–2005 was "in the unorganized sector, mainly by export-oriented industries such as garments, textiles, leather and diamond cutting" which held 23.0% of factory sector employment in 2003–2006 and 32.2% of unregistered manufacturing sector employment in 2005–2006 (Thomas, 2013: 690). Here, yet again, it is the informal (or unorganized) sector that offers jobs to people, the payment from which in turn supports the domestic demand.

Industries that are dependent on mass domestic consumption demand—food products, beverages, and tobacco products—were also a significant source of labor absorption which held 22.2% of factory sector employment in 2003–2006 and 28.9% of unregistered manufacturing sector employment in 2005–2006. However, it is alarming that while these industries had generated 2.05 million new jobs in India between 1983 and 1993–1994, they lost a total of 0.3 million jobs during the period 1999–2000 to 2004–2005 (Thomas, 2013: 681). This reversal in employment growth in the Indian food industry since the late 1990s possibly reflects the slowdown in the agricultural and rural economy. From the early 1990s, "agricultural production, productivity, and value of output have decelerated for almost all crops" in India due to policy change (Mishra & Reddy 2011: 48). It is necessary to note, nevertheless, that "the pace of workforce transformation depends on agriculture productivity to sustain non-agricultural employment" (Nagaraj, 2011: 77). This point is important as nearly 60% of India's GDP is driven by domestic private consumption, as compared to 40% in China (World Economic Forum, 2019: 8).

It is crucial for the Indian economy to keep up the vitality of the domestic consumption market and related industries, which function as a transformational pivot connecting the livelihood-supporting, low-value-added, huge agrarian economy with the profit-seeking, high-value-added, high-tech economy. In other words, the post-peasant socio-economy needs careful articulation of various sectors and different modes of production in order for there to be a healthy circulation of income, demand, and job opportunities, thus enabling labor absorption and structural industrial transformation.

In this way, when we say "jobless growth", we are witnessing the balancing off of the capital-intensification of high-tech formal industry requiring less labor on the one hand, and the growing job market in the informal sector. The engine of economic growth lies in the former, whereas the livelihood basis for the post-peasant masses

---

[18] Tejani admits, "A caveat to our results are known weaknesses of the estimation of services GDP in India, especially with respect to the output of the private corporate sector and the informal segment of the tertiary sector" (2016: 867–868).

lies in the latter. While there is less space for entry of workers in the high-tech formal sector, there is growing space for casual labor and small-scale enterprises in the informal sector. Employment in the latter is often unstable and unreliable, but nevertheless provides the people with some source of income.

1.10   Reassembling Diversities: Reconvergence to the South Asian Path of Development

In this precarious and unstable economic environment for the non-elite masses, how do people seek risk mitigation and life chance expansion? Against the image of one-way proletarianization of ex-peasants who are exploited as cheap laborers in the informal sector, it is more often the case that the post-peasant households diversify their source of income by combining various sources. For example, a household in Garh Manitiri combined agriculture, small-scale poultry, term employment in a private company, cashew nut growing, and urban migration of a young member. Other sources of income found in the village are government employment (if a member is educated and lucky), casual labor, shopkeeping, offering tutorials to students, contract jobs, or illicit liquor business. Arguably, the strategy of livelihood diversification represents, beyond the postcolonial divergence, the reconvergence of household strategy to the South Asian path of diversity-driven development.

The traditionalized structure of kinship, caste, and religion is loosened today, but personal–kin–caste-religious networks play important roles. People often depend on these "intimate networks" to seek education and jobs in the expanding lifeworld (Tokita-Tanabe, 2021). This explains both the persistence and change in socio-economic relationships. The economy is still embedded in social relationships, but the social relationships are no longer in a fixed structure. Rather, they function as networks to support a new dynamic movement of people, information, and money.

Also, we note that there are born new combinations of diverse materials, skills, and knowledge, that are enabled by new encounters of diverse social groups in the open economic environment, to produce a large variety of goods and services on a small scale according to the wide range of different needs arising from a vibrant market. The competitiveness of the small-scale unorganized sector is not only due to its ability to respond to diverse needs that large-scale production finds difficult to fulfil (Datt & Ravallion, 2011; Krishna, 2011), but also because of the new innovations that are taking place through "reassembling diversities".

For example, Kazuyuki Kubota's study shows how the leather industry in Dharavi, a huge slum with numerous enterprises and workshops in the outskirts of Mumbai, responds flexibly to small or large orders for a wide range of products from low to high quality (Kubota, in press, 2021). There is a loose network of workshops and factories (located also in slum areas), employing a range of workers from medium-to high-skilled, some capable of mass-producing simple products and others capable of producing technically demanding designs for export. Design and manufacture of leather goods in the workshops is mainly based on the knowledge and skills accumu-lated by the Chambars, a leather caste Dalit community, and a group of Muslim leather craftsmen, combined with the knowledge of modern design, demand, and marketing of the educated classes. Kubota reports that it is the educated Dalit entrepreneurs owning leather workshops in Dharavi who play a pivotal role of mediating high-level artisan skills accumulated by the Chambars with the knowledge of the designers and exporters from outside to produce value-added products. The new combination of these diverse skills and knowledge is leading to innovation of new products with value-added design and quality.

Kaoru Kawanaka also describes how a variety of products are made in small lots in the export industry of ladies' garments in Delhi by utilizing diverse skills and knowledge and combining richly varied materials (Kawanaka, 2017, 2018). A wide range of woven cotton fabrics and accessories made by artisans of various localities is put together to create high-quality fashionable products. There are only a limited number of skilled tailors and master artisans who are permanently employed; and other tailors, who are in circular migration between the village and the city, are seasonally employed. This is a way to adapt to the seasonal changes in demand, and to meet the requirements of the seasonal workers who wish to have a basis in the village and also diversify their source of income. When it comes to production, one highly skilled tailor takes the responsibility of the entire sewing process, while giving simple parts to less skilled tailors, and completes each garment one by one. This cell production system, rather than the line production system seen in knit fabric manu-facture, is suited to tailoring the delicate Indian woven cotton fabrics which require subtle adjustments in the tailoring process. Division of labor between skilled and semi-skilled workers, as well as allocation and control of work by managerial master artisans, enables efficient production and skill learning. A network of tailors built on links between urban and rural areas supports access to jobs, mobility between facto-ries, and skill learning. Workers acquire skills gradually on the job in this circulatory process, rather than through training by companies.[19]

In contemporary India, as diverse post-peasant agents seek to secure their liveli-hood and increase their life chances, there is an expansion of people's participa-tion in market economy and democratic politics. In this process, diverse skills and knowledge accumulated in various social groups meet with each other and also with modern knowledge and technology. This process is leading to a transformation of some informal industries, represented by fabric and leather, which have uniquely Indian design but appeal to the global market. While capital-intensive high-tech formal industry, such as IT, represents one bright aspect of the Indian economy, the beneficiaries are mostly limited to the elite. The labor-intensive and labor-absorbing informal sectors, such as fabric and leather, represent another kind of hope for the post-peasant mass based Indian economy. They cater to the global and domestic

---

[19] Companies do not train these workers or sort them according to type of work. The conventional explanation for this is that India's woven-garment industry consisting of small and medium-sized enterprises is inefficient and dependent on protectionism, but this does not seem to be the only picture according to Kawanaka.

market demand with a wide range of products from low to high quality, and also offer
job opportunities to various artisans and laborers with varying skills and different
degrees of connection with the rural agrarian economy.

There are plural economic sectors and modes of production with different degrees
of capital intensity and labor intensity as well as varying emphasis on profit and
livelihood in India. The key to sustainable development of the Indian economy lies
in mediating these various sectors and modes with a balance between the rural and
the urban, agricultural and non-agricultural, informal and formal, and livelihood and
profit.

1.11   Conclusion

India has always been a meeting place and assemblage of diversities, where the existence of diversities is affirmed. As regards the development path, previous studies
have discussed the capital-intensive Western path and the labor-intensive East Asian
path. Both paths presume stability of the natural environment, and focus on how
to use endowed resources more efficiently to maximize production. In South Asia,
however, a unique socio-economic system has developed, which takes into consideration unstable changes in the natural environment, and secures livelihood in ways that
is compatible with environmental uncertainty. Through the maintenance of diverse
groups and exchanges among them, the South Asian path of development has directed
human efforts towards the diversification and accumulation of cultural resources in
the form of specialized skill and knowledge rather than just the maximization of
overall production which often leads to standardization. This South Asian path, which
can be called "diversity-driven", has historically sought to ensure the maintenance
of diversity without denying the plurality of human ways of life and heterogeneity of
the world, and to increase the richness of society as a whole through the intersection,
coexistence, and assembling of these diversities.

We contend that the perspective of the South Asian path of diversity-driven development explains important aspects of the present economic dynamism in India where
the post-peasant masses are diversifying sources of income to both secure livelihood
and increase life chances in the market economy and democratic politics. Also, there
is a new reassembling of diversities where varied skill and knowledge meet and
give rise to innovations in the glocal connections. The Indian economy is characterized by the prominence of the capital intensive, high-value-added industries such
as IT as well as the hugeness of the labor intensive, low-value-added industries
such as food, fabric, and leather in the manufacturing sector, and trade, restaurants,
communication, and transport in the service sector that support the non-agricultural
income and expanding lifeworld of the post-peasant masses. The South Asian path
of development cannot be characterized as either capital intensive or labor intensive based on the regionally particular factor endowments. Its characteristics rather
lie in the coexistence and connection of extreme varieties of modes of production.
In this environment, the potentiality and hope of the Indian economy, though rife

with conflict and friction, lie in the patient and creative articulation and connection between various sectors and different modes of production that satisfy the needs of both the security of human livelihood and the expansion of life chances in the globalizing socio-economy.

Needless to say, the reality of the situation in "diversity-driven" India has its negative aspects, such as hierarchy and disparity that persists and is the target of heavy criticism today. This point should indeed be taken seriously. However, diversity should never be reduced or translated to hierarchy and disparity in both real terms and in our understanding.

It is my contention that the study of the South Asian path of development has a deep significance for today's world as it leads us to ask—instead of the production-centered question of what kind of society can produce more efficiently that often leads to the idea of standardization—perhaps a more vital question related to the future of humanity: how humans can secure their livelihood in the age of precarity and uncertainty,[20] and how they can make the existence of diverse others a source of richness for society as a whole.

References

Ali, T. O. (2018). *A local history of global capital: Jute and peasant life in the Bengal delta*. Princeton: Princeton University Press.

Appadurai, A. (1993). Number in the colonial imagination. In C. Breckenridge & P. van der Veer (Eds.), *Orientalism and the postcolonial predicament: Perspectives on South Asia* (pp. 314–339). Philadelphia: University of Pennsylvania Press.

Austin, G. (2017). *Economic development and environmental history in the Anthropocene: Perspectives on Asia and Africa*. London: Bloomsbury Academic.

Austin, G., & Sugihara, K. (Eds.). (2013). *Labour-intensive industrialization in global history*. London: Routledge.

Bayly, C. A. (1983). *Rulers, townsmen and bazaars: North Indian society in the age of british expansion, 1770–1870*. Cambridge: Cambridge University Press.

Berkemer, G., & Frenz, M. (Eds.). (2003). *Sharing sovereignty: The little Kingdom in South Asia*. Berlin: Klaus Schwartz Verlag.

Bray, F. (1986). *The rice economies: Technology and development in Asian societies*. Oxford: Bail Blackwell.

Chatterjee, P. (2008a). Democracy and economic transformation in India. *Economic and Political Weekly, 43*(16), 53–62.

Chatterjee, P. (2008b). Peasant cultures of the twenty-first century. *Inter-Asia Cultural Studies, 9*(1).

Cohn, B. S. (1987). The census, social structure and objectification in South Asia. In *An anthropologist among the historians and other essays* (pp. 224–254). New Delhi: Oxford University Press.

Datt, G., & Ravallion, M. (2011). Has India's economic growth become more pro-poor in the wake of economic reforms? *The World Bank Economic Review, 25*(2), 157.

De, S. C. (1952a). The cowry currency in India. *Orissa Historical Research Journal, 1*(1), 1–10.

De, S. C. (1952b). Cowry currency in Orissa. *Orissa Historical Research Journal, 1*(2), 10–21.

---

[20] Precarity and uncertainty pose a serious challenge to humanity in the age of the Anthropocene (Austin, 2017).

Dumont, L. (1970). *Homo hierarchicus: The caste system and its implications*. Chicago: Chicago University Press.

Economic Survey. (2011–12). Reterived 26th October, 2021, from https://www.indiabudget.gov.in/economicsurvey/.

Fujita, K. (2002). Indo Nōgyō ron: Gijutsu, Seisaku, Kōzōhenka (Theory of agriculture in India: Technology, policy and structural change). In H. Esho (Ed.), *Gendai Minami Ajia 2: Keizai Jiyūka no Yukue (Contemporary South Asia 2: Future of economic liberalization)* (pp. 97–119). Tokyo: University of Tokyo Press.

Fujita, K. (2015). Dokuritsugo Indo no Keizai Hattenkeiro: Tayōsei to Kaisōsei no Gabanansu (Economic development path in independent India: Governance of diversity and disparity). In A. Tanabe, K. Sugihara, & K. Wakimura (Eds.), *Gendai Indo 1: Tayōsei Shakai no Chōsen (Contemporary India 1: The challenge of diversity society)* (pp. 279–303). Tokyo: University of Tokyo Press.

Gadgil, M., & Guha, R. (1992). *This fissured land: An ecological history of India*. New Delhi: Oxford University Press.

Gandhi, A., Harriss-White, B., Haynes, D. E., & Schwecke, S. (2020). *Rethinking markets in modern India: Embedded exchange and contested jurisdiction*. Cambridge: Cambridge University Press.

Hayami, Y. (1988). *Japanese agriculture under siege: The political economy of agricultural policies*. Basingstoke: Macmillan.

Heimann, J. (1980). Small change and ballast: Cowry trade and usage as an example of Indian Ocean economic history. *South Asia: Journal of South Asian Studies, 3*(1), 48–69.

Hossain, H. (1979). The alienation of weavers: Impact of the conflict between the revenue and commercial interests of the east India company, 1750–1800. *Indian Economic and Social History Review, 16*(3), 323–345.

IndiaStat.com. Reterived 20th , 2013, from https://www.indiastat.com/.

Ishii, Y. (1978). History and Rice-Growing. In Y. Ishii (Ed.), *Thailand: A rice-growing society* (pp. 15–39). Honolulu: University Press of Hawaii.

James, K. S. (2011). India's demographic change: Opportunities and challenges. *Science, 333*, 576–580.

Kanda, S. (2015). Kingendai Indo no Enerugī: Shijō no Keisei to Riyō no Chikisei (Energy in modern India: Market formation and regionality of use). In A. Tanabe, K. Sugihara, & K. Wakimura (Eds.), *Gendai Indo 1: Tayōsei Shakai no Chōsen (Contemporary India 1: The challenge of diversity society)* (pp. 85–110). Tokyo: The University of Tokyo Press.

Kanda, S. (2017). *Shio to Indo: Shijō, Shōnin, Igirisu Higashi Indo Gaisha (Salt and India: Markets, merchants and the English east India company)*. Nagoya: The University of Nagoya Press.

Kannan, K. P., & Raveendran, G. (2009). Growth sans employment: A quarter century of jobless growth in India's organised manufacturing. *Economic and Political Weekly, 44*(10), 80–91.

Kantowsky, D. (1982). Max weber on India and Indian interpretations of weber. *Contributions to Indian Sociology, 16*(2), 141–174.

Kawanaka, K. (2017). Gendai Indo no Apareru Sangyō: Hōseikō Nettowāku to Jōkyōtekiōteki Seisan (Apparel industry in New Delhi, India: Network of tailors and situationally-adaptive production organization). *Ph.D. thesis submitted to the Graduate School of Asian and African Area Studies, Kyoto University*.

Kawanaka, K. (2018). Derī Apareru Sangyō niokeru Hōseikō no Idō Patān (Mobility patterns of migrant tailors in the apparel export industry of Delhi, India). *Nihon Kansei Kōgakkai Ronbunshi (Transactions of Japan Society of Kansei Engineering), 17*(1), 63–69.

Kotani, H. (2014). Makkusu Uēbā no Nōgyō Seidoshi Kōsō to Indo: Indotekina Hatten ni Koyūnamono (Max weber's conception of the history of agricultural institutions and India: What is unique about Indian development). *Shisō, 1087*, 69–88.

Krishna, A. (2011). Poverty knowledge and poverty action in India. In A. Gupta and K. Sivaramakrishnan (Eds.), *The State in India after liberalization: Interdisciplinary perspectives* (pp. 111–132). London: Routedge.

Kubota, K. (2021). Gendai Indo Munbaī niokeru Kawaseihin Sangyō: Suramu Kōbō Nettowāku wo tsūjita Inobēshon (The leather industry in contemporary Mumbai, India: Innovation through a network of slum workshops). *Ph.D. thesis submitted to the Graduate School of Asian and African Area Studies, Kyoto University.*

Kubota, K. (in press). Munbaī Dārāvī no Hikaku Sangyō no Hen'yō: Chanbāru Shokunin no Nettowāku to Soshikika ni chakumokushite (The transformation of leather industry in Dharavi, Mumbai: With a focus on the network and organisation of chambhar craftsmen). *Mahārāshutora (Mahararshtra)* 13.

Kulke, H. (1995). Introduction. In H. Kulke (Ed.), *The state in India 1000–1700* (pp. 1–47). New Delhi: Oxford University Press.

Markovits, C. (2000). *The global world of Indian merchants, 1750–1947: Traders of Sind from Bukhara to panama.* Cambridge: Cambridge University Press.

Mishra, S., & Narasimha Reddy, D. (2011). Persistence of crisis in Indian agriculture: Need for technological and institutional alternatives. In D. M. Nachane (Ed.), *India development report 2011* (pp. 48–58). New Delhi: Oxford University Press.

Mizushima, T. (2015). Yōyū suru Toshi Nōson eno Shikaku (A perspective on the fusion of the urban and the rural). In T. Mizushima & H. Yanagisawa (Eds.), *Gendai Indo 2: Yōyū suru Toshi Nōson (Contemporary India 2: The fusion of the urban and the rural)* (pp. 3–24). Tokyo: The University of Tokyo Press.

Mosse, D. (2003). *The rule of water: Statecraft, ecology, and collective action in South India.* New Delhi: Oxford University Press.

Nagaraj, R. (2011). Industrial performance, 1991–2008: A review. In D. M. Nachane (Ed.), *India development report 2011* (pp. 69–80). New Delhi: Oxford University Press.

Nakamura, H. (1984). *Kyōdōtai no Keizai Kōzō: Rōdō no Chikuseki to Kōkan (The economic structure of community: Accumulation and exchange of labor).* Tokyo: Shinhyōron.

Neyazi, T. A., Tanabe, A., & Ishizaka, S. (Eds.). (2014). *Democratic transformation and the vernacular public arena in India.* London: Routledge.

Oishi, T. (2015). Kan'indoyōsekai to Indojin Shōnin Kigyōka no Nettowāku (The Indian Ocean rim world and the network of the Indian merchants and enrepreneurs). In A. Tanabe, K. Sugihara, & K. Wakimura (Eds.), *Gendai Indo 1: Tayōsei Shakai no Chōsen (Contemporary India 1: The challenge of diversity society)* (pp. 169–196). Tokyo: The University of Tokyo Press.

Okahashi, H. (2015). Kūkankōzō no Keisei to Hendō (The formation and transformation of the spatial structure). In H. Okahashi & K. Tomozawa (Eds.), *Gendai Indo 4: Daitō suru Shinkeizai Kūkan (The emerging new economic space)* (pp. 29–51). Tokyo: The University of Tokyo Press.

Parthasarathi, P. (2001). *The transition to a colonial economy: Weavers, merchants and kings in South India, 1720–1800.* Tokyo: Cambridge University Press.

Perlin, F. (1984). Growth of money economy and some questions of transition in late pre-colonial India. *Journal of Peasant Studies, 11*(3), 96–107.

Perlin, F. (1986). Monetary revolution and societal change in the late medieval and early modern times-a review article. *Journal of Asian Studies, 45*(5), 1037–1049.

Perlin, F. (1987). Money-use in late pre-colonial India and the international trade in currency media. In J. F. Richards (Ed.), *The imperial monetary system of Mughal India* (pp. 232–373). New Delhi: Oxford University Press.

Pomeranz, K. (2000). *The great divergence: China, Europe, and the making of the modern world economy.* Princeton, N.J.: Princeton University Press.

Pomeranz, K. (2004). South and East Asia in global economic history: An ongoing dialogue. *Economic and Political Weekly, 39*(49), 5268–5272.

Riello, G., & Parthasarathi, P. (2011). *The spinning world: A global history of cotton textiles, 1200–1850.* Oxford: Oxford University Press.

Riello, G., & Roy, T. (2009). *How India clothed the world: The world of South Asian textiles, 1500–1850.* Leiden: Brill.

Roy, T. (2004). Economic history: An endangered discipline. *Economic and Political Weekly, 39*(29), 3238–3243.

Roy, T. (2005). *Rethinking economic change in India: Labour and livelihood*. London: Routledge.

Roy, T. (2007). A delayed revolution: Environment and agrarian change in India. *Oxford Review of Economic Policy, 23*(2), 239.

Rudner, D. W. (2020). *Caste and capitalism in colonial India*. Berkeley: University of California Press.

Sarma, J. S. (1978). India—a drive towards self-sufficiency in food grains. *American Journal of Agricultural Science, 60*(5), 859–864.

Sato, T., & Sugihara, K. (2015). Kankyō no Tayōsei to Bunka no Tayōsei (Environemental diversity and cultural diversity). In A. Tanabe, K. Sugihara, & K. Wakimura (Eds.), *Gendai Indo 1: Tayōsei Shakai no Chōsen (Contemporary India 1: The challenge of diversity society)* (pp. 39–60). Tokyo: The University of Tokyo Press.

Schultz, T. W. (1953). *The economic organization of agriculture*. New York: McGraw-Hill.

Sen, A. (1999). *Development as freedom*. Oxford: Oxford University Press.

Sengupta, A., Kannan, K. P., & Raveendran, G. (2008). India's common people: Who are they, how many are they and how do they live? *Economic and Political Weekly, 43*(11), 49–63.

Singer, M. (1966). Religion and social change in India: The max weber thesis, phase three. *Economic Development and Cultural Change, 14*(4), 497–505.

Stein, B. (1989). Eighteenth century India: Another view. *Studies in History (n.s.), 5*(1), 1–26

Sugihara, K. (2003). The East Asian path of economic development. In G. Arrighi, T. Hamashita, & M. Selden (Eds.), *The resurgence of East Asia: 500, 150 and 50 year perspectives* (pp. 78–123). London: Routledge.

Sugihara, K. (2004). East Asian path. *Economic and Political Weekly, 39*(34), 3855–3858.

Sugihara, K. (2007). The second noel Butlin lecture: Labour-intensive industrialisation in global history. *Australian Economic History Review, 47*(2), 121–154.

Sugihara, K. (2008). Multiple paths of economic development in global history. In *Multiple paths of economic development in global history, proceedings of the symposium in commemoration of the executive committee meeting of the IEHA* (pp. 1–29). Kyoto University Global COE Program on Sustainable Humanosphere and Osaka University Grants-in-Aid for Scientific Research Project on Global History: Center for Southeast Asian Studies, Kyoto University.

Sugihara, K. (2010). Minamiajiagata Hattenkeiro no Tokushitsu (The characteristics of the South Asian path of development). *Minamiajiakenkyū (The Journal of the Japanese Association for South Asian Studies), 2010*(22), 170–184.

Sugihara, K. (2012). Nettai Seizonken no Rekishiteki Shatei (The historical scope of the tropical humanosphere). In K. Sugihara, K. Wakimura, K. Fujita, & A. Tanabe (Eds.), *Rekishi no nakano Nettai Seizonken: Ontai Paradaimu wo Koete (The torpical humanosphere in history: Beyond the temperate paradigm)*. Kyoto: Kyoto University Press.

Sugihara, K. (2015). Shokuminchiki niokeru Kokunai Shijō no Keisei (The formation of domestic market in the colonial era). In A. Tanabe, K. Sugihara, & K. Wakimura (Eds.), *Gendai Indo 1: Tayōsei Shakai no Chōsen (Contemporary India 1: The challenge of diversity society)* (pp. 197–222). Tokyo: The University of Tokyo Press.

Sugihara, K. (2020). *Sekaishi nonakano Higahi Ajia no Kiseki (The East Asian miracle in global history)*. Nagoya: The University of Nagoya Press.

Tamanoi, M. (1983). Reconsidering the concept of post-peasantry: The transformation of the Masoveria system in old Catalonia. *Ethnology, 22*(4), 295–305.

Tanabe, A. (2006). Introduction. In M. Kimura & A. Tanabe (Eds.), *The state in India: Past and present* (pp. 1–34). New Delhi: Oxford University Press.

Tanabe, A. (2015). Kāsuto Shakai kara Tayōsei Shakai e: Gendai Indoron no Paradaimu Tenkan (From caste society to diversity society: Paradigm shift in India studies). In A. Tanabe, K. Sugihara, & K. Wakimura (Eds.), *Gendai Indo 1: Tayōsei Shakai no Chōsen (Contemporary India 1: The challenge of diversity society)* (pp. 3–36). Tokyo: The University of Tokyo Press.

Tanabe, A. (2017). Conditions of 'Developmental Democracy': New logic of inclusion and exclusion in globalizing India. In M. Mio, & A. Dasgupta (Eds.), *Looking beyond the state: Changing forms of inclusion and exclusion in India*. London: Routledge.

Tanabe, A. (2018). Spirituality as the source of human creativity: Insights from India. In S. Yamash'ta, T. Yagi, & S. Hill (Eds.), *The Kyoto manifesto for global economics: The platform of community, humanity, and spirituality* (pp. 179–193). Singapore: Springer.

Tanabe, A. (2021a). *Caste and equality in India: A historical anthropology of diverse society and vernacular democracy*. London: Routledge.

Tanabe, A. (2021b). From sharing risks to taking risks: The system of entitlements and its fragmentation in eighteenth and nineteenth century Orissa. In K. Fujita & T. Mizushima (Eds.), *Sustainable development in India: Groundwater irrigation, energy use, and food production* (pp. 38–65). London: Routledge.

Tanabe, A. (2022). Varieties of money in early modern India: Connecting diversities in market, society and polity. *Choiki Bunka Kagaku Kiyo (interdisciplinary Cultural Studies), 26*, 127–152.

Tanabe, A., & Fujita, K. (2021). Transformation of the socio-economic structure in a village society in Odisha. In: K. Fujita (Ed.), *Mid-term report of the grant-in-aid research project "New Stage of South Asian Agriculture and Rural Economy:Integrated Study on the Dynamism of Mobility in Land and Labor" (FY2016–21)* (pp. 89–123). Kyoto: The Center for Southeast Asian Studies.

Tejani, S. (2016). Jobless growth in India: An investigation. *Cambridge Journal of Economics, 40*(3), 843–870.

Thomas, J. J. (2013). Explaining the 'Jobless' growth in Indian manufacturing. *Journal of the Asia Pacific Economy, 18*(4), 673–692.

Todd, E. (1987). *The causes of progress: Culture, authority, and change* (trans. Boulind, R.). Oxford: Basil Balckwell.

Tokita-Tanabe, Y. (2021). Reimagining familial relationships: Intimate networks and kinship practices in Odisha, India. *Contemporary South Asia, 29*(1), 66–80.

Varshney, A. (1995). *Democracy, development, and the countryside*. Cambridge: Cambridge University Press.

Wakimura, K. (2009). Kinben Kamumei wa Okottanoka? Indoshi ni okeru "Tochi Kishōka" (Was there an industrious revolution?: Land scarcity in Indian history) " In M. Oshima (Ed.), *Tochi Kishōka to Kinben Kakumei no Hikakushi (Comparative history of land scarcity and industrious revolution)* (pp. 251–274). Kyoto: Minerva Shobō.

Washbrook, D. (1993). Land and labour in late eighteenth-century South India: The golden age of Pariah? In P. Robb (Ed.), *Dalit movements and the meanings of labour in India* (pp. 68–86). New Delhi: Oxford University Press.

Washbrook, D. (1988). Progress and problems: South Asian economic and social history c.1720–1860. *Modern Asian Studies, 22*(1), 57–96.

Weber, M. (1958). *The religion of India: The sociology of hinduism and buddhism* (trans. Gerth, H.).

Wittfogel, K. A. (1957). *Oriental despotism: A comparative study of total power*. New Haven: Yale University Press.

Wong, R. B. (1997). *China transformed: Historical change and the limits of European experience*. Ithaca: Cornell University Press.

Wong, R. B. (2004). Asia in the future of economic history. *Economic and Political Weekly, 39*(52), 5669–5672.

World Economic Forum. (2019). *Future of Consumption in Fast-Growth Consumer Markets: INDIA*. https://www3.weforum.org/docs/WEF_Future_of_Consumption_Fast-Growth_Consumers_markets_India_report_2019.pdf.

Yanagisawa, H. (2014). *Gendai Indo Keizai: Hatten no Engen Kiseki Tenbō (The contemporary Indian economy: Origins, trajectories, and prospects of development)*. Nagoya: The University of Nagoya Press.

Yanagisawa, H. (2015). Hikitsuzuku Kadai: Kakusashakai no Kōzō (The persistent agenda: The structure of disparate society). In T. Mizushima & H. Yanagisawa (Eds.), *Gendai Indo 2: Yōyū suru Toshi Nōson (Contemporary India 2: The fusion of the urban and the rural)* (pp. 325–329). Tokyo: The University of Tokyo Press.

Chapter 2
Economic Growth and Structural Change: The Case of India

Kazuo Mino

Abstract Structural transformation of the Indian economy has two distinctive features: (i) the employment share of the agricultural sector has not declined much, although its income share has been rapidly decreasing with economic growth and; (ii) the service sector started expanding before the income share of the manufacturing sector has not increased enough. In this chapter, we mainly focus on the first feature by examining a two-sector development model with labor market frictions. Our model exhibits an unbalanced decline in the employment and income shares of the agricultural sector.

2.1 Introduction

Currently, India has the fifth-largest GDP and the second-largest population in the world. During the last three decades, the presence and influence of India in the global economy have significantly increased. In particular, India's rapid economic growth after the late 1990s has been attracting considerable attention. As well as other emerging economies, the recent economic growth in Indian economy has been associated with the continuing transformation of industrial structure. As is well known, the structural change of a growing economy displays a similar pattern: as an economy grows, the income and employment shares of the agricultural sector continue declining, while those of the service sector continue rising. Moreover, the income and employment shares of the manufacturing sector first rise, and then they start falling. Figure 2.1 shows the typical patterns of changes in the GDP and employment shares of each sector.[1] As an example from the real data. Figure 2.2 displays changes in

---

[1] Figure 2.1 is taken from a numerical example examined by Hori et al. (2015).

K. Mino (✉)
Institute of Economic Research, Kyoto University, Yoshida Honmachi, Sakyo-ku, Kyoto, Japan
e-mail: mino@kier.kyoto-u.ac.jp

© Springer Nature Singapore Pte Ltd. 2022
K. Mino and T. Yagi (eds.), *The Cultural Basis of Economic Growth in India*,
Creative Economy, https://doi.org/10.1007/978-981-15-9305-5_2

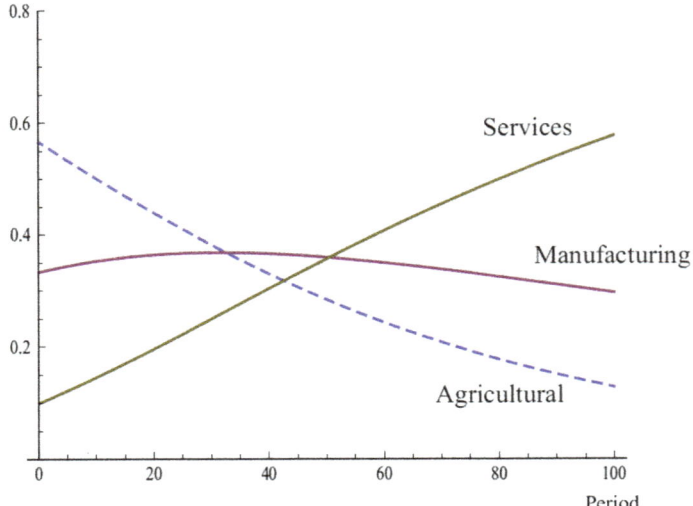

Fig. 2.1 The typical profile of structural change

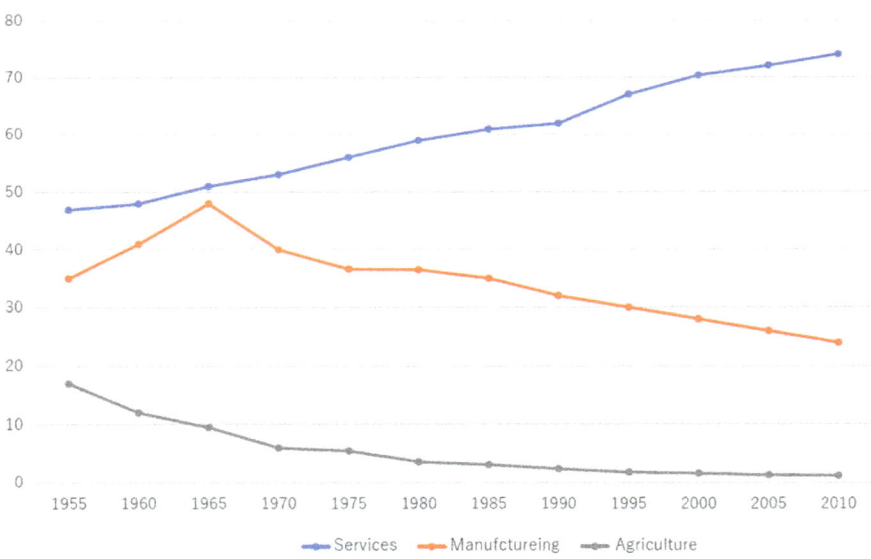

Fig. 2.2 The structural change in Japan from 1955 to 2010

the GDP share of each industry in Japan. (The profile of changes in the employment shares exhibit a similar pattern.)[2]

The structural change of the Indian economy exhibits such a profile. However, a close inspection reveals that there are two prominent features which are not observed in the growth processes of East Asian countries such as Japan, China (PRC), Taiwan, and South Korea who experienced rapid economic growth. The first feature of the relation between growth and structural change in India is that while the income share of the agricultural sector has been decreasing, the employment share of that sector has not been declining much. As shown in the next section, the continuing shrink of the GDP share of the agricultural sector has not been associated with a proportional decrease in its employment share. As a result, the average income of workers in agriculture has relatively decreased. Despite the recent income expansion, India's per capita GDP in 2018 was 158th in the world, so that India is still classified as a poor country according to the world economic outlook issued by the International Monetary Fund (IMF). The large employment share and low wages in the agricultural sector is the main cause of the low per capita income in India.

The second feature observed in India's data is that compared to the emerging economies in East Asia, the GDP and employment shares of the manufacturing sector shows a relatively low level of expansion. In general, an emerging economy expands the manufacturing industry before the service sector starts a rapid expansion. However, In the case of India, the service sector started a high level of growth before the manufacturing industries sufficiently expanded. Consequently, a substantial decrease in the GDP share of the agricultural sector has been mostly absorbed by a rapid expansion of the service sector rather than that of the manufacturing sector.

In this paper, we first summarize the basic facts about growth and structural change in India after the 1950s. We then construct a simple model that may capture the prominent features of the structural transformation of the Indian economy mentioned above. In our model economy, there are two production sectors, agricultural and non-agricultural. We first confirm that as assumed in the standard modeling of growth and structural change, if the labor market realizes an efficient allocation of the labor force between the two production sectors, we obtain the conventional outcomes. Namely, rises in productivity both in the agricultural and non-agricultural sectors shift the labor force from the agricultural sector to the non-agricultural sectors. Consequently, the decrease in the income share of the agricultural sector is associated with a proportional decline in its employment share.

We then introduce a cost of labor shift between the two sectors: a worker in the agricultural sector must pay an additional learning cost to work in the non-agricultural sector. This cost of labor shift reflects the skills needed for non-agricultural production, and it decreases with the ability owned by an agent. We assume that the learning ability is distributed according to a stationary distribution function. We also assume that each agent determines to work in the non-agricultural sector, if and only if the

---

[2] The linkage between economic growth and structural change has been a major topic in growth economics. Herrendorf et al. (2014) presents a detailed survey on this topic. See also Jorgenson and Timmer (2011).

real wage in the non-agricultural sector exceeds the real wage in the agricultural
sector plus the learning cost for working in the non-agricultural sector. We show that
in the presence of labor market frictions, a higher level of agricultural productivity
raises the employment share of agriculture: an opposite outcome to that obtained in
the standard setting. Moreover, while a rise in the productivity of the manufacturing
sector reallocates the labor force from the agricultural to the manufacturing sectors,
its impact is relatively small, compared to that held in the standard model with a
frictionless labor market.

This chapter mostly focuses on the first feature of the Indian structural change,
that is, unbalanced declines of the GDP share and the employment share of the
agricultural sector. However, when discussing the possible extension of the base
model, we show that a three-sector version of the base model would explain that the
growth of the manufacturing sector in India has achieved a relatively low level of
expansion.

The rest of the chapter is organized as follows. Section 2.2 summarizes the basic
facts about growth and structural change in India. Section 2.3 considers the baseline
analytical framework without labor market frictions. Section 2.4 presents our main
discussion that treats a growth model in which there are frictions of labor allocation
between the different production sectors. Section 2.5 treats possible extensions of
our model. Section 2.6 gives economic implication of our model analysis. Section 2.7
concludes.

2.2 Background Facts

Before presenting our model that is suitable for discussing growth and structural
change in India, we summarize the basic facts about India's growth and structural
change after the Second World War.

2.2.1 Economic Growth in India

Before its independence in 1947, the per capita income in India had stagnated for
nearly ten centuries including the British colonial era from 1858 to 1947: the per
capita income was almost the same over 1000 years.[3] Thus, modern development and
growth in India started after independence. From economic as well as political viewpoints, the era after independence is commonly divided into the before-liberalization
period from 1947 to 1991, and the after-liberalization period, 1991 and thereafter.
The graphs in Fig. 2.3 show the changes in population, per capita income, real growth
rate of GDP, and investment GDP ratio in India from 1950 to 2019. Those graphs

---

[3] Roy (2002) presents a useful overview of India's economic history before the independence.

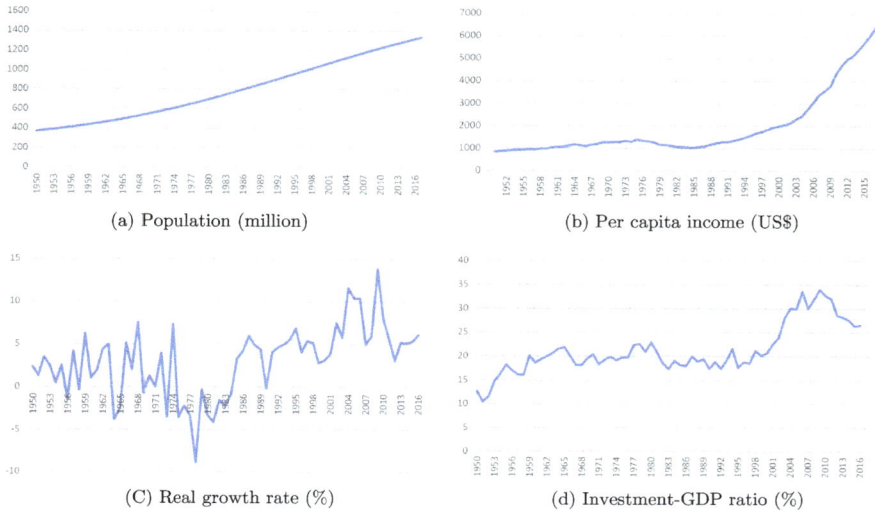

Fig. 2.3 a–d Changes in population, per-capita GDP, real growth rate, investment-GDP ratio in India from 1950 to 2019

reveal that, except for population, the per capita income as well as the growth rate of GDP started increasing after liberalization.

As pointed out by Basu (2018), the Indian economic policy during the pre-liberalization period was heavily influenced by British social democracy and the planned economy of the Soviet Union. As a result, economic policies in this era were characterized by economic interventionism, a large-scale government-run public firms, business regulation, and central planning. India's Five-Year Plans followed the central planning of the Soviet Union. However, India's interventionism is more modest than the extreme Soviet style central command system. The policy of concentrating simultaneously on capital-intensive heavy industry and subsidizing low-skill cottage industries. Although modern economic growth started after the independence, the average growth rates of GDP and per capita income during the pre-liberalization period were still modest.

Economic liberalization in India was initiated in 1991 by Prime Minister Narasimha Rao and Finance Minister Manmohan Singh. The collapse of the Soviet Union, which was India's major trading partner during the pre-liberalization period, and a rapid increase in oil prices caused by the Gulf Wars, gave rise to a major balance-of-payments crisis in India. To cope with the crisis, India asked for a $1.8 billion loan from the International Monetary Fund (IMF), and the IMF demanded the Indian government to realize a large-scale economic de-regulation in return for the loan. Responding to the IMF's requirement, the Rao government conducted substantial economic reforms in 1991. The reforms included lowering tariffs and interest rates, terminating many public monopolistic firms, as well as allowing foreign direct investment (FDI) in many sectors. Moreover, in the process of subsequent reforms during the 1990s, the Indian government conducted financial liberalization. As a result of those reforms, the Indian economy started prolonged economic growth, together with rises in life expectancy and literacy rates. In particular, India experienced high growth rates, averaging 9% from 2003 to 2007. The growth rate then dropped to 5.6% due to the 2007–2008 global financial crisis. However, in 2013, the GDP growth rate accelerated to 6.4% from the previous year's 5.5%. The acceleration continued in 2014 and 2015, with growth rates of 7.5% and 8.0% respectively. In 2015, India grew faster than China for the first time since 1991. However, the growth rate subsequently decelerated, to 7.1% and 6.6% in 2016 and 2017, respectively, mainly because of the 2016 Indian banknote demonetization and rises in goods and services taxes.[4]

2.2.2 Structural Change in India

When discussing the relationship between economic growth and industrial structural change in India, it is useful to compare India's profile with that of China (People's Republic of China: PRC). China and India are the two largest emerging economies in the world. These two economies have been following largely similar patterns of growth and development. In particular, both India and China started continuing rapid expansion of their GDP after the substantial economic reforms in the 1980s and 1990s. However, as pointed out in Sect. 2.1, the structural change in the Chinese economy has been exhibiting the conventional pattern of structural transformation, whereas India's structural change has been showing irregularities.

China is the world's most populous country and has the second-largest GDP. In parallel with the graphs in Fig. 2.3, the graphs in Fig. 2.4 show changes in population, per-capita income, growth rate of real GDP, and investment to GDP ratio in China from 1950 to 2019. Additionally, Table 2.1 compares the key magnitudes of both countries in 2018.[5]

The economic structure of India and China changed as a result of substantial economic reforms. In the early 1980s, the industrial structure in India was still dominated by agriculture: the employment share and the GDP (value-added) share of the agricultural sector were repetitively 69.4 and 37.6% in 1980. This situation gradually changed due to a series of economic reforms that started in the early 1990s. In 2010, the employment share of the agricultural sector accounted for 52.80% of employment and 15.20% of GDP. On the other hand the employment share of the industrial sector was 13.45% of employment in 1981, and it increased to 19.90% in 2010. At the same time, the GDP share of the service sector increased from 37.87% to 58.27% from 1980 to 2010. Such an increase in the GDP share was associated with an increase in the sector's employment share, which changed from 17.20% in 1981

---

[4] See Bhalla and Surjit (2011), Datt and Ravallion (2002), and Shimizu (2009) for further discussion on economic growth in India after the independence.

[5] Song et al. (2011) constructs a model that depicts recent economic growth in China.

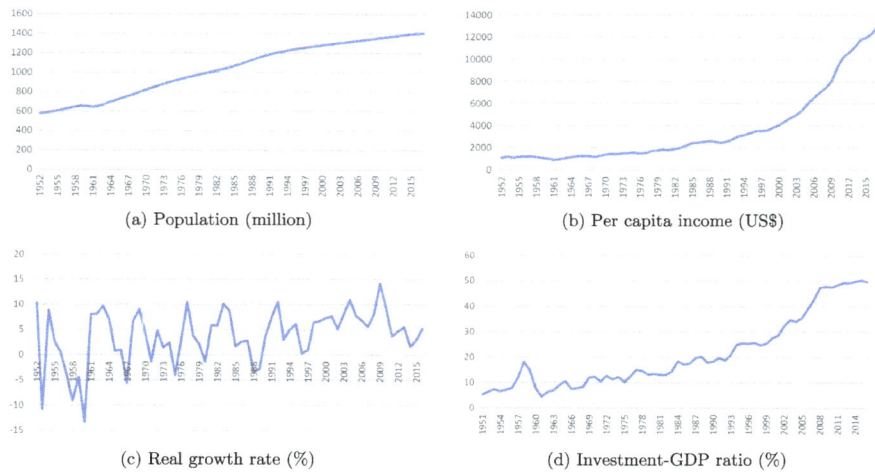

(a) Population (million)

(b) Per capita income (US$)

(c) Real growth rate (%)

(d) Investment-GDP ratio (%)

Fig. 2.4 **a–d** Changes in population growth, per-capita income, growth rate of real GGP, nvestment-GDP ratio in China from 1950 to 2019

Table 2.1 China and India in 2018 (*Source* IMF World Economy Outlook)

	Population	Share of the global GDP	Per capita GDP
China	11.39 billion	2nd	$8600 (75th in the world)
India	13.31 billion	6th	$1998 (145th in the world)

to 27.35% in 2010. The expansion of the service sector absorbs largely medium and highly skilled labor. As mentioned earlier, the rough sketch of the industrial structural transformation in India demonstrates prominent features: (i) the employment share of the agriculture sector has not been declined much despite a continuing decrease in the income share of that sector, and (ii) the service sector started expanding before the manufacturing sector grew substantially.

The profile of structural change in China basically similar to that in India. However, as Table 2.2 shows, there are substantial quantitative differences. As for the GDP share of the agricultural sector, the change in China was similar to that in India: its share dropped from 32% in 1981 to 9.3% in 2010. Note that, in contrast to India, the employment share of agriculture also decreased substantially from 59 to 32% in 2010. As mentioned in Sect. 2.1, the proportional falls in the GDP and employment shares of the agricultural sector is a typical profile of structural change in many countries. Furthermore, compared to those in China, the GDP and employment shares of the manufacturing sector in India were relatively low. And the GDP and employment shares of services started continuing expansion before the manufacturing sector grew substantioally.

Table 2.2 GDP shares andeEmployment shares in India and China (*Source* GGDC 10 Sector Data)

	Real GDP share (%)						
	India				China		
	1960	1990	2010		1960	1990	2010
Agriculture	53.7	31.5	16.1	Agriculture	42.1	22.4	9.3
Manufacturing	21.4	30.4	32.7	Manufacturing	29.2	45.3	48.1
Servies	24.9	38.1	51.2	Servies	28,7	32.3	42.6
	Employment share (%)						
	1960	1990	2010		1960	1990	2010
Agriculture	71.9	66.4	54.7	Agriculture	72.3	58.2	31.9
Manufaturing	11.7	13.2	19.5	Manufaturing	15.5	22.3	28.5
Services	16.4	20.4	25.8	Services	12..2	19.5	39.6

Like India, China was dominated by the agricultural industry: the agricultural sector accounted for 58.0% of employment and 32.5% of real GDP in 1981. Due to the substantial reforms initiated by Deng Xiaoping that started in 1978, the economic situation in China completely changed to rapid and widespread industrialization. By 2010, the employment share of the agricultural sector declined to 31.9% and its GDP share to 9.3%. The manufacturing sector's employment share increased 1.13 times from 25.4% in 1981 to 28.8% in 2010; and its income share increased 1.07 times from 45.5% in 1981 to 48.8% in 2010. The increase in the GDP share of the manufacturing sector from1991 to 2001 was partly due to changes in ownership in the mid-1990s. On the other hand, the expansion of the service sector's employment share was much higher than its GDP share from 1981 to 2010. During this period, the employment share of the service sector increased 2.4 times from 16.4% to 39.3%, whereas its GDP share increased 1.9 times from 22.0% to 41.7%. As Table 2.2 shows, the service sector's shares of both employment and GDP in China were initially lower than those of India. However, in the process of a series of economic reforms, the Chinese government enhanced the market economy and allowed private ownership. Additionally, China participated in the World Trade Organization in 2001. This lead to rapid increases in exports and FDI, which contributed to China's rapid growth of income and employment in the 2000s.

The patterns of changes in the employment and income shares in both India and China demonstrate that economic activities have shifted from the agricultural sector to the industrial and service sectors. Thus, the linkage between economic growth and industrial structural change in both countries basically follows that of other countries that had experienced modern economic growth and development. The expansion of the service sector in both countries was mainly attributed to rapid urbanization, a rising standard of living as well as an increase in the number of middle- and upper-income households. In particular, an increase in foreign demand for the demand for information technology and software services accelerated growth of the services sector in India. However, as mentioned earlier, India's employment

share of the agricultural sector was still 53%, which is much higher than China's
share (32%) in 2010. Then, what is the main reason of such a slow decline of the
employment share of the agricultural sector in India? Of course, there are prominent
differences between the two countries. First, as for economic reforms, the Chinese
government implemented stronger reforms than the Indian government. The strong
democratic traditions in India make it difficult to undertake reforms as serious as
those conducted in China. For example, the government's strategies of labor reform
and tax reform conducted taken by the Chinese government were more efficient
than those conducted in India Moreover, compared to those in China, the economic
reforms in India have been less focused on manufacturing industries than on services
such as banking, transport, and telecommunications as well as software services. Due
to the differences in the economic reforms, the per capita GDP became substantially
higher in China than in India.

Although we do not deny the importance of institutional as well as political differences in India and China may give rise to the difference in growth-structural change
profiles, in the model analysis conducted below, we present an alternative exposition
emphasizing that the labor market frictions decreasing the speed of sectoral shift of
labor may be larger in India than in China.[6]

2.3 The Baseline Model Without Labor Market Frictions

2.3.1 Modeling Structural Change

In the foregoing studies on the relation between economic growth and structural
change, researchers have employed two alternative approaches. The one is based on
the assumption that there are divergences in productivity change among the different
production sectors. If the growth rate of the total factor productivity (TFP) of the non-
agricultural sector is higher than that of the agricultural sector and if the preferences
of consumers are homothetic, then the relative price of agricultural goods increases,
which promotes substitution from agricultural goods for non-agricultural goods in
consumption demand so that the expenditure share of the non-agricultural goods
rises. As a consequence, the consumption demand for non-agricultural goods grows
faster than the demand for agricultural goods, which raises the relative income as
well as employment shares of the non-agricultural good sector. This approach was
initiated by Baumol (1967) and a recent sample includes Echevarria (1997), Ngai and
Pissarides (2007), and Acemoglu and Guerrieri (2008). The second approach is based
on the demand-induced structural change due to the presence of non-homothetic
preferences. For example, Kongsamut et al. (2001) use a Stone-Geary utility function
to consider the dynamics of sectoral labor reallocation. Foellmi et al. (2008) introduce
a hierarchic utility function to obtain nonlinear Engel curves for the various products,

---

[6] Mallick (2017) presents a detailed study on the comparison of structural changes in China and
India.

which generates consumption cycles. Provided that demand functions only depend on the relative position of the product in the hierarchy, they also show that structural change is consistent with the Kaldor facts. Hori et al. (2015) also derive the same outcome by using a model with commodity specific habit formation in consumption.[7]

Moreover, several authors such as Matsuyama (1991) and Guillo et al. (2010) combine those alternative models of structural change. Among others, Matsuyama (1992) presents a highly tractable model of structural transformation that incorporates non-homothetic preferences as well as sectoral unbalanced productivity change. Our baseline model without labor market frictions follows Matsuyama (1992).[8]

2.3.2 Setup

Production

Consider a closed economy with two production sectors: one sector produces agricultural goods and the other produces non-agricultural goods. According to the conventional classification of commodities, non-agricultural goods involve manufacturing goods as well as services. The production function of the agricultural sector in period t is specified as

$$Y_{a,t} = A_t F\left(N_{.a,t}\right), \tag{2.1}$$

where $Y_{a,t}$ and $N_{a,t}$ respectively denote the output and labor input of the agricultural sector, and A_t represents the total factor productivity (TFP) of that sector. We assume that labor is necessary to produce and the marginal productivity is diminishing. Thus, $F\left(N_{a,t}\right)$ satisfies

$$F(0) = 0, \quad F'\left(N_{a,t}\right) > 0, \quad F''\left(n_{a,t}\right) < 0.$$

Similarly, the production function of the non-agricultural sector is

$$Y_{m,t} = M_t G\left(N_{m,t}\right), \tag{2.2}$$

where $Y_{m,t}$, $N_{m,t}$ and M_t denote output, labor input and TFP of the non-agricultural sector, respectively. It is also assumed that

$$G(0) = 0, \quad G'\left(N_{m,t}\right) > 0, \quad G''\left(N_{m,t}\right) < 0.$$

---

[7] See also Herrendorf et al. (2013) for a further discussion of the role of preference structure in structural transformation of a growing economy.

[8] Matsuyama (1992) is based on a two-sector model of economic development examined by Matsuyama (1991). A useful discussion on the modeling of structural transformation is given by Chap. 21 in Acemoglu (2009).

Final goods and factor markets are assumed to be competitive. Hence, the representative firms in the agricultural and the non-agricultural sectors respectively selects its labor input to maximize profits

$$\pi_{a,t} = A_t F\left(N_{.a,t}\right) - w_t N_{a,t},$$
$$\pi_{m,t} = p_t M_t G\left(N_{m,t}\right) - w_t N_{m,t},$$

where p_t is the price of non-agricultural goods in terms of agricultural goods, $w_{a,t}$ and $w_{m,t}$ are wage rate held in the agricultural and the non-agricultural goods sectors in terms of the agricultural good. Profit maximization gives the following first-order conditions:

$$w_{a,t} = A_t F'\left(N_{a,t}\right), \quad w_{m,t} = p_t M_t G'\left(N_{m,t}\right). \tag{2.3}$$

We assume that the labor market is perfectly competitive and labor can freely shift between the two sectors. Therefore, the competitive real wages (in terms of the agricultural good) satisfy the following:

$$w_{a,t} = w_{m,t} = w_t. \tag{2.4}$$

As a result, from (2.3) we obtain

$$p_t = \frac{A_t F'\left(N_{a,t}\right)}{M_t G'\left(N_{m,t}\right)}. \tag{2.5}$$

Namely, the relative price, p_t, equals the relative magnitudes of marginal productivity of labor.

Consumption

In Matsuyama's model, it is assumed that the representative household lives forever, and it determines the entire path of the optimal consumption plan at the outset. In the baseline model, we consider a non-overlapping generations economy in which agents in each generation live for one period. This setting is employed just for simplifying model manipulation. In Sect. 2.5, we show that the model can be extended to a more general environment in which agents in each generation live for two periods.

The agents are homogeneous and constitute a continuum with a mass of the population, N. We assume that the population stays constant over time. The agents in each cohort constitute a representative household. The household consumes the agricultural and non-agricultural goods, and the utility function of the household who lives in period t is given by

$$U_t = \beta \log\left(c_{a,t} - \gamma\right) + \log\left(c_{m,t}\right), \quad \gamma > 0, \quad \beta > 0, \tag{2.6}$$

where $c_{a,t}$ and $c_{m,t}$ respectively denote the consumption levels of agricultural good and non-agricultural good of the representative household. Here, a positive constant

γ represents the basic consumption of the agricultural good, and β shows a relative weight on the felicity generated by agricultural good consumption relative to the felicity of the non-agricultural good consumption.

The household maximizes U_t by selecting $c_{a,t}$ and $c_{m,t}$ subject to the flow budget constraint

$$c_{a,t} + p_t c_{m,t} = I_t,$$

where I_t is the total income of the household. Since we have assumed that the production technology of both sectors exhibits diminishing returns in labor input, the household receives the quasi profits as well as wage payments. Hence, I_t equals the total value of outputs:

$$I_t = w_t n_{a,t} + w_t n_{m,t} + \pi_{a,t} + \pi_{m,t}. \tag{2.7}$$

The condition for the optimal selection of agricultural and non-agricultural goods consumption is that the marginal rate of substitution between two goods equals the relative price so that we obtain

$$\frac{c_{a,t} - \gamma}{c_{m,}} = p_t. \tag{2.8}$$

Equilibrium Conditions

We have assumed that the population of each generation is N, and thus the aggregate consumption of each good is expressed as $C_{i,t} = N c_{i,t}$ $(i = a, m)$. Hence, (2.8) yields

$$C_{a,t} = N\gamma + p_t C_{m,t}. \tag{2.9}$$

We consider a closed economy, and, hence, the market equilibrium conditions of the final goods market are

$$C_{i,t} = Y_{i,t}, \quad i = a, m. \tag{2.10}$$

In addition, it is assumed that the labor is fully employed, so that the labor market equilibrium condition is

$$N_{a,t} + N_{m,t} = N. \tag{2.11}$$

Using, (2.5), (2.9) and (2.10), we obtain the following condition:

$$F\left(N_{a,t}\right) - \frac{\gamma N}{A_t} + \frac{F'\left(N_{a,t}\right)}{G'\left(N - N_{a,t}\right)} G\left(N - N_{a,t}\right) \tag{2.12}$$

This equation determines the equilibrium level of $N_{a,t}$ under a given level of A_t. Using (2.12), we find the following:

$$\frac{dN_{a,t}}{dA_t} = -\frac{G'}{(F'G' - F'')A_t^2} < 0, \qquad \frac{dN_{a,t}}{dN} = \frac{G'}{(F'G' - F'')} > 0.$$

Hence, as long as

$$F(N) - \frac{\gamma N}{A_t} > 0,$$

there is a unique equilibrium level of $N_{a,t}$, and it is expressed as

$$N_{a,t} = L(A_t; N). \quad L_A(.) < 0, \quad L_N(.) > 0 \tag{2.13}$$

In words, a rise in the productivity of the agricultural sector lowers labor allocation to the agricultural sector, while a higher population increases the labor input of the agricultural sector.

Note that in this formulation, the productivity level of the non-agricultural sector, M_t, does not affect the labor allocation between the two sectors. This outcome stems from the logarithmic utility function assumed in (2.6). To see this, suppose that the utility function is given by

$$U_t = \beta \frac{(c_{a,t} - \gamma)^{1-\eta}}{1 - \eta} + \frac{c_{m,t}^{1-\eta}}{1 - \eta}, \quad \eta > 0, \quad \eta \neq 1.$$

Then the first-order condition for an optimum becomes

$$c_{a,t} - \gamma = p_t^{\frac{1}{\eta}} c_{m,t}.$$

Thus, Eq. (2.12) is replaced with

$$F(N_{a,t}) = \frac{N\gamma}{A_t} + \left[\frac{F'(N_{a,t})}{G'(N - N_{a,t})}\right]^{\frac{1}{\eta}} \left(\frac{M_t}{A_t}\right)^{1-\frac{1}{\eta}} G(N - N_{a,t}).$$

This equation means that if $\eta > 1$, then a higher A_t decreases the equilibrium level of $N_{a,t}$. However, the level of M_t affects the equilibrium value of $N_{a,t}$.

2.3.3   Growth and Structural Change

Technical Progress

Following Matsuyama (1991), we assume that there is learning by doing in the non-agricultural sector. The total factor productivity in the non-agricultural sector changes according to

$$M_{t+1} = \theta Y_{m,t} + (1 - \delta) M_t, \quad \theta > 0, \quad \delta \in [0, 1), \tag{2.14}$$

where δ is the rate of depreciation of knowledge in the non-agricultural good production. The above expression means that the current level of TFP of the non-agricultural sector is determined by the cumulative production level of the non-agricultural goods:

$$M_t = \theta \sum_{j=1}^{\infty} (1 - \delta)^j Y_{m,t-j}.$$

Since we have assumed that each generation lives for one period, the accumulated knowledge, M_t, is transferred from one generation to the next through intergenerational externalities: $t + 1$-*th* generation can learn the knowledge M_t that is left by the t-*th* generation.

From (2.2) and (2.14), the growth rate of TFP in the non agricultural good sector is expressed as,

$$\frac{M_{t+1} - M_t}{M_t} = \theta G \left(N - L \left(A_t, \, N \right) \right). \tag{2.15}$$

If there is no continuing technical change in the agricultural sector, A_t stays constant over time. In this case, (2.15) gives the balanced growth rate of the non-agricultural output. Since a rise in A depresses $L\,(.)$, a rise in TFP of the agricultural sector accelerates expansion of the non-agricultural sector. Moreover, an increase in the population , N, also raises productivity growth due to the scale effect.

Structural Change
Note that from (2.5) the relative price satisfies

$$p_t = \frac{A_t F' \left(L \left(A_t \right) \right)}{M_t G' \left(N - L \left(A_t \right) \right)}. \tag{2.16}$$

Thus, A_t stays constant and M_t continues rising according to (2.16), the price of non-agricultural goods continues decreasing, which means that the agricultural good becomes expensive relative to the non-agricultural goods. In contrast, if the agricultural productivity increases substantially, (2.16) shows that p_t may rise, so that the agriculture goods become less expensive relative to the non-agriculture goods. Those results fit well to our intuition concerning resource allocation and price changes in the neoclassical environment.

Finally, note that the GDP share of the agricultural sector is

$$\mu_t = \frac{Y_{a,t}}{Y_{a,t} + p_t Y_{m,t}} = \frac{F\left(L\left(A_t, N\right)\right) G'\left(L\left(A_t, N\right)\right)}{F\left(L\left(A_t, N\right)\right) G'\left(L\left(A_t, N\right)\right) + F'\left(L\left(A_t, N\right)\right)}.$$

We see that $\frac{d\mu_t}{dA} < 0$. Consequently, a rise in the productivity of the agricultural sector decreases not only the labor employment of the agricultural sector but also its GDP share of that sector. It is to be noted that the continuous rise in TFP of the non-agricultural sector does not affect the labor allocation between the two sectors nor the GDP share of each sector.[9]

Summary

To sum up, the baseline model without labor market frictions presents the following results:

(i) A rise in the productivity of the agricultural sector lowers both the employment and income share of that sector.
(ii) The price of non-agricultural goods relative to the agricultural good will decline as the productivity of the non-agricultural sector rises.
(iii) Under the presence of the learning-by-doing effect in the non-agricultural sector, a rise in the productivity of the agricultural sector raises the growth rate of non-agricultural output.

Those findings fit well to the profiles of growth and industrial structural change observed in many East Asian countries, including China.[10]

2.4 The Model with Labor Market Frictions

Matsuyama's (1992) model discussed so far successfully captures the role of agricultural productivity in economic development in a coherent manner. However, in Matsuyama's neoclassical setting, the labor force freely sifts between the agricultural and non-agricultural sectors. As a result, the real wages in both sectors have the same value, and in the process of economic growth, both the employment and GDP shares of the agricultural sector uniformly decline. As emphasized in Sect. 2.2, these outcomes do not fit well with the linkage between economic growth and structural

---

[9] In this chapter, we focus of growth and structural change in a closed economy. Matsuyama (1992) also examines a small open economy in which a rise in the agricultural productivity may shrink the manufacturing good sector. This is because a higher productivity in the agricultural sector strengthens the comparative advantage in the agriculture goods under free trade. Since India is not a small country, such a conclusion may not hold.

[10] Duarte and Restuccia (2010) explore the relation between structural change and aggregate productivity of the economy from an empirical viewpoint.

transformation observed in the Indian economy. In this section, we modify the baseline, neoclassical model to depict the growth-and structural change relationship that is characteristic of the Indian economy.

2.4.1 Setup

Production

The production side of the economy is the same as before. The final goods and factor markets are competitive so that the labor demand in each sector is determined by

$$A_t F' \left(N_{a,t} \right) = w_{a,t}, \quad p_t M_t G' \left(N_{m,t} \right) = w_{m,t}. \tag{2.17}$$

Again, $w_{i,t}$ $(i = a, m)$ denotes the real wage in terms of the agricultural good. If the labor market is perfectly competitive, it holds that $w_{a,t} = w_{m,t}$, leading to the condition given by (2.5). However, as discussed below, we assume that there are frictions in the labor market, under which (2.5) fails to hold.

Households' Behavior

Unlike the previous model, we assume that agents are heterogeneous. At the outset of her life, each agent draws her ability from a given distribution function. We denote ϕ_i as agent i's ability drawn from the following cumulative distribution function of ability:

$$\text{Prob} \left(x \leq \phi \right) = \Gamma \left(\phi \right). \tag{2.18}$$

Here, the cumulative distribution function satisfies

$$\Gamma \left(\phi_{\min} \right) = 0, \quad \Gamma' \left(\phi \right) > 0, \quad \lim_{\phi \to \phi_{\max}} \Gamma \left(\phi \right) = 1,$$

where $\phi_{\min}$ denotes the minimum level of ability. As discussed below, in our model, an agent's 'ability' has a broad meaning. It may reflect the agent's learning ability, skills, family background, social status, and health status. as well as the flexibility that allows the agent to adjust to a new environment. Our key assumption is that an agent should pay an additional learning cost to work in the non-agricultural sector. The agent selects to work in the agricultural sector, if the wage in the agricultural sector, $w_{a,t}$ exceeds the discounted wage in the non-agricultural sector, $w_{m,t} / \left(1 + \psi_i \right)$, where ψ_i denotes agent i's discount factor which is determined by

$$\psi_i = \frac{\delta}{\phi_i}, \quad \delta > 0. \tag{2.19}$$

In contrast, if $w_{za,t} < w_{m,t}/(1+\psi_i)$, the agent works in the non-agricultural sector. Hence, the cutoff level of ψ^* is given by

$$(1+\psi^*)\, w_{a,t} = w_{m,t}. \tag{2.20}$$

Hence, from (2.19) and (2.21), the cutoff level of ability is determined by the following condition:

$$\phi_t^* = \frac{\delta w_{a,t}}{w_{m,t} - w_{a,t}}. \tag{2.21}$$

We assume that $w_{m,t} > w_{a,t}$ for all $t \geq 0$. If an agent draws $\phi_i < \phi_t^*$, then she works in the agricultural good sector, while an agent with $\phi_i \geq \phi_t^*$ chooses to work in the non-agricultural sector. (We assume that an agent with $\phi_i = \phi_t^*$ works in the non-agricultural sector.) As a result, in each period, an amount of $\Gamma(\phi^*)\,N$ agents work in the agricultural sector, and $[1 - \Gamma(\phi^*)]N$ agents engage in the job of the non-agricultural sector.

We denote the consumption of agricultural and non-agricultural goods by the agents working in the agricultural sector as $c_{a,t}^a$ and $c_{m,t}^a$, respectively. Similarly, $c_{a,t}^m$ and $c_{m,t}^m$ represent consumption levels of the agents who work in the non-agricultural sector. The utility function of type j $(= a, m)$ agent is specified as

$$u_t^i = \frac{\left(c_{a,t}^j\right)^{1-\sigma}}{1-\sigma} + \frac{\left(c_{m,t}^j\right)^{1-\sigma}}{1-\sigma}. \quad 0 < \sigma < 1, \quad j = a.m. \tag{2.22}$$

In what follows, we assume that the elasticity of substitution between the agricultural and non-agricultural goods, which is $1/\sigma$, is higher than one. The budget constraint is

$$c_{a,t}^j + p_t c_{m,t}^j = I_t^j, \quad j = a, m,$$

where I_t^j is the income of type j agents. The first-order conditions for utility maximization gives

$$c_{a,t}^j = p_t^{\frac{1}{\sigma}} c_{m,t}^j.$$

The utility maximization yields the following demand functions:

$$c_{a,t}^j = \frac{I_t^j}{1 + p^{1-\frac{1}{\sigma}}}, \quad c_{m,t}^j = \frac{I_t^j p_t^{-\frac{1}{\sigma}}}{1 + p^{1-\frac{1}{\sigma}}} \left(= \frac{I_t^j}{p_t^{\frac{1}{\sigma}} + p}\right). \tag{2.23}$$

Note that under our assumption of $0 < \sigma < 1$, a rise in the relative price of the non-agricultural good, p_t, raises the consumption demand for agricultural goods, while it depresses the demand for the non-agricultural goods.

Market Equilibrium Conditions

Denoting the aggregate demand for both goods by type j agents as $C_{a,t}^{j}$ and $C_{m,t}^{j}$, these variables are defined by

$$C_{s,t}^{a} = \Gamma\left(\phi^*\right) N c_{s,t}^{a}, \quad C_{s,t}^{m} = \left[1 - \Gamma\left(\phi^*\right)\right] N c_{s,t}^{m}, \quad s = a, m. \tag{2.24}$$

From (2.23) and (2.24), the aggregate demand of the whole agents are respectively given by

$$C_{a,t} = C_{a,t}^{a} + C_{a,t}^{m} = \frac{I_t^a \Gamma\left(\phi^*\right) N I_t^a + I_t^m \left[1 - \Gamma\left(\phi^*\right)\right] N I_t^m}{1 + p^{1-\frac{1}{\sigma}}},$$

$$C_{m,t} = C_{m,t}^{a} + C_{m,t}^{m} = \frac{p_t^{-\frac{1}{\sigma}}}{1 + p^{1-\frac{1}{\sigma}}} \left\{{}^a\Gamma\left(\phi^*\right) N I_t^a + I_t^m \left[1 - \Gamma\left(\phi^*\right)\right] N I_t^m\right\}.$$

Hence, the market equilibrium condition for each good is given by

$$A_t F\left(\Gamma\left(\phi^*\right) N\right) = \frac{I_t^a \Gamma\left(\phi^*\right) N I_t^a + I_t^m \left[1 - \Gamma\left(\phi^*\right)\right] N I_t^m}{1 + p^{1-\frac{1}{\sigma}}}, \tag{2.25}$$

$$M_t G\left(\left(1 - \Gamma\left(\phi^*\right)\right) N\right) = \frac{p_t^{-\frac{1}{\sigma}}}{1 + p^{1-\frac{1}{\sigma}}} \left\{I_t^a \Gamma\left(\phi^*\right) N I_t^a + I_t^m \left[1 - \Gamma\left(\phi^*\right)\right] N I_t^m\right\} \tag{2.26}$$

These equations mean that the relative price satisfies the following condition:

$$p_t = \left[\frac{M_t G\left(\left(1 - \Gamma\left(\phi^*\right)\right) N\right)}{A_t F\left(\Gamma\left(\phi^*\right) N\right)}\right]^{-\sigma}. \tag{2.27}$$

Equation (2.27) means that if ϕ^* is fixed, a rise in the relative productivity, M_t/A_t, lowers the price of the non-agricultural goods relative to the agricultural goods. This property is the same as the behavior of the relative price in the frictionless economy shown by (2.16).

2.4.2 Technical Progress and Structural Change

The Equilibrium Level of Cutoff

Using (2.19), (2.20), and (2.21), we obtain

$$\phi_t^* = \frac{\delta A_t F'\left(\Gamma\left(\phi^*\right) N\right)}{p_t M_t G'\left(\left(1 - \Gamma\left(\phi^*\right)\right) N\right) - A_t F'\left(\Gamma\left(\phi^*\right) N\right)}.$$

Fig. 2.5 Existence of the equilibrium level of cutoff

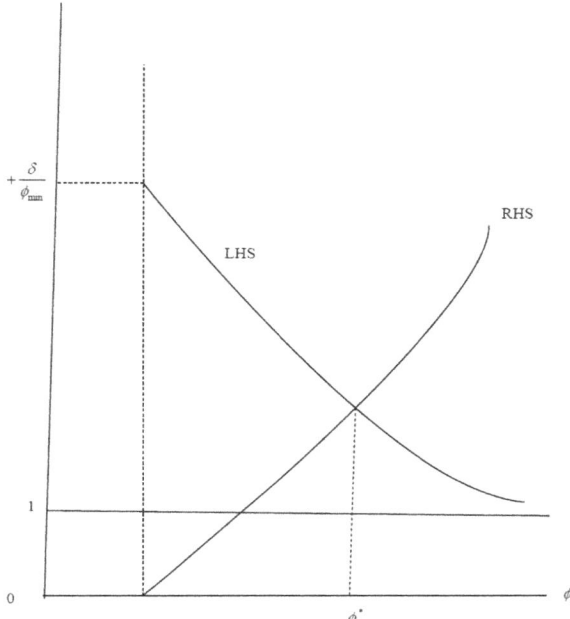

Substituting (2.27) for the above leads to the following:

$$\frac{\delta}{\phi_t^*} + 1 = \left(\frac{M_t}{A_t}\right)^{1-\sigma} \left[\frac{F((\Gamma(\phi^*)\,N)}{G((1-\Gamma(\phi^*))\,N)}\right]^{\sigma} \left[\frac{G'((1-\Gamma(\phi^*))\,N)}{F'(\Gamma(\phi^*)\,N)}\right]. \quad (2.28)$$

We see that the right-hand-side of (2.28) monotonically decreases with ϕ^*. Hence, as Fig. 2.5 depicts, there is a unique cutoff level of ϕ that fulfills the threshold condition of the occupational choice of agents.

It is also seen that a rise in M_t/A_t shifts the graph of the right-hand-side of (2.28). Thus, a rise in the productivity of the non-agricultural sector relative to the agricultural sector lowers the cutoff level of ϕ^*, meaning that the labor force shifts from the agricultural sector to the non-agricultural sector. Note that, in contrast to Matsuyama's model discussed in the previous section, a higher A_t increases the labor input in the agricultural sector. The equilibrium value of the cutoff is thus expressed as

$$\phi_t^* = \Phi\left(\frac{M_t}{A_t}\right), \quad \Phi'(.) < 0. \quad (2.29)$$

Structural Change

If the productivity rise in the non-agricultural sector grows faster than in the agricultural sector, then M_t/A_t continues rising so that the employment share of the agricultural sector will decrease. The pace of reduction in the employment share of the agricultural sector, however, depends on the shape of the distribution function of agents' ability, $\Gamma(\phi)$. It has been pointed out that the distribution of learning ability can be described by a Pareto distribution rather than a normal distribution. We thus specify $\Gamma(\phi)$ by a Pareto distribution function such as

$$\Gamma(\phi) = 1 - \left(\frac{\phi}{\phi_{\min}}\right)^{-\eta}, \quad \eta > 1, \quad \phi_{\min} > 0. \tag{2.30}$$

In the above, η is a shape parameter and $\phi_{\min}$ is a given level of minimum ability held by the agents. As is well known, the magnitude of the shape parameter expresses the degree of heterogeneity. If η is large, the share of agents who hold relatively high ability is small. On the other hand, if η is close to unity, the tail of the distribution function, $1 - \Gamma(\phi) = 1 - \Gamma(\phi) = \left(\frac{\phi}{\phi_{\min}}\right)^{-\eta}$ is 'fat', which means that the share of agents with high ability is relatively large.

To see the relationship between the degree of heterogeneity of agents and changes in the employment share due to a productivity change, we rewrite (2.28) as

$$\phi^* = \frac{\sigma}{\left(\frac{M_t}{A_t}\right)^{1-\sigma} \left[\frac{G((1-\Gamma(\phi^*))N)}{F((\Gamma(\phi^*)N)}\right]^{-\sigma} \left[\frac{G'((1-\Gamma(\phi^*))N)}{F'(\Gamma(\phi^*)N)}\right] - 1} \tag{2.31}$$

If η is large so that agents are less heterogeneous, then a change in ϕ^* has a relatively small effect on $\Gamma(\phi^*)$. Therefore, the graph of the right-hand side of (2.31) is less steep. In contrast, if η is close to 1.0 and the heterogeneity among the agents is high, the graph of the right-hand side of (2.31) is relatively steep. Since we have assumed that $0 < \sigma < 1$, if the productivity gap between the agricultural and non-agricultural sectors is widened, i.e. M_t/A_t increases, then the graph of the left-hand side of (2.31) becomes steeper. Then, as Fig. 2.6 demonstrates, a fall in the employment share of the agricultural sector due to a rise in M_t/A_t yields a larger fall in ϕ^* under a high level of η than under a low level of η. In words, a more heterogeneous economy gives rise to less decrease in the employment share of the agricultural sector as a result of a rise in the productivity gap between the agricultural and non-agricultural sectors.

On the other hand, the relative price between the agricultural and non-agricultural goods is given by

$$p_t = \frac{A_t F'\left(\Gamma\left(\phi_t^*\right) N\right)}{\left(1 - \frac{\sigma}{\phi_t^*}\right) M_t G'((1 - \Gamma(\phi_t^*)) N)}$$

Since a rise in M_t/A_t decreases ϕ^*, if η is large so that $\Gamma(\phi^*)$ is less sensitive to a change in ϕ^*, $G(.)/F(.)$ does not change much, and, hence, a fall in p_t mostly reflects a direct effect through a decrease in $(M_t/A_t)^{-\sigma}$. However, if η is small, then a

Fig. 2.6 The effect of a rise in M_t/A_t

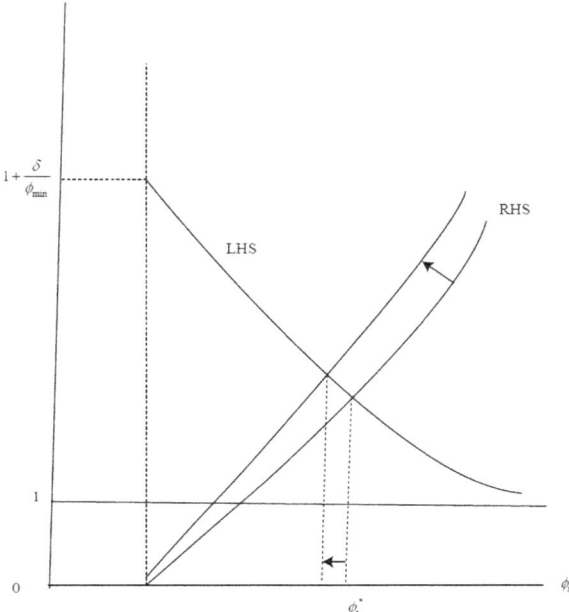

fall in ϕ^* yields a relatively large decrease in $G\,(.)\,/F\,(.)$, and, hence, a rise in M_t/A_t presents a relatively large decrease in the relative price between the agricultural and the non-agricultural goods. Additionally, the income share of the agricultural sector is given by

$$
\mu_t = \frac{AF\,(\Gamma\,(\phi^*)\,N)}{AF\,(\Gamma\,(\phi^*)\,N) + p_t M_t G\,((1 - \Gamma G\,(\phi^*))\,N)}
$$

$$
= \frac{1}{1 + \left(\frac{M_t}{A_t}\right)^{1-\sigma}\left[\frac{G((1-\Gamma(\phi^*))N)}{F(\Gamma(\phi^*)N)}\right]^{1-\sigma}}. \tag{2.32}
$$

Again, if η is large so that $G\,(.)\,/F\,(.)$ is relatively insensitive to a change in ϕ^*, the decrease in the income share, μ_t, mainly reflects the direct effect of a rise in M_t/A_t. Conversely, a low level of η enhances the effect of a change in M_t/A_t on μ_t by adding the indirect effect through the rise in $G\,(.)\,/F\,(.)$ caused by the reduction in ϕ^*.

In sum, in the context of our model, the economy in which the agents are relatively heterogeneous, a rise in the productivity gap between the agricultural and the non-agricultural sectors, M_t/A_t, gives rise to a relatively large decrease in the relative price of agricultural good and the income share of the agricultural sector as well as a relatively small reduction in the employment share of the agricultural sector.

Growth

As well as in the model without labor market frictions, we assume that A_t stays constant and that by the learning-by-doing effect, M_t changes according to (2.14). Then, in our setting, the TFP of the non-agricultural sector changes according to

$$M_{t+1}\theta G M_t \left(\left(1 - \phi_t^*\right) N\right) + (1 - \delta) M_t.$$

Then, from (2.29), the growth rate of the TFP of the non-agricultural sector is given by

$$\frac{M_{t+1} - M_t}{M_t} = \theta G \left(\left(1 - \Phi \left(\frac{M_t}{A}\right)\right)\right) - \delta. \qquad (2.33)$$

As M_t/A increases, $\phi_t^* = \Phi\left(M_t/A\right)$ falls, meaning that the TFP of the non-agricultural sector continues rising. Note that since $G\left(L_m\right)$ exhibits diminishing returns, the growth rate of TFP of the non-agricultural sector continues to decrease. As shown above, if the agents are highly heterogeneous, ϕ_t^* is less sensitive to a change in M_t/A. Therefore, in our model, economic growth due to technical progress in the non-agricultural sector is more prominent in the economy with homogeneous agents than the economy in which the agents are highly heterogeneous.

Summary

The model with labor market frictions presents the following outcomes:

 (i) If the productivity of the non-agricultural sector grows faster than that of the agricultural sector, then both employment and income shares of the agricultural sector decline. However, a fall in the employment share of the agricultural sector relatively slow if the heterogeneity in the ability of each agent is high.
 (ii) In the presence of the learning-by-doing effect in the non-agricultural sector, a rise in the relative productivity, M_t/A_t, raises the rate of expansion of the non-agricultural output.
(iii) As M_t/A_t increases, the price of the non-agricultural goods generally decreases.

Consequently, if the heterogeneity among the agents is high, our model with labor market friction exhibits not only generally observed patterns of growth and structural change but also a profile that is characteristic to the Indian economy.

2.5   Extensions

The baseline model with labor market frictions discussed so far have imposed restrictive assumptions. In this section, we show that some of those restrictions can be eliminated.

2.5.1 Endogenous Technical Progress in the Agricultural Productivity

Following Matsuyama (1992), We have assumed that continuing productivity increase is present in the non-agricultural sector alone. We now assume that there are learning-by-doing effects in the agricultural sector as well as in the non-agricultural sector.[11] Thus we assume:

$$M_{t+1} = \theta_m Y_{m,t} + (1 - \delta_m)M_t, \quad \theta_m > 0, \quad 0 < \delta_m < 1,$$
$$A_{t+1} = \theta_a Y_{a,t} + (1 - \delta_a)A_t, \quad \theta_a > 0, \quad 0 < \delta_a < 1.$$

The above formulation of the learning-by-doing effect is in parallel with that in the non-agricultural sector. Let us define: $x_t = M_t / A_t$. Then it holds that

$$\frac{M_{t+1}}{M_t} = \theta_m G \left[N - N\Gamma \left(\Phi \left(x_t \right) \right) \right] + 1 - \delta_m, \tag{2.34}$$

$$\frac{A_{t+1}}{A_t} = \theta_a F \left[N\Gamma \left(\Phi \left(x_t \right) \right) \right] + 1 - \delta_a. \tag{2.35}$$

From (2.34) and (2.35), the complete dynamic system of the economy can be expressed as

$$\frac{x_{t+1}}{x_t} = \frac{M_{t+1}}{M_t} \cdot \frac{A_t}{A_{t+1}} = \frac{\theta_m G \left[N - N\Gamma \left(\Phi \left(x_t \right) \right) \right] + 1 - \delta_m}{\theta_a F \left[N\Gamma \left(\Phi \left(x_t \right) \right) \right] + 1 - \delta_a}. \tag{2.36}$$

We see that the right-hand-side of (2.36) monotonically decreases with x_t. In the steady-state equilibrium in which x_t stays constant, it holds that

$$\theta_m G \left[N - N\Gamma \left(\Phi \left(\bar{x} \right) \right) \right] + 1 - \delta_m = \theta_a F \left[N\Gamma \left(\Phi \left(\bar{x} \right) \right) \right] + 1 - \delta_a,$$

The left-hand side of the above equitation monotonically increases with x, while its right hand side monotonically increases with x. Hence, there exists a unique level of $\bar{x}$. As Fig. 2.7 shows, there is a unique level of $\bar{x}$, and it holds global instability. This means that once the economy falls into a development stage by some exogenous shocks, x_t continues rising, which yields a continuing shift of labor force from the agricultural sector to the non-agricultural sector. However, as shown above, if the distribution of agent's ability follows a Pareto distribution and if the heterogeneity of agents' ability is relatively small, then the employment share of the agricultural sector does not decrease as fast as the income share of that sector.

---

[11] As to detailed empirical studies on sectroal technical change, see Herrendorf and Valentinyi (2012) and Herrendorf et al. (2015).

Fig. 2.7 Convergence to the
balanced growth equilibrium

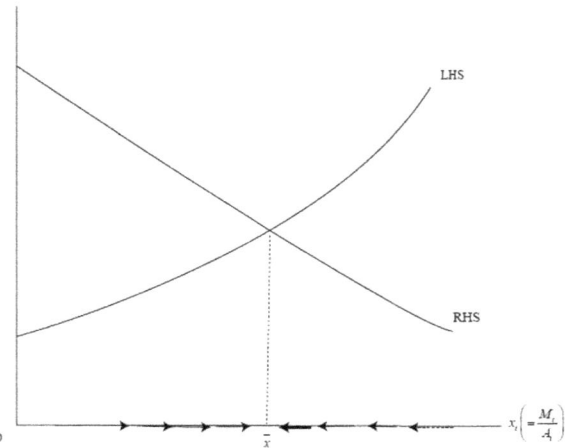

2.5.2 A Three-Sector Model

For simplicity of analysis, we have assumed that there are two types of industries
in our model economy. It is straightforward to extend our model to the standard
three-sector setting in which there are three types of industries: the agricultural,
manufacturing, and service industries.[12] In this extended framework, the production
function of each sector is given by

$$Y_{a,t} = A_t F\left(L_{a,t}\right), \quad Y_{m,t} = M_t G\left(L_{m,t}\right), \quad Y_{c,t} = S_t H\left(L_{s,t}\right).$$

Here, $Y_{s,t}$ and $L_{s,t}$ respectively denote output and labor input of the service sector.
Hence, the full employment condition of labor is now replaced with

$$L_{a,t} + L_{m,t} + L_{s,t} = N.$$

We assume that labor can freely shifts between the manufacturing and service
sectors. Therefore, the competitive wages in both sector is equalized to satisfy the
following condition:

$$p_t N_t G'\left(L_{m,t}\right) = q_t S_t H'\left(L_{s,t}\right),$$

where q_t is the price of services in terms of agricultural good. As before, a shift of
labor from the agricultural to the other two sectors is associated with learning costs.
Thus the cutoff condition is given by

---

[12] A well-cited contribution to the standard three-tsector model without labor market frictions is
Kongsamut et al. (2001).

$$\left(1 + \frac{\sigma}{\phi_t^*}\right) w_{t,a} = w_{m,t} = w_{s,t},$$

where $w_{s,t}$ denotes the wage in terms of the agricultural good sector paid in the service sector. Again, agents who draw $\phi < \phi^*$ works in the agricultural sector, and agents with $\phi \geq \phi^*$ work in the other sectors. This means that the labor force allocated to the manufacturing and the service sectors is determined by

$$L_{m,t} + L_{s,t} = \left[1 - \Gamma\left(\phi_t^*\right)\right] N.$$

The allocation of labor between the manufacturing and the service sector is determined by condition $p_t M_t G'\left(L_{m,t}\right) = q_t S_t H'\left(L_{s,t}\right)$.

The optimization problem of agents who work in the agricultural sector is given by

$$\max U_t^j = \frac{\left[(c_{a,t}^j - \gamma_a)^{\mu_a} \left(c_{m,t}\right)^{\mu_m} \left(c_{s,t} + \gamma_s\right)^{\mu_s}\right]}{1 - \sigma}, \quad \sigma, \gamma_a, \gamma_s > 0$$

subject to

$$c_{a,t}^j + p_t c_{m,r}^j + q_t c_{m,t}^j = I_t^j \quad j = a, m, s.$$

A positive parameter, γ, is introduced to express that services are superior to manufacturing goods, so that an income expansion increases the expenditure share of services relative to that of manufacturing goods. As before, the structural transformation between the agricultural goods sector and the other two sectors stems from the unbalanced productivity growth.

Given this setting, a rise in the relative productivity between the agricultural and the manufacturing as well as service sectors, M_t/A_t and S_t/A_t shifts labor from the agricultural to the non-agricultural sectors. But the speed of decline in the employment share would be slow if the distribution of agents' ability exhibits a Pareto distribution with a relatively low value of the shape parameter. On the other hand, a continuing shift of labor from the manufacturing to the service sectors is generated by the presence of a non-homothetic preference between the manufacturing goods and services. In particular, if the non-homotheticity of the preference over the manufacturing goods and services (the magnitude of γ) is large, then an income rise yields a rapid shift of labor from the manufacturing good sector to the service sector. This means that the income and employment shares of the service sector starts expanding before those shares of the manufacturing sector become sufficiently large. As a result, (i) if the heterogeneity among the workers are relatively high, and (ii) if the productivity of services is relatively high, then the three-sector version of our baseline model may illustrate the pattern of growth and structural transformation that are characteristic of the Indian economy.

2.5.3 Capital Accumulation

It is not difficult to generalize our non-overlapping generation model to the standard Diamond's (1965) two-period-lived overlapping generations (OLG) setting with capital accumulation. We now reformulate the model with labor market frictions discussed so far in the context of a two-period lived OLG model with capital.

Production

The production functions of the agricultural and the non-agricultural sectors are respectively given by

$$Y_{a,t} = A_t F\left(L_{t,a}\right),$$
$$Y_{m,t} = M_t G\left(K_t, L_{m,t}\right),$$

where K_t is a stock of the aggregate capital. Here, we assume that capital is employed by the non-manufacturing sector alone. We assume that function $G\left(K_r, L_{a,t}\right)$ is homogeneous of degree one with respect to capital and labor. Letting r_t be the rate of return to capital, the factor prices are satisfied in the following manner:

$$w_{t,a} = A_t F'\left(L_{a,t}\right),$$
$$w_{m,t} = p_t M_t G_L\left(K_t, L_{a,t}\right)$$
$$r_t = p_t G_K\left(K_t, L_{a,t}\right).$$

The cutoff condition for the labor allocation is the same as that of the model without capital:

$$\phi_t^* = \frac{\sigma}{p_t M_t G_L\left(K_t, L_{a,t}\right) - A_t F'\left(L_{a,t}\right)}.$$

A difference from the model without capital is that the cutoff level of agents' ability depends on the capital stock as well.

Following Diamond (1965), we assume that all agents live for two periods, young and old. The young agents fully devote their available time to work, whereas the old agents do not work.

Consumption

For notational simplicity, we assume that the population of each cohort, N_t, stays constant over time, and it is normalized to unity. Letting c_t^j and x_{t+1}^j be type j ($j = a, m$) agent' consumption in their young and old agents who are bone at the beginning of period t, the utility function of each type of agent is given by

$$u_t^j = \frac{\left(c_{a,t}^j\right)^{1-\sigma}}{1-\sigma} + \frac{\left(c_{m,t}^j\right)^{1-\sigma}}{1-\sigma}$$

$$+ \frac{1}{1+\rho}\left[\frac{\left(x_{a,t+1}^j\right)^{1-\sigma}}{1-\sigma} + \frac{\left(x_{m,t+1}^j\right)^{1-\sigma}}{1-\sigma}\right], \quad 0 < \sigma < 1, \quad j = a.m.$$

where $\rho\,(> 0)$ denotes the time preference rate. For analytical simplicity, we use a logarithmic utility function. Note that since the old agents do not work, the type of an agent, i.e. $j = a$ or $j = m$ is determined according to the sector in which the agent works in her young age.

The budget constraint for a type j agent at her young age is

$$c_{a,t}^j + p_t c_{m,t}^j + s_t^j = w_t^j, \quad j = a, m,$$

where s_t^j denotes the saving of the young agent of type j. Similarly, the agent's budget constraint in her old age is

$$x_{a,t+1}^j + p_{t+1}x_{m,t+1}^j = (1 + r_{t+1})\,s_t^j,$$

where r_{t+1} is the rate of return to capital (real interest rate) held in period $t + 1$. Combining the budget constraints in both ages, we obtain the intertemporal budget constraint of the agent in such a way that

$$c_{a,t}^j + p_t c_{m,t}^j + \frac{x_{a,t+1}^j + p_{t+1}x_{m,t+1}^j}{1 + r_{t+1}} = w_{j,t}, \quad j = a, m. \tag{2.37}$$

To derive the optimal consumption, define the expenditure of the household in each period as follows:

$$c_{a,t}^j + p_t c_{m,t}^j = E_t^j, \quad E_{t+1}^j = x_{a,t+1}^j + p_{t+1}x_{m,t+1}^j. \tag{2.38}$$

The optimal choice of consumption of the type j household yields the following conditions:

$$\frac{c_{a,t}^j - \gamma}{c_{m,t}^j} = p_t, \quad j = a, m \tag{2.39}$$

$$\frac{x_{a,t+1}^j - \gamma}{x_{m,t+1}^j} = \frac{p_{t+1}}{1 + r_{t+1}}, \quad j = a, m. \tag{2.40}$$

Using (2.38), (2.39) and (2.40), we find that the levels of optimal consumption are given by

$$c_{a,t}^j = \frac{E_t^j}{1 + p_t^{1-\frac{1}{\sigma}}}, \qquad c_{m,t}^j = \frac{E_t^j}{p_t^{\frac{1}{\sigma}} + p_t}, \tag{2.41}$$

$$x_{a,t+1}^j = \frac{E_{t+1}^j}{1 + p_{t+1}^{1-\frac{1}{\sigma}}}, \qquad x_{m,t+1}^j = \frac{E_{t+1}^j}{p_{t+1}^{\frac{1}{\sigma}} + p_{t+1}} \tag{2.42}$$

From (2.41) and (2.42), we find that the indirect utility expressed in the expenditures in both periods can be written as

$$\hat{u}_t^j = \frac{\left(\frac{E_t^j}{1+p_t^{1-\frac{1}{\sigma}}}\right)^{1-\sigma}}{1-\sigma} + \frac{\left(\frac{E_t^j}{p_t^{\frac{1}{\sigma}}+p_t}\right)^{1-\sigma}}{1-\sigma}$$
$$+ \frac{1}{1+\rho}\left[\frac{\left(\frac{E_{t+1}^j}{1+p_{t+1}^{1-\frac{1}{\sigma}}}\right)^{1-\sigma}}{1-\sigma} + \frac{\left(\frac{E_{t+1}^j}{p_{t+1}^{\frac{1}{\sigma}}+p_{t+1}}\right)^{1-\sigma}}{1-\sigma}\right], \quad j = a.m.$$

Consequently, the optimization problem for the type j household is to maximize $\hat{u}_t^j$ subject to

$$E_t^j + \frac{E_{t+1}^j}{1 + r_{t+1}} = w_t^j, \quad j = a, m.$$

by selecting E_t^j and E_{t+1}^j. The optimal levels of consumption expenditures must satisfy the Euler equation such that

$$(E_t^j)^{-\sigma} = \xi\left(1 + p_t^{1-\frac{1}{\sigma}}\right)^{1-\sigma}, \quad \left(E_{t+1}^j\right)^{-\sigma} = \xi\frac{1}{1+r_{t+1}}\left(p_{t+1}^{\frac{1}{\sigma}} + p_{t+1}\right)^{1-\sigma},$$

where ξ is a Lagrangian multiplier. Hence, the Euler equitation is expressed as

$$\left(\frac{E_{t/+1}^j}{E_t^j}\right)^{\sigma} = (1 + r_{t+1})\left(\frac{1 + p_t^{1-\frac{1}{\sigma}}}{p_{t+1}^{\frac{1}{\sigma}} + p_{t+1}}\right)^{1-\sigma}, \quad .j = a, \ m. \tag{2.43}$$

Market Equilibrium Conditions

We have assumed that $N_t = 1$ for all $t \geq 0$, and thus the population working in the agricultural and non-agricultural sectors in period t are respectively given by $\Gamma\left(\phi_t^*\right)$ and $1 - \Gamma\left(\phi_t^*\right)$. Therefore, the cutoff condition in the baseline model, given by (??) is replaced by

$$\phi_t^* = \frac{\sigma A_t F'\left(\Gamma\left(\phi^*\right)\right)}{p_t M_t G_N\left(\left(1 - \Gamma\left(\phi^*\right)\right), K_t\right) - A_t F'\left(\Gamma\left(\phi_t^*\right)\right)}. \tag{2.44}$$

The only difference from the cutoff condition in the baseline model is that the equilibrium level of ϕ_t^* now depends on capital stock, K_t, as well. The market equilibrium conditions for the agricultural and non-agricultural goods are respectively given by

$$
\begin{aligned}
A_t F\left(\Gamma\left(\phi^*\right) N\right) &= \Gamma\left(\phi_t^*\right) c_{a,t}^a + \left[1 - \Gamma\left(\phi_t^*\right)\right] c_{a,t}^m \\
&= \frac{\Gamma\left(\phi_t^*\right) E_{,t}^a + \left[1 - \Gamma\left(\phi_t^*\right)\right] E_t^m}{1 + p^{1-\frac{1}{\sigma}}},
\end{aligned}
\tag{2.45}
$$

$$
M_t G\left(\left(1 - \Gamma\left(\phi^*\right)\right) N\right) = \Gamma\left(\phi_t^*\right) c_{a,t}^a + \left[1 - \Gamma\left(\phi_t^*\right)\right] c_{a,t}^m
$$
$$
\frac{p_t^{-\frac{1}{\sigma}}}{1 + p^{1-\frac{1}{\sigma}}}\left\{\Gamma\left(\phi_t^*\right) E_t^a + \left[1 - \Gamma\left(\phi_t^*\right)\right] E_t^m\right\}. \tag{2.46}
$$

As well as in the baseline model. these equations mean that the relative price satisfies the following condition:

$$
p_t = \left[\frac{M_t G\left(\left(1 - \Gamma\left(\phi_t^*\right)\right), K_t\right)}{A_t F\left(\Gamma\left(\phi^*\right)\right)}\right]^{-\sigma}. \tag{2.47}
$$

Since only young agents save, the equilibrium condition for the asset market is

$$
\begin{aligned}
K_{t=1} &= \Gamma\left(\phi_t^*\right) s_t^a + \left[1 - \Gamma\left(\phi_t^*\right)\right] s_t^m \\
&= w_{a,t} - C_t^a - p_t C_{a,t}^a + w_{m,t} - C_{a,t}^m - p_t C_{m,t}^m,
\end{aligned}
\tag{2.48}
$$

where $C_{j,t}^a = \Gamma\left(\phi_t^*\right) c_{j,t}^a$ and $C_{j,t}^m = \left[1 - \Gamma\left(\phi_t^*\right)\right] c_{j,t}^m$ $(j = a, m)$.

Working of the Model

While we do not present a detailed analysis of this model, the working of the model can be summarized as follows. First, the cutoff condition (2.44) means that the equilibrium level of ϕ_t^* is written as

$$
\phi_t^* = \hat{\Phi}\left(\frac{M_t}{A_t}, K_t\right). \tag{2.49}
$$

As a result, the equilibrium relative price determined by (2.47) is expressed as

$$
p_t = \Pi\left(\frac{M_t}{A_t}, K_t\right). \tag{2.50}
$$

Consequently, substituting (2.49) and (2.50) into (2.48), we see that the evolution of capital stock is expressed as follows:

$$K_{t+1} = A_t F' \left[\Gamma \left(\Omega \left(\frac{M_t}{A_t}, K_t \right) \right) \right] - \frac{\Omega \left(\frac{M_t}{A_t}, K_t \right) E_t^a}{1 + \Pi \left(\frac{M_t}{A_t}, K_t \right)^{1-\frac{1}{\sigma}}} - \frac{\left[1 - \Omega \left(\frac{M_t}{A_t}, K_t \right) \right] E_t^m}{1 + \Pi \left(\frac{M_t}{A_t}, K_t \right)^{1-\frac{1}{\sigma}}}$$

$$\Pi \left(\frac{M_t}{A_t}, K_t \right) M_t G_N \left[1 - \Omega \left(\frac{M_t}{A_t}, K_t \right), K_t \right] - \frac{\Omega \left(\frac{M_t}{A_t}, K_t \right) E_t^a}{\Pi \left(\frac{M_t}{A_t}, K_t \right)^{\frac{1}{\sigma}} + \Pi \left(\frac{M_t}{A_t}, K_t \right)} \qquad (2.51)$$

$$- \frac{\left[1 - \Omega \left(\frac{M_t}{A_t}, K_t \right) \right] E_t^a}{\Pi \left(\frac{M_t}{A_t}, K_t \right)^{\frac{1}{\sigma}} + \Pi \left(\frac{M_t}{A_t}, K_t \right)},$$

where E_t^a and E_t^m follow the Euler equation (2.43), in which r_{t+1} is given by

$$r_{t+1} = M_t G_K [\Gamma (\Omega \left(\frac{M_t}{A_t}, K_t \right).$$

If A_t and M_t stay constant, it is easy to see that (2.43) and (2.51) constitute a complete dynamic system with respect to K_t, E_t^a and E_t^m. Although the model structure more complex than the baseline model, if we set $\sigma = 1$ (logarithmic utility) and specify $G(.) = K_t^\alpha N^{1-\alpha} = K_t^\alpha$, the system is substantially simplified, and we can examine the convergence process of capital to its steady-state level. Also, we can examine the transitional as well as the long-run impacts of permanent changes A_t and M. As far as in such a simplified setting, the main conclusions obtained in the baseline model without capital generally hold in the model with capital and two-period lived households.

2.6 Discussion

When characterizing the structural transformation of the Indian economy, we have emphasized labor market frictions due to the presence of adjustment costs and agent heterogeneity. In the existing literature, some authors have provided alternative expositions about the structural change that is characteristic of the Indian economy. Before discussing the economic implications of our findings, let us consider alternative expositions about India's structural transformation.[13]

---

[13] Several authors also inspect the low productivity growth in developing countries from different perspectives: see, for example, Gollin et al. (2014), Herrendorf and Valentinyi (2012), Restuccia et al. (2008).

2.6.1 Alternative Views

Sectoral Differences in the Financial Markets

When exploring the reason behind the slow movement of labor from the agricultural to the other sectors in India, Leukhina et al. (2018) focus on the sectroal difference in the financial market. The authors claim that the rural areas in India have established networks of friends and family that effectively insures against income fluctuations. On the other hand, cities provide no formal or informal insurance. Hence, households have fewer incentives to migrate to cities so that a large body of labor force remains abundant and cheap in agriculture. Additionally, the incentives for switching to large-scale capital-intensive methods of farming stay weak in the agricultural sector.

Based on their idea, Leukhina et al. (2018) construct a model of a two-sector economy consisting of an urban area and a rural area. In the urban area, non-agricultural goods are produced by the use of capital and labor, and the households face uninsured labor income risk. The rural actor produces agricultural goods by use of labor and land, and the households in that area have access to complete insurance against their income risks. It is assumed that the urban area has a constant-returns-to-scale tecology under which labor and capital are substitutes for each other, while in the rural production technology labor and land are complements The authors numerically analyze their model and find that there are large-scale productivity and wage gaps between the urban and rural areas in their calibrated model. The authors conclude that a complete financial market supported by the rural network is the main obstacle that prevents the Indian economy from realizing efficient allocation of labor force between the agricultural and non-agricultural sectors.

In this paper, we simply assume that sectorsal shift or labor is associated with adjustment costs. The study by Leukhina et al. (2018) presnts a plausible microfoundation for such a presence of such adjustment costs in the Indian labor market.[14]

Difference in Human Capital Intensity

Some authors focus on the technological gap between the agricultural and non-agricultural sectors rather than the misallocation of labor. For example, Herrendorf and Schoellman (2018) inspect the data of 13 countries ranging from rich (Canada, United States) to poor (India, Indonesia) and find that wages are considerably lower in agriculture than in the other sectors. Furthermore, the agriculture sector employs less-educated workers and provides ower returns to human capital. The authors construct a multi-sector model in which workers differ in observed and unobserved characteristics and sectors differ in their human-capital intensities. They assume that there are barriers to the reallocation of labor out of agriculture to the other sectors. Hence, in their model, there are two main reasons why wages are lower in agriculture: agricultural workers have lower ability and agriculture is less human capital intensive. The first reason is captured by the presence of barriers to labor allocation in their model. Herrendorf and Schoellman (2015) estimate the barriers to labor

---

[14] See also Herrendorf and Schoellman (2018) for further investigation on this topic.

mobility for the sampled 13 countries and find they are much smaller than what the macro-development studies typically assume. Based on their finding, the authors claim that a productivity gap caused by the difference in human capital intensity between non-agricultural and agricultural sectors is the main cause of the sectroal wage gap. However, Herrendorf and Schoellman (2015) also suggest that productivity gaps may result from barriers that affect commodity markets rather than the labor market.[15]

2.6.2 Implications of the Model Analysis

It has been often argued that India has a great cultural diversity, which plays an important role in India's economic development. India and other South Asian countries are among the largest recipients of monthly transfers from their workers in foreign countries. Owing to their religious, ethnic, and social diversity, more than 30 million Indians access and transfer their income from countries such as Saudi Arabia, the UAE, Malaysia, Singapore, the US, Canada, the UK, and Australia. Regional languages and minority religions have established themselves as global community networks: typical examples are the Tamils in Malaysia and the Sikhs in Canada. Such internal connections provide them with access to education and jobs, partly through professional visa arrangements. In addition, Indian civilization values of tolerance, cosmopolitanism, and multiculturalism gives a unique character to Indian culture. Indian people belong to a variety of religions. While 94% of the world's Hindus live in India, there are also substantial populations of Muslims, Christians, Sikhs, Buddhists. This religious diversity is India's strength in the sense that diversity generates rich music art and literature. It also gives an opportunity for Indian people to increase people-to-people contacts across the globe.

The cultural diversity mentioned above is obviously a strength of the Indian economy in many aspects. At the same time, cultural diversity may also yield negative effects on development. The model of this paper captures such a negative side of Indian economy. We argued that diversity in Indian society may play a negative role in efficient resource allocation. In our model, the degree of heterogeneity of agents' ability represents part of the diversity. If, as mentioned earlier, the ability assumed in the model follows a Pareto distribution, the smaller the value of the Pareto coefficient, ϕ, and the closer it is to 1, the greater the heterogeneity of the workers and the greater the proportion of workers who remain in the agricultural sector. Thus, if the heterogeneity of workers represents part of the cultural and social diversity of India, then the other high level of diversity will hinder the movement of labor from the strikebreakers to the non-agricultural sector. Moreover, the disparity in the average level of education between rural and urban areas can be an obstacle to labor migration from the agricultural to the non-agricultural sector. Of course, our model fails

---

[15] Several authors also inspect the low productivity growth in developing countries: see, for example, Gollin et al. (2014), Herrendorf and Valentinyi (2012), Restuccia et al. (2008).

to describe the direct and indirect merits of cultural diversity for long-run growth in India, and hence, our finding may emphasize the negative side of diversity in India too much.

2.7 Conclusion

A distinctive feature of the industrial structural transformation in India in the past three decades is that the employment share of the agricultural sector has not declined much compared to its decrease in the value-added share. Such an unbalanced structural change gives rise to continuing reduction in income per worker in agriculture and persistent low productivity in labor input in that sector. This paper argued that the slow reduction in the employment share of the agricultural sector may be the presence of high adjustment costs of the sectral labor shift. We constructed a simple model of growth and structural change with labor market frictions and revealed that a high adjustment costs of sectoral labor shift and a high degree of heterogeneity among workers may yield a slow reduction of the employment share of the agricultural sector in the process of long-term economic growth. Of course, labor markets are not perfect as assumed in the standard neoclassical growth models even in the advanced countries. We aguned that labor market imperfection gives a larger effect on the structural change in India compared to the East Asian countries. Our model analysis suggested that the imperfection in the labor mark partially stems from a degree of cultural diversity in the Indian society.

Although we are not against the many authors who claim that cultural diversity in India has played a relevant role in the recent growth and development of the Indian economy. However, we also claim that cultural diversity in India may be a source of inefficient allocation of labor in India. We guess that further development and growth of the Indian economy would depend on a subtle balance between the negative and positive roles of diversity that have been characterizing the cultural background of India's long-term growth.

References

Acemoglu, D. (2009). *Introduction to modern economic growth*. MIT Press.

Acemoglu, D., & Guerrieri, V. (2008). Capital deepening and Nonbalanced economic growth. *Journal of Political Economy, 116,* 467–498.

Aziz, J. (2008). Deconstructing China's and India's growth: The role of financial policies. Working Paper No. 24, Indian Council for Reseadh on International Economic Relations.

Basu, K. (2018). A short History of India's economy: A chapter in the Asian Drama. WIDER Working Paper, No. 2018/124, United Nations University.

Banerjee, V., & Moll, B. (2010). Why does misallocation persist? *American Economic Journal: Macroeconomics, 2*(1), 189–206.

Baumol, W. (1967). Macroeconomics of unbalanced growth: The anatomy of the urban crisis. *American Economic Review, 57*, 415–426.

Bhalla, & Surjit, B. (2011). Inclusion and growth in India: Some facts, some conclusions. Working Paper No.39, Asia Research Centre, London School of Economics and Political Science.

Buera, F., & Kaboski. (2012). The rise of the service economy. *American Economic Review, 102*, 2540–2569.

Buera, Francisco, J., & Kaboski, J. P. (2009). Can traditional theories of structural change t the data? *Journal of the European Economic Association, 7*, 469–477.

Boppart, T. (2014). Structural change and the Kaldor facts in a growth model with relative price effects and non-Gorman preferences. *Econometrica, 82*, 2167–96.

Chattopadhyay, S. (2016). Slow structural change in India: Is it related to rising relative price of agriculture? a partial equilibrium model. *Theoretical Economics Letters, 6*, 401–406.

Datt, G., & Ravallion, M. (2002). India's economic growth leaving the poor behind? *Journal of Economic Perspective, 16*, 89–108.

Diamond, P. (1965). National debt in a neoclassical growth model. *American Economic Review, 55*, 1126–1150.

Duarte, M., & Restuccia, D. (2010). The role of the structural transformation in aggregate productivity. *Quarterly Journal of Economics, 125*, 129–173.

Echevarria, C. (1997). Changes in sectoral composition associated with economic growth. *International Economic Review, 38*, 431–452.

Foellmi, R., & Zweimüler, J. (2008). Structural change, Engel's consumption cycles and Kaldor's facts of economic growth. *Journal of Monetary Economics, 55*, 1317–1328.

Guillo, M., Papageorgiou, C., & Perez-Sebastian, F. (2010). A unified theory of structural change. *Forthcoming in Journal of Economic Dynamics and Control.*

Gollin, D., Lagakos, D., & abd Waugh. (2014). The agricultural productivity gap. *Quarterly Journal of Economics, 129*, 939–993.

Herrendorf, B., Rogerson, R., & Valentinyi, À. (2013). Two perspectives on preferences and structural transformation. *American Economic Review, 103*, 2752–89.

Herrendorf, B., & Schoellman, T. (2018). Wages, human capital, and barriers to structural transformation. *American Economic Journal: Macroeconomics, 10*(2), 1–23. https://doi.org/10.1257/mac.20160236.

Herrendorf, B., & Valentinyi, À. (2012). Which sectors make poor countries so unproductive? *Journal of the European Economic Association, 10*, 323–341.

Herrendorf, B., Rogerson, R., & Valentinyi, À. (2014). Growth and structural transformation. In *Handbook of Economic Growth*, Vol. 2B, ed. by P. Aghion & S. N. Durlauf. North-Holland, pp. 855–941

Herrendorf, B., & Herrington, C., Alentinyi, À. (2015). Sectoral technology and structural transformation. *American Economic Journal: Macroeconomics, 7*, 104–133.

Herrendorf, B., & Schoellman, T. (2015). Why is measured labor productivity so low in agriculture? *Review of Economic Dynamics, 18*, 1003–1022.

Hori, T., Ikefuji, M., & Mino, K. (2015). Conformism and structural change. *International Economic Review, 56*, 939–961.

Ichikawa, K., Fujimoto, T., Sakamaki, T., Saito, Y., & Sato, T. (2019). Economic growth and industrial stricture in India, (in Japanese), ESRI Research Note No.44, The Japanese Cabinet Office.

Jorgenson, D. W., & Timmer, M. P. (2011). Structural change in advanced nations: A new set of stylised facts. *Scandinavian Journal of Economics, 113*, 1–29.

Kongsamut, P., Rebelo, S., & Xie, D. (2001). Beyond balanced growth. *Review of Economic Studies, 68*, 869–882.

Leukhina, O., Raghav, P., & Rahman, M. (2018). Why is agricultural productivity so low in poor countries? The case of India. unpublished manuscript.

Mallick, J. (2017). Structural change and productivity growth in India and thePeople's Republic of China. ADBI Working Paper No. 656, Asian Development Bank Institute.

Matsuyama, K. (1991). Increasing returns, industrialization, and indeterminacy of equilibrium. *Quarterly Journal of Economics, 106,* 617–650.

Matsuyama, K. (1992). Agricultural productivity, comparative advantage, and economic growth. *Journal of Economic Theory, 58,* 317–334.

Ngai, R., & OPissarides, C. (2007). Structural change in a multisector model of growth. *American Economic Review, 97*(1), 429–43.

Nathan, M., & Lee, N. (2013). Cultural diversity, innovation, and entrepreneurship: Firm-level evidence from London. *Economic Geography, 89,* 367–394.

Restuccia, D., Yang, D.-T., & Zhu, X. (2008). Agriculture and aggregate productivity: A quantitative cross-country analysis. *Journal of Monetary Economics, 55,* 234–250.

Roy, T. (2002). Economic history and modern India: Redefining the link. *Journal of Economic Perspectives, 16,* 109–130.

Sato, T. (2016). Development of Indian industries: An overview, (in Japanese), RIBE Discussion Paper No. 2026_J04, Research Institute of Business and Economics, Kobe University.

Shimizu, S. (2009). Economic growth in India, (in Japanese), Business Report on Pasicifiv Rim Vol. 9, NO.33, Japan Research Institute.

Song, Z., Storesletten, K., & Zilibotti, F. (2011). Growing like China. *American Economic Review, 101,* 196–233.

Chapter 3
Happiness and Social Capital in India

Yoshio Itaba

Abstract Numerous studies have examined happiness in Europe, America, and East Asia, but few studies have focused on developing countries. Furthermore, it was found that social capital is an important determinant of happiness in happiness studies. Therefore, this study aims to examine happiness and how it relates to social capital in India. Most studies about India were small-scale and used data limited to demographic conditions (e.g., women, rural, urban, the elderly). The present chapter examines nationwide data and broad demographic conditions as well as social capital, which is important but has not yet been considered in an Indian happiness study. The analysis confirms that our results fit the usual patterns that are found in the happiness literature. However, there are some specific findings in the case of India. For example, there is no significant education–happiness relationship in the estimation. Happiness had a positive and statistically significant correlation with top-level managers, executives, and the self-employed. Social capital had a strong positive correlation with happiness. Our results clearly confirmed the presence of a positive relationship between social capital and happiness. In that sense, social capital was a big predictor of happiness. Finally, we estimated the determinants of social capital.

3.1 Introduction

In its 2013 book *Guidelines on Measuring Subjective Well-being*, the Organization for Economic Co-operation and Development (OECD) defined "Subjective Well-Being" (SWB) as "good mental states, including all of the various evaluations, positive and negative, that people make of their lives and the affective reactions of people to their experiences" (OECD, 2013, p. 8). This report also stated that "subjective well-being covers a wider range of concepts than just happiness."

According to the OECD guidelines, there are four reasons to pay attention to SWB:

Y. Itaba (✉)
Faculty of Economics, Doshisha University, Kyoto, Japan
e-mail: yitaba@mail.doshisha.ac.jp

© Springer Nature Singapore Pte Ltd. 2022
K. Mino and T. Yagi (eds.), *The Cultural Basis of Economic Growth in India*,
Creative Economy, https://doi.org/10.1007/978-981-15-9305-5_3

1. To complement other outcomes: SWB can provide information on social outcomes and affairs that other conventional indicators such as unemployment rate do not provide.
2. To better understand the drivers of SWB: Analysis of SWB can provide information on the relative importance of different factors that affect a person's well-being.
3. To support policy evaluation and cost–benefit analysis, particularly when they involve nonmarket outcomes: SWB can complement other social and economic indicators as a measure of policy outcomes. SWB has advantages over cost–benefit analyses such as the contingent valuation method.
4. To help identify potential policy problems: Analysis of SWB can provide information about human behavior and decision-making that leads to an appropriate policy.

Other terms similar to SWB are "satisfaction with life" or "quality of life". To date, these terms appear to have been used interchangeably. In this chapter, the term "happiness" is mainly used.

Numerous studies have examined happiness in Europe, America, and East Asia, but few studies have focused on developing countries. Therefore, this study aims to examine happiness and how it relates to social capital in India. The main studies pertaining to SWB in India.

Agrawal et al. (2011) explored determinants of life satisfaction in an urban sample ($n = 1,099$) of Bangalore in South India. Life satisfaction, as developed by Diener et al. (1985), is not a single-scale measure that is usually used in the literature but is instead predicted by income, age, and education. Important predictors of life satisfaction differ between men and women.

Ghosh, Millet, Subramanian and Pramanik (2017), examined the extent of contextual variation between neighborhoods across multiple dimensions of elderly health. Their data included a nationally representative sample of 6,560 Indian adults aged 50 years and older.

Linsen et al. (2011) focused on the effects of relative income and conspicuous consumption on SWB, using data on 697 individuals from 375 rural low-income households in India.

White et al. (2014) focused on a new approach of "Inner Wellbeing" which aimed to capture what people think and feel they can be and do, using data on individuals in rural communities in the global South. Their sample size was small.

White et al. (2012) explored the relationship between religion and well-being. The extent to which religions provide welfare depends upon communities and organizations. Respondents were 1,200 heads of household.

Polit (2005) focused on the effects of perceived marginality (e.g., social inequality in connection with caste status) on people's well-being in three villages in the Central Himalayas in North India between 2002 and 2005. The research instrument was an interview.

Hafen et al. (2011) examined relationships among the big five personality traits, emotional intelligence, and happiness. Participants included 205 university students in India. The results were nearly the same as those in their previous work.

Ghosh, Lahiri and Datta (2017) investigated the happiness of young women in rural Bengal with an emphasis on their marital life. Total sample size was 654 married women.

Lakshmanasamy (2010) empirically analyzed the relationship between income and happiness in India using primary sample data of 315 respondents. Respondents were mostly middle and upper-middle income households. They reported that the correlates of happiness were both absolute income and relative income.

Most studies were small-scale and used data limited to demographic conditions (e.g., women, rural, urban, the elderly). The present chapter examines nationwide data and broad demographic conditions as well as social capital, which is important but has not yet been considered in an Indian happiness study.

This chapter is constructed as follows. Section 3.1 describes the data and examines the relationship between happiness and related variables. Section 3.2 estimates the relationship between happiness and economic–demographic variables using an ordered logit model, from which several interesting results were derived. In particular, it was found that social capital is an important determinant of happiness in India. Section 3.3 focuses on the determinants of social capital, and the conclusions are presented in the final section.

3.2 Data Description

The present analysis utilized data compiled in the research project "Research on India", funded by Kakenhi (No. 16KT0089; Chief Researcher, Prof. Kazuo Mino). Some of the items in the present survey were used in my previous survey described in Itaba (2016).

3.2.1 Survey Outline

The following is the outline of the survey conducted in the project:

A. Survey title: "Research on India"
B. Survey period: October 2017
C. Survey method: Online survey (Goo Research)
D. Sample number: 4,046.

3.2.2   Descriptive Statistics of Survey Results

Table 3.1 shows the descriptive statistics of the variables. The descriptive statistics for social capital will be given in Sect. 2.1 These variables are used in the following happiness analysis, with short remarks provided for some of them.

SWB can be defined as the positive evaluation of one's life that is associated with good feelings (Pinquart & Sörensen, 2000, p. 187). Two aspects of SWB were investigated in this chapter: *happiness* and *life satisfaction.*

3.2.3   Happiness

Happiness was measured by the following question: "On a scale from 0 to 10, please rate your overall level of happiness." Possible responses ranged from 0 (extremely unhappy) to 10 (extremely happy). Figure 3.1 shows the overall distribution of happiness, which had an average score of 7.6. Reported happiness decreased in India from 2006 to 2016, with an average happiness level of 4.2 in 2016.[1] Therefore, reported happiness in this chapter was rather higher compared to its usual value.

The question concerning life satisfaction was "How satisfied are you on the whole?" Responses were coded on a five-point rating scale from 1 to 5. Figure 3.2 shows the overall distribution of life satisfaction, where the average score of 4.14 is a little higher compared to the average level of happiness after doubling responses of life satisfaction. There was a significant correlation between happiness and life satisfaction (0.51). However, this coefficient was not so high compared to the 0.69 reported in Lakshmanasamy (2010), which used a three-point rating scale from 1 to 3. Furthermore, the life satisfaction distribution was highly positively skewed opposed to the happiness distribution. These two terms, *happiness* and *life satisfaction*, are usually used interchangeably. Strictly speaking, there is a slight difference in some cases. According to Veenhoven (2012, p. 6), "the term 'life-satisfaction' is mostly used for 'overall happiness', but refers in some cases particularly to its cognitive component and is than synonymous with 'contentment'". *Happiness* and *life satisfaction* questions would not have the same connotation in the questionnaire. Hence, each question might measure slightly different matters. We therefore focused mainly on happiness and discuss life satisfaction as a complement to happiness.

3.2.4   Social Capital

The literature on determinants of happiness has focused mainly on internal factors such as income and marital status. But other important external factors are present

---

[1] Veenhoven (2012) , Happiness in India (IN), World Database of Happiness, Erasmus University Rotterdam, The Netherlands. Viewed on 2019–03-04 at http://worlddatabaseofhappiness.eur.nl.

Table 3.1 Summary of variables used in the empirical analysis

Nominal variable (question)	Variable discription	Freq.	%	Obs.	Mean	Std. Dev.	Min.	Max.
Gender	Male(=1)	59.7	59.7	4,046	1.40	0.49	1	2
	Female(=2)	40.3	40.3					
Marital status	Single(=1)	1393	34.4	4,046	1.68	0.54	1	4
	Married(=2)	2572	63.6					
	Divorced(=3)	45	1.1					
	Widowed(=4)	36	0.9					
Education	Below HSC/SSC(=1)	322	8.0	4,013	2.73	0.60	1	3
	Attended college but has not graduated(=2)	440	11.0					
	College graduate or higher(=3)	3251	81.0					
Child	Don't have(=0)	1255	31.0	4,046	0.69	0.46	0	1
	Have(=1)	2791	69.0					
House	House(no)(=0)	1210	29.9	4,046	0.70	0.46	0	1
	House(owned)(=1)	2836	70.1					
Health	Unhealthy(=1)	158	3.9	4046	3.83	1.61	1	5
	If pressed to say, I would say "unhealthy."(=2)	259	6.4					
	Normal level of health(=3)	1395	34.5					
	If pressed to say, I would say "healthy."(=4)	520	12.9					
	Healthy(=5)	1714	42.4					
Age	Less tha 20(=1)	401	9.9	4,046	0.70	0.46	0	1
	20 to 29 years old(=2)	1060	26.2					
	30 to 39 years old(=3)	1031	25.5					

(continued)

Table 3.1 (continued)

Nominal variable (question)	Variable discription	Freq.	%	Obs.	Mean	Std. Dev.	Min.	Max.
	40 to 49 years old(=4)	763	18.9					
	50 to 59 years old(=5)	497	12.3					
	60 or above(=6)	294	7.3					
City size	Large-sized cities (population of one million or larger)(=1)	2470	62.6	3,945	1.59	0.91	1	4
	Medium-sized cities (population of less than one million)(= 2)	925	23.4					
	Small-sized cities(=3)	251	6.4					
	Towns or villages(=4)	299	7.6					
Income	None (no income)(=1)	450	12.3	3,662	3.40	2.19	1	15
	Less than $4,999(=2)	951	26.0					
	$5,000 to $9,999(=3)	908	24.8					
	$10,000 to $19,999(=4)	671	18.3					
	$20,000 to $29,999(=5)	274	7.5					
	$30,000 to $39,999(=6)	139	3.8					
	$40,000 to $49,999(=7)	81	2.2					
	$50,000 to $59,999(=8)	63	1.7					
	$60,000 to $69,999(=9)	25	0.7					
	$70,000 to $79,999(=10)	26	0.7					
	$80,000 to $99,999(=11)	20	0.5					
	$100,000 to $119,999(=12)	15	0.4					
	$120,000 to $139,999(=13)	12	0.3					

(continued)

Table 3.1 (continued)

Nominal variable (question)	Variable discription	Freq.	%	Obs.	Mean	Std. Dev.	Min.	Max.
	$140,000 to $159,999(=14)	12	0.3					
	$160,000 or more(=15)	15	0.4					
Work status	Top level manager, executive(= 1)	1001	24.7	4,046	3.55	2.21	1	8
	Regular employee(=2)	924	22.8					
	Civil servant(=3)	80	2.0					
	Contract /fixed-term /Part-time employee/home-based work(=4)	459	11.3					
	Self-employed(=5)	632	15.6					
	Student(=6)	505	12.5					
	Unemployed (includes homemakers) (=7)	293	7.2					
	Other(=8)	152	3.8					
Happiness	0(Very Unhappy) (=0)	9	0.2	4,046	7.61	1.78	0	10
	1(=1)	22	0.5					
	2(=2)	42	1.0					
	3(=3)	66	1.6					
	4(=4)	104	2.6					
	5(=5)	213	5.3					
	6(=6)	378	9.3					
	7(=7)	786	19.4					
	8(=8)	1100	27.2					
	9(=9)	834	20.6					
	10 (Very Happy) (=10)	492	12.2					

(continued)

Table 3.1 (continued)

Nominal variable (question)	Variable discription	Freq.	%	Obs.	Mean	Std. Dev.	Min.	Max.
Life satisfaction	Not satisfied(=1)	244	6.0	4,046	4.14	1.168	1	5
	If pressed to say, I would say "not satisfied"(=2)	187	4.6					
	Cannot say either way(=3)	485	12.0					
	If pressed to say, I would say "satisfied"(=4)	960	23.7					
	Satisfied(=5)	2170	53.6					

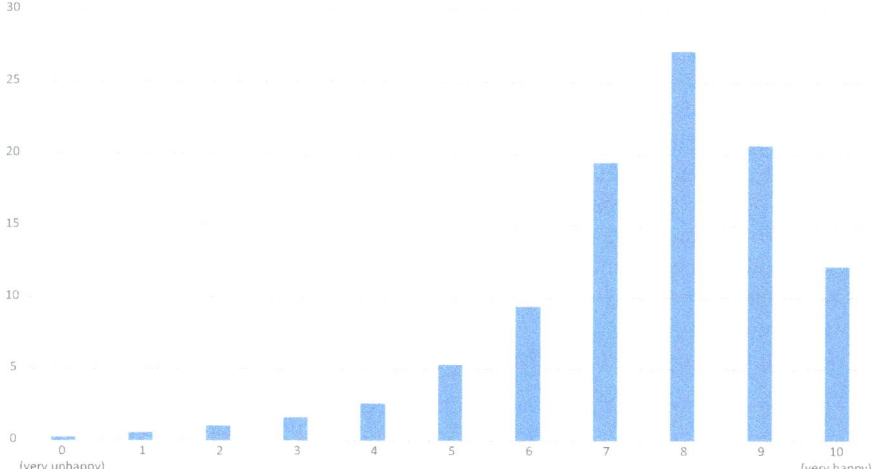

Fig 3.1 Happiness (n = 4,046)

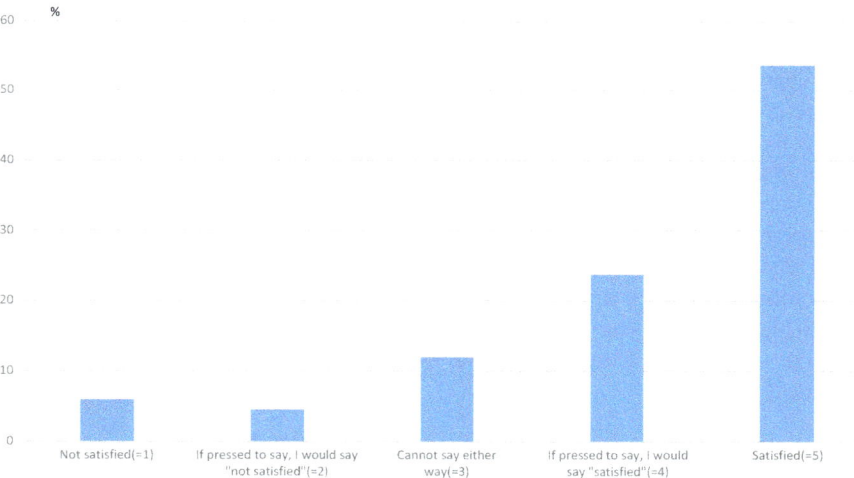

Fig. 3.2 Life satisfaction (n = 4,046)

as well such as the environment around people. Social capital is the representative external factor.

Social capital can be broken down and operationalized into a number of sub-dimensions. One distinction is between cognitive and structural social capital. Structural social capital refers to externally observable behaviors and actions within the network such as roles, rules, precedents, and procedures. Cognitive social capital refers to people's perceptions of the level of interpersonal trust as well as norms of reciprocity within the group, which includes norms, values, attitudes, and beliefs (Villalonga-Olives & Kawachi, 2015, p. 47).

Another distinction is between bridging social capital and bonding social capital.[2] These two types of social capital are recognized by Putnam (2000). Bridging social capital refers to relationships with people from other communities, cultures, or socioeconomic backgrounds (Oztok et al., 2015, p. 20). Bonding social capital refers to strong ties of attachment between relatively homogeneous individuals (Oztok et al., 2015, p. 20). Whereas bonding social capital bonds actors covered by it, bridging social capital bridges actors with other actors outside (Sato, 2013, p. 3). Furthermore, it is said that bonding social capital is inward-looking and bridging social capital is outward-looking.

The following six questions about social capital were asked:

1. (Generalized trust) "On a scale from 0 to10, how much do you basically trust your fellow Indians?" Generalized trust is defined as general beliefs about the extent to which other people can be trusted. It is essential for cooperative relationships (Ostrom, 2000), thriving democracies (Putnam, 1993; Tavits, 2006), and economic growth (Knack & Keefer, 1997).[3] This question was answered on a scale from 0 to 10, where 0 is *extremely dissatisfied* and 10 is *extremely satisfied*.

2. (Direct reciprocity) "Do you think that the person you helped might also help you in the future? Choose the appropriate response." This question measures direct reciprocity, with responses on a scale from 1 to 3. Although cooperation has been observed in the past behavior of a known partner under direct reciprocity, cooperation has also been observed in anonymous social experiences under generalized reciprocity. Therefore, the following question measures generalized reciprocity.

3. (Generalized reciprocity) "Do you think that when you help a person in trouble, someone will also help you whenever you are in trouble?"

4. (Structural social capital: extent of relationship) "How often do you meet with your neighbors? Please select the best response for each of the following questions."

   A. How frequently do you meet with your neighbors?
   B. How many neighbors do you meet with?

5. (Structural social capital: neighborhood activities) This question relates to neighborhood activities that you participate in. "Do you currently participate in any of the following activities?

   A. Activities designed to promote relationships between people in the area (such as neighborhood groups and associations)

---

[2] Szreter and Woolcock (2004). This paper also introduced linking social capital, which describes relationships across individuals who occupy different statuses of power within a social hierarchy.

[3] See Dawson (2017).

B.   Sports, hobbies, and amusement activities (such as various types of sporting activities and artistic and cultural activities)

C.   Volunteer, NPO, civic, and other similar types of activities

D.   Other organizational activities (such as political activities and religious activities)

6.   (Particularized trust) "Do you have anyone you can consult with or rely on regarding any problems or worries you may have in daily life?" Please select how much you can rely on the person(s) for each item below.

A.   Your neighbors

B.   Your immediate family members

C.   Other relatives

D.   Friends and acquaintances

E.   Doctors and counselors

F.   Schoolteachers and cram school tutors

G.   Your own caste members

H.   Your own religious group members.

Particularized trust is defined as beliefs about the extent to which only specific individuals associated with a certain network or networks can be trusted.

Table 3.2 presents the results of the social capital questions. The average of generalized trust (question 1) was 8.4, which is higher than that in Japan. The average values for questions 2, 3, and 4 were also higher than in Japan. Neighborhood activities (question 5) in which respondents participated were mainly A. activities designed to promote relationships between people in the area (such as neighborhood groups and associations) and B. sports, hobbies, and amusement activities (such as various types of sporting activities and artistic and cultural activities). For question 6, respondents mainly relied on B. immediate family and D. friends and acquaintances.

Principal component analysis was used to obtain factors for each respondent using an orthogonal rotation (i.e., a varimax rotation) in order to reduce the social capital dataset to a more manageable size. Four factors were derived from the rotated factor matrix, which is a matrix of factor loadings of each variable. Table 3.3 shows the varimax-rotated four-factor component matrix. Variables are listed in order of size of their loadings. There are four factors. Questions that loaded highly on factor 1 seemed to relate to structural social capital. Therefore, factor 1 was labeled as structural social capital. Questions that loaded highly on factor 2 seemed to relate to particularized trust, such as family members, friends, and acquaintances. Therefore, factor 2 was labeled as particularized trust (neighborhood) factors. Questions that loaded highly on factor 3 seemed to relate to particularized trust, such as caste members, religious group members, schoolteachers, and cram school tutors. Therefore, factor 3 was labeled as particularized trust (religious and educational). Questions that loaded highly on factor 4 seemed to relate to reciprocity and generalized trust. Therefore, factor 4 was labeled as reciprocity and generalized trust.

Structural social capital, particularized social capital (N, neighbors), and particularized social capital (RE, religion and education) are bonding social capital whereas

Table 3.2 Results of social capital questions

Nominal variable (question)	Variable description	Freq.	%		Mean	Std. Dev.	Skewness
1. On a scale of 0–10, please rate how much you basically trust your fellow Indians?	0 (I do not trust people at all)(=1)	21	0.5		8.40	2.003	−1.097
Generalized trust	1(=2)	45	1.1				
	2(=3)	62	1.5				
	3(=4)	94	2.3				
	4(=5)	108	2.7				
	5(=6)	316	7.8				
	6(=7)	378	9.3				
	7(=8)	746	18.4				
	8(=9)	990	24.5				
	9(=10)	802	19.8				
	10 (I trust people a great deal)(=11)	484	12.0				
	total	4046	100.0				
2. Do you think that the person you helped might also help you in the future? Choose the appropriate	I disagree(=1)	181	4.5		2.49	0.583	−0.626
Direct reciprosity	Cannot say either way(=2)	1717	42.4				

(continued)

Table 3.2 (continued)

Nominal variable (question)	Variable description	Freq.	%	Mean	Std. Dev.	Skewness
	I agree (=3)	2148	53.1			
3. Do you think that when you help a person in trouble, someone will also help you whenever you are in	I disagree(=1)	188	4.6	2.57	0.581	−0.995
Generalized reciprosity	Cannot say either way(=2)	1353	33.4			
	I agree (=3)	2505	61.9			
4. How often do you meet with your neighbors? Please select the best response for each of the following questions						
A. How frequently do you meet your neighbors?	Never (=1)	128	3.2	2.91	0.795	−0.219
	Hardly ever (greetings only) (=2)	1088	26.9			
	We stand around and talk on a daily basis (=3)	1844	45.6			

(continued)

Table 3.2 (continued)

Nominal variable (question)	Variable description	Freq.	%		Mean	Std. Dev.	Skewness
	We consult with each other and lend each other daily supplies, etc. We cooporate with each other to make our lives better (=4)	986	24.4				
B. How many neighbors do you meet?	No one. I don't even know who my next door neighbors are(=1)	134	3.3		2.96	0.884	−0.203
	I know and interact with a few people in my neighborhood (=2)	1270	31.4				
	I know and interact with a decent amount of people in my neighborhood(=3)	1281	31.7				
	I know and interact with many people in my neighborhood(=4)	1361	33.6				
					Mean	Std. Dev	Skewness

(continued)

Table 3.2 (continued)

Nominal variable (question)	Variable description	Freq.	%		Mean	Std. Dev.	Skewness
		Never(=1)	Hardly ever(=2)	Yes, occasionally(=3)	Yes, often(=4)			
5. This question is about neighborhood activities that you participate in. Do you currently participate in any of the following activities?								
A. Activities designed to promote relationships between people in the area (such as neighbourhood groups and associations)	291(7.2%)	713(17.6%)	945(48.1%)	097(27.1%)	2.95	0.856	−0.595
B. Sports, hobby, and amusement activities (such as various types of sporting activities, and artistic and cultural activities)	382(9.4%)	909(22.5%1)	742(43.1%)	1013(25%)	2.84	0.909	−0.428
C. Volunteer, NPO, civic, and other similar types of activities	630(15.6%)	224(30.3%)	1495(37%)	397(17.2%)	2.56	0.950	−0.110

(continued)

Table 3.2 (continued)

Nominal variable (question)	Variable description	Freq.	%			Mean	Std. Dev.	Skewness
D. Other organizational activities(such as political activities and religious activities)	720(17.8%)	089(26.9%)	1540(38.1)	697(17.2)		2.55	0.974	−0.151
						Mean	Std. Dev	Skewness
6. Do you have anyone that you can consult with or rely on regarding any problems or worries that you may have in daily life? For each of the items below, please select how much you can rely on the	Not at all(1=)	Hardly at all(2=)	Cannot say either way(3=)	To a certain extent(4=)	Deeply(=5)			
A. Your neighbors	606(15%)	708(17.5%)	739(8.3%)1	663(41.1%)	330(8.2%)	3.10	1.225	−0.413
B. You immediate family members	218(5.4%)	330(8.2%)	129(10.6%)1	422(35.1%)	647(40.7%)	3.98	1.151	−1.125
C. Other relatives	398(9.8%)	595(14.7%)	i05(19.9%)1	793(44.3%)	455(11.2%)	3.32	1.153	−0.600
D. Friends and acquaintances	203(5%)	378(9.3%)	459(11.3%)1	920(47.5%)	086(26.8)%	3.82	1.084	−1.022
E. Doctors and counselors	389(9.6%)	556(13.7%)	786(19.4%)1	622(40.1%)	593(17.1%)	3.41	1.199	−0.575

(continued)

Table 3.2 (continued)

Nominal variable (question)	Variable description	Freq.	%			Mean	Std. Dev.	Skewness
F. School teachers and cram school tutors	754(18.6%)	779(19.3%)	907(22.4%)	1213(30%)	393(9.7%)	2.93	1.273	−0.126
G. Your own caste members	821(20.3%)	790(19.5%)	922(22.8%)	1133(28%)	380(9.4%)	2.87	1.283	−0.060
H. Your own religious group members	850(21%)	664(16.4%)	889(22%)	158(28.6%)	485(12%)	2.94	1.329	−0.124

Table 3.3 Rotated factor matrix

	Factor 1	Factor 2	Factor 3	Factor 4
	Structural	Particularized (N)	Particularized (RE)	Reciprocity and generalized trust
5.A. Activities designed to promote relationships between people in the area (such as neighborhood groups and associations)	0.801	−0.035	−0.008	−0.023
5.B. Sports, hobby, and amusement activities (such as various types of sporting activities, and artistic and cultural activities)	0.762	−0.009	−0.058	−0.027
5.C. Volunteer, NPO, civic, and other similar types of activities	0.746	−0.103	0.118	−0.096
4.B. How many neighbors do you meet?	0.687	0.039	−0.060	0.085
4.A. How frequently do you meet your neighbors?	0.667	0.167	−0.146	0.099
5.D. Other organizational activities(such as political activities and religious activities)	0.599	−0.164	0.234	−0.049
6.B. You immediate family members	−0.066	0.908	−0.167	−0.047
6.D. Friends and acquaintances	−0.074	0.774	0.001	−0.010
6.C. Other relatives	−0.077	0.598	0.279	0.085
6.A. Your neighbors	0.220	0.564	0.092	0.003
6.E. Doctors and counselors	0.004	0.451	0.379	−0.130
6.G. Your own caste members	−0.011	−0.009	0.875	0.043
6.H. Your own religious group members	−0.013	−0.062	0.866	0.080
6.F. School teachers and cram school tutors	0.045	0.110	0.718	−0.049

(continued)

Table 3.3 (continued)

	Factor 1	Factor 2	Factor 3	Factor 4
	Structural	Particularized (N)	Particularized (RE)	Reciprocity and generalized trust
2. Direct reciprosity	−0.016	−0.119	0.077	0.849
3. Generalized reciprocity	−0.078	−0.028	0.020	0.845
1. Generalized trust	0.202	0.217	−0.073	0.505

Note: Extraction Method:Principal Component Analysis. Rotation Method: Varimax with Kaiser Normalization. Rotation converged in 6 iterations

Table 3.4 Correlation coefficients between happiness and social capital

	Happiness
Structural	0.3367*
Particularized (N)	0.2418*
Particularized (RE)	0.0839*
Reciprocity and generalized trust	0.3365*

* denotes significance at the 5%

reciprocity and generalized trust are bridging social capital when considering questions that loaded on each factor. Hereafter we will label these types of social capital as STRUCTURAL, PARTICULARIZED(N), PARTICULARIZED(RE), and RECIPROCITY AND GENERALIZED TRUST.

This analysis revealed four scales in the social capital questionnaire. Table 3.4 shows correlation coefficients between happiness and these four factors. All correlation coefficients are positive and significant, with structural social capital and reciprocity and general trust strongly correlated with happiness.

3.2.5 Other Variables

The average age of survey respondents was 32 years, and 59.7% were men and 40.3% were women. Average income was about $7,500, which is rather higher than the GNI per capita in U.S. dollars of $1,830 in 2017.[4] The distribution of marital status was 29.3% single, 63.6% married, 1.1% divorced, and 0.9% widowed. The relationship between marriage and happiness has been widely studied and there is a general consensus that marriage has a positive effect on happiness.

Education level was divided into three categories: below higher secondary certificate/state secondary certificate (HSC/SCC), attended college but has not graduated,

[4] Viewed on 2019/09/05 at https://data.worldbank.org/indicator/NY.GNP.PCAP.CD?locations=IN.

Table 3.5 Average of happiness by city size

	Average of happiness
Large-sized cities	8.76
Medium-sized cities	8.56
Small-sized cities	8.26
Towns or villages	8.11

and college graduate or higher. The third category, college graduate or higher, was 81%.

City sizes were divided into four types: large-sized cities (population of 1 million or more), medium-sized cities (population of less than 1 million), small-sized cities, and towns or villages. The largest number of respondents lived in large-sized cities. Table 3.5 shows the average level of happiness by city size.

3.2.6 Happiness Analysis

This section describes the results of estimating ordered probity equations in which individual's well-being levels are regressed on a set of personal characteristics.

Our basic economic model was based on the orthodox manner. The basic regression estimated is as follows:

$$y_i = a + b_1 x_{i1} + b_2 x_{i2} + ...b_k x_{ik} + e_i, i = 1, ..., n$$

where y_i is happiness for each respondent i, x_{ij} (j = 1, ..., k) are explanatory variables, and i indexes the n sample observations. The explanatory variables include those mentioned in the data section. The term e_i is a random disturbance. The appropriate specification is an ordered logit model because responses to the happiness question are ordinal rather than cardinal in nature.

Table 3.6 shows results for the whole sample (1) with columns (2) and (3) breaking down the data into different subsamples, where the dependent variable is happiness. Columns (4), (5), and (6) of Table 3.6 present the same results for life satisfaction, which will be discussed as a complement to happiness.

From the findings in Table 3.6, happiness has a positive and statistically significant correlation with female dummy, house (owned) dummy, health, no of income, top level manager, executives, self-employed, STRUCTURAL, PARTICULARIZED(N), RECIPROCITY AND GENERALIZED TRUST, and city size, whereas happiness does not have a statistically significant relationship to marital status, age, and education level for the whole sample.

We can confirm that our results fit the usual patterns that are found in the happiness literature, including Praag et al. (2003), Blanchflower and Oswald (2004), and Stutzer and Frey (2012). There are some specific findings in the case of India.

Table 3.6 Results of estimation (happiness and life satisfaction)

| | | Dependent Variables | | | | | |
| | | Happiness | | | Life satisfaction | | |
	Variables	Whole sample (1)	Male (2)	Female (3)	Whole sample (4)	Male (5)	Female (6)
Marital status	Single	Reference			Reference		
	Married	0.0853	0.0174	0.1936	0.4325	0.4912	0.3589
		[0.75]	[0.12]	[1.06]	[3.59]**	[3.12]**	[1.85]
	Divorced	0.067	−0.7073	0.6323	0.1784	−0.3297	0.4616
		[0.20]	[−1.41]	[1.45]	[0.50]	[−0.60]	[0.96]
	Widowed	−0.0255	−1.381	0.9169	0.5076	−0.1614	1.0697
		[−0.07]	[−2.65]**	[1.98]*	[1.24]	[−0.28]	[1.78]
Gender	Male	Reference			Reference		
	Female	0.1574			0.2445		
		[2.36]*			[3.29]**		
Age	Age	−0.0891	−0.1686	−0.0536	−0.326	−0.697	0.376
		[−0.63]	[−0.92]	[−0.21]	[−2.08]*	[−3.49]**	[1.34]
	Age squared	0.0136	0.0241	0.0124	0.0726	0.1186	−0.0221
		[0.74]	[1.05]	[0.36]	[3.50]**	[4.60]**	[−0.56]
House	House (owned) dummy	0.1739	0.106	0.2534	0.1403	0.1402	0.1067
		[2.51]*	[1.16]	[2.36]*	[1.87]	[1.42]	[0.91]
Child	Child dummy	0.0546	0.1322	−0.1165	−0.0684	−0.013	−0.1552
		[0.54]	[1.04]	[−0.69]	[−0.64]	[−0.10]	[−0.86]

(continued)

Table 3.6 (continued)

		Dependent Variables					
		Happiness			Life satisfaction		
		(1)	(2)	(3)	(4)	(5)	(6)
Health	Health	0.5334	0.5112	0.5866	0.4633	0.4657	0.4763
		[17.88]**	[13.40]**	[12.03]**	[14.63]**	[11.52]**	[9.15]**
Education	HSC/SSC	Reference			Reference		
	Attended college but has not graduated	−0.2639	−0.1593	−0.4605	0.1632	0.3288	−0.1176
		[−1.75]	[−0.85]	[−1.75]	[1.02]	[1.67]	[−0.42]
	College graduate or higher	−0.1692	−0.154	−0.2249	−0.0429	0.1398	−0.3644
		[−1.32]	[−0.95]	[−1.03]	[−0.32]	[0.83]	[−1.58]
Income	NI of income	0.15	0.337	−0.0785	0.2221	0.3513	0.0738
		[2.03]*	[3.37]**	[−0.69]	[2.62]**	[3.06]**	[0.57]
Work status	Top level manager, executive	0.2433	0.1797	0.3753	0.1238	0.1166	0.1547
		[2.77]**	[1.63]	[2.54]*	[1.25]	[0.95]	[0.91]
	Regular employee	Reference			Reference		
	Civil servant	0.2847	0.335	−0.0867	0.0455	0.0865	−0.3384

(continued)

Table 3.6 (continued)

		Dependent Variables					
		Happiness			Life satisfaction		
		(1)	(2)	(3)	(4)	(5)	(6)
		[1.21]	[1.25]	[−0.17]	[0.18]	[0.30]	[−0.61]
	Contract /fixed-term /Part- time employee/home-based work	0.1497	0.1637	0.1336	0.0621	0.1894	−0.0952
		[1.33]	[1.02]	[0.82]	[0.50]	[1.07]	[−0.54]
	Self-employed	0.3564	0.193	0.6526	0.057	0.0551	0.0594
		[3.53]**	[1.51]	[3.92]**	[0.52]	[0.40]	[0.32]
	Student	0.0625	0.1307	−0.0921	0.0055	−0.1196	0.2775
		[0.41]	[0.68]	[−0.35]	[0.03]	[−0.58]	[0.98]
	Unemployed (includes homemakers)	0.1521	0.2493	0.0052	0.0643	0.1119	−0.0843
		[1.05]	[0.94]	[0.03]	[0.40]	[0.38]	[−0.40]
	Other	0.2309	0.1162	0.2703	0.3905	0.333	0.2789
		[1.21]	[0.49]	[0.83]	[1.69]	[1.11]	[0.75]
Social capital	STRUCTURAL	0.512	0.523	0.5052	0.2814	0.3114	0.2395
		[13.02]**	[10.19]**	[8.13]**	[6.66]**	[5.67]**	[3.54]**

(continued)

Table 3.6 (continued)

		Dependent Variables					
		Happiness			Life satisfaction		
		(1)	(2)	(3)	(4)	(5)	(6)
	PARTICULARIZED(N)	0.321	0.2757	0.3957	0.2884	0.2324	0.3738
		[8.60]**	[5.82]**	[6.45]**	[7.20]**	[4.54]**	[5.72]**
	PARTICULARIZED(RE)	−0.0648	−0.0594	−0.0664	−0.0769	−0.0299	−0.1311
		[−1.78]	[−1.23]	[−1.17]	[−1.91]	[−0.56]	[−2.10]*
	RECIPROCITY AND GENERALIZED TRUST	0.5542	0.5789	0.4892	0.2116	0.2146	0.1936
		[15.34]**	[12.67]**	[8.18]**	[5.55]**	[4.46]**	[3.04]**
City size	Large-sized cities	0.2546	0.1789	0.4335	0.0131	−0.1461	0.3192
		[1.98]*	[1.16]	[1.80]	[0.09]	[−0.85]	[1.24]
	Medium-sized cities	0.243	0.1184	0.4789	0.0735	−0.1644	0.4932
		[1.80]	[0.73]	[1.92]	[0.50]	[−0.91]	[1.84]
	Small−sized cities	0.1365	0.2077	−0.0011	0.1053	−0.073	0.3903
		[0.79]	[1.00]	[−0.00]	[0.57]	[−0.32]	[1.17]
	Towns or villages	Reference			Reference		

(continued)

Table 3.6 (continued)

	Dependent Variables					
	Happiness			Life satisfaction		
	(1)	(2)	(3)	(4)	(5)	(6)
cut1	-4.4892	-4.5475	4.6317	-0.8624	-1.3142	-0.1781
	[-9.62]**	[-7.71]**	[-5.93]**	[-2.56]*	[-3.09]**	[-0.31]
cut2	-3.2098	-3.402	-3.1512	-0.1464	-0.5914	0.5369
	[-8.92]**	[-7.33]**	[-5.27]**	[-0.44]	[-1.40]	[0.93]
cut3	-2.4077	-2.5158	-2.461	0.8645	0.4155	1.5705
	[-7.25]**	[-5.96]**	[-4.36]**	[2.59]**	[0.99]	[2.73]**
cut4	-1.6622	-1.7926	-1.6768	2.2494	1.8512	2.9079
	[-5.21]**	[-4.42]**	[-3.09]**	[6.70]**	[4.38]**	[5.03]**
cut5	-0.9658	-1.1819	-0.8536			
	[-3.09]**	[-2.97]**	[-1.60]			
cut6	-0.1482	-0.2695	-0.1534			
	[-0.48]	[-0.69]	[-0.29]			
cut7	0.7697	0.6478	0.7808			

(continued)

Table 3.6 (continued)

	Dependent Variables					
	Happiness			Life satisfaction		
	(1)	(2)	(3)	(4)	(5)	(6)
	[2.50]*	[1.66]	[1.48]			
cut8	2.0666	1.9265	2.1336			
	[6.67]**	[4.90]**	[4.04]**			
cut9	3.6113	3.4649	3.7255			
	[11.51]**	[8.71]**	[6.96]**			
cut10	5.2272	5.1028	5.3339			
	[16.38]**	[12.60]**	[9.81]**			
N	3566	2143	1423	3566	2143	1423
ll	−5793.1274	−3485.33	−2282.59	−3927.7057	−2351.3397	−1558.457
r2_p	0.1223	0.1188	0.1359	0.0933	0.1017	0.0907
df_m	26	25	25	26	25	25
chi2	1614.4034	939.5383	718.1525	808.4873	532.3641	310.8016
p	0	0	0	0	0	0

Note: t statistics in brackets. *<0.05, ** p<0.01

3.2.7 Education

Our estimation did not show a significant education–happiness relationship, consistent with the results in Lakshmanasamy (2010, 315 respondents). Our result is not surprising, given its consistency with the literature that shows a negative or absent education–happiness relationship Clark and Oswald (1996). There is a view that happiness depends upon the gap between real conditions and aspirations. Happiness is not likely to increase with a higher education level, because education raises aspiration targets. Another reason to account for the lack of relationship between education and happiness is that education is instrumental. Education becomes insignificant when other variables are included as repressors. Therefore, education acts mainly through its effects on variables such as income and social capital.

3.2.8 Work Status

Happiness has a positive and statistically significant correlation with top-level manager, executive, and self-employed (reference variable is "regular employee"). These results are reasonable. The self-employed have greater independence and autonomy compared with the employed. This accounts for greater happiness in the self-employed (Benz & Frey, 2004, p. 98; Andersson, 2008). In general, greater freedom in the work environment, such as the opportunity to "be your own boss" is an important source of happiness at work (Benz & Frey, 2004, p. 98). These conditions can also apply to top-level manager and executive.

3.2.9 Marital Status

Being married was not associated with happiness in all cases. Being married is likely to have a statistically significant and positive correlation with happiness compared with being single due to the wide range of marital benefits, including increased earnings, insurance against adverse life events, and gains from economies of scale and specialization within the family.[5] However, happiness did have a positive and statistically significant correlation with being married for the whole sample and male respondents when applying life satisfaction as the dependent variable instead of happiness (see columns (4) and (5)). Young women in particular did not rate their marriage as happy in each case (see column (6)) due to poverty as well as "husband-related" (e.g., extramarital affairs, alcoholism, abuse) and "in-law-related" reasons.[6] These reasons might not apply to the present study because our data included much older married women. Future research is needed to determine the reasons.

---

[5] Stutzer and Frey (2006).

[6] Ghosh, Lahiri and Datta (2017, p. 123).

3.2.10 Age

Age was not significant in the three cases (see columns (1), (2), and (3)). There is a well-defined U-shape between happiness and age in the literature (e.g., Blanch-flower & Oswald, 2008). Age also has a positive and statistically significant corre-lation with happiness in another Indian happiness study (Lakshmanasamy, 2010). However, age was not significant even after applying age as the sole repressor in the present study. Even so, age did have a U-shape over life cycle when applying life satisfaction as the dependent variable instead of happiness for the whole sample and male respondents (see columns (4), (5), and (6)). Survey-based measures are sensi-tive to question type. Therefore, measurement methods might account for the stated difference, because happiness was measured on an 11-point integer rating from 0 to 10 whereas life satisfaction was measured on a 5-point integer rating from 1 to 5.

3.2.11 City Size

Large cities, medium-sized cities, and small cities were positively correlated with happiness (reference variable is "town and village"). But only large cities had a statistically significant correlation with happiness. As indicated by Albouy (2008), happiness does not tend to depend upon city size when controlling for the full set of individual, household, and area characteristics.

There are pros and cons in the case of large cities. The pros are gains from the reduced cost of moving goods across space, labor-market pooling, the benefits of moving people across firms, and the large flow of ideas, all of which creates human capital at the individual level and facilitates innovation. The cons are commuting costs and high land prices. The props outweighed the cons for large cities in the present study.

3.2.12 Social Capital

STRUCTURAL, PARTICULARIZED(N), and RECIPROCITY AND GENERAL-IZED TRUST had a positive and statistically significant correlation with happiness in the three cases. Contrary to what might be expected, PARTICULARIZED (RE) was not significantly correlated with happiness.

Relationships exist between social capital and social outcomes such as better health, low crime rates, and effective government administration (e.g., Putnam, 1993; Helliwell & Putnam, 1995; Ichino & Maggi, 2000). As for the effects of social capital on happiness and SWB, most previous studies provided evidence of a positive relationship (e.g., Bartolini et al., 2016; Helliwell, 2006; Orlowski & Wicker, 2015; Pinquart & Sörensen, 2000).

How does social capital affect happiness? There are many channels through which increases in social capital improve happiness. For example, benefits come through greater efficiency in economic outcomes and government. Networks also improve cooperation both within and among communities. Therefore, those who are connected are more likely to feel happier than those who are not.

The present analysis concludes that social capital is associated with a high level of both happiness and life satisfaction, although some demographic factors are differently associated with both. We now proceed to an analysis of determinants of social capital.

3.3   Social Capital and Hypothesis

There are recent theoretical contributions in the literature on social capital. Glaeser et al. (2002) provided a simple model that analyzed an individual's decision to accumulate social capital. Chou (2006) considered three channels through which social capital can affect economic growth, human capital, financial development, and collaboration between firms. Beugelsdijk and Smulders (2009) analyzed a model of economic growth, bonding social capital, and bridging social capital. Roseta-Palma et al. (2010) sophisticated the analysis of Beugelsdijk and Smulders (2009). Agénor and Dinh (2013) generalized Routledge and von Amsberg (2003), Chou (2006), Bofota et al. (2012), and Growiec (2012) and focused on the macroeconomic effects of social capital, insisting that the key benefit of social capital is to help promote imitation.

The present study used the model of social capital formation by Glaeser et al. (2002) (the GLS model) because it facilitates empirical analysis, although more sophisticated models exist.

The GLS model treats social capital as an individual characteristic and is similar to the model of human capital. Individual social capital is represented as the stock variable, S. Each individual receives a per-period utility flow of S $R(\widehat{S})$, which is the flow pay-off to the individual, where $\widehat{S}$ is the aggregate per-capita social capital, $R(\widehat{S})$ is a differentiable function with aggregate per-capita social capital as its argument, and $R'(\widehat{S}) > 0$ is assumed. The social capital stock follows the dynamic budget constraint,

$$S_{t+1} = \delta\varphi S_t + I_t$$

$(1 - \delta)$ is the depreciation rate. φ is defined as $(1 - \theta) + \theta\lambda$, where θ is the probability that an individual leaves the community and λ is the proportion of which the value of social capital falls when an individual leaves the community. Therefore, φ represents the depreciation factor arising from mobility. The level of investment I_t needs a time cost $C(I_t)$, where $C(\,\cdot\,)$ is increasing and convex. The opportunity cost of time is the wage rate w. It is assumed that individuals have a known lifespan of T periods and that they discount the future with discount factor β.

The individual's maximization problem is as follows:

$$\max_{I_0,\ldots,I_t} \sum_{t=0}^{T} \beta^t [S_t R(S_t) - wC(I_t)]$$

$$s.t. S_{t+1} = \delta\varphi S_t + I_t, \forall t$$

The individual maximizes his objective function, taking aggregate per capita social capital, $\hat{S}$, as fixed. The first-order condition associated with this investment problem is given by

$$wC'(I_t) = \frac{1 - (\beta\delta\varphi)^{T-t+1}}{1 - \beta\delta\varphi} R(\hat{S})$$

This first-order condition implies the following comparative static results. The left (right) side of the above equation is the marginal cost (marginal benefit) of social capital investment. Social capital investment (I) rises with β (discount factor), $R(\hat{S})$ (occupational returns of social skills), and $\hat{S}$ (aggregatesocialcapital) because an increase in these variables raises the marginal benefit. In contrast, social capital investment (I) decreases with θ (mobility), $(1-\delta)$ (rate of social capital depreciation), $(1-\lambda)$ (rate of social capital depreciation due to relocation), and t (age) because an increase in these variables lowers the marginal benefit. Because an increase in w (opportunity cost of time) raises the marginal cost, social capital investment declines.

3.3.1 Empirical Analysis of Social Capital

In order to examine the hypotheses previously proposed, OLS was utilized to conduct the estimations. The estimated equation takes the following form

$$SC_i = a + b_1 x_{i1} + b_2 x_{i2} + \ldots b_k x_{ik} + u_i, i = 1, \ldots, n$$

where SC_i is social capital for each respondent i, x_{ij} ($j = 1, \ldots, k$) are explanatory variables, and i indexes the n sample observations. The explanatory variables include those mentioned in the data section. The term u_i is a random disturbance.

Estimate results are shown in Table 3.7. A regression was conducted for each type of social capital. The parameters are presented, with ** and * in Table 3.7 to indicate significance at the 1% and 5% significance levels, respectively. The adjusted R-squared is around 0.1 (which is relatively high in studies of this kind.)

Table 3.7 Estimation results (social capital)

	Variables	Structural	Particularize (N)	Particularized (RE)	Reciprocity and generalized trust
Gender	Male	Reference			
	Female	−0.0552	0.0674	−0.1014	−0.021
		[−1.67]	[1.98]*	[−2.90]**	[−0.62]
Age	Less than 20	0.0119	0.0486	0.0756	0.035
		[0.15]	[0.58]	[0.89]	[0.42]
	20–29 years old	0.1353	−0.08	0.1132	0.1048
		[2.60]**	[−1.49]	[2.05]*	[1.95]
	30–39 years old	Reference			
	40–49 years old	−0.2638	0.0272	−0.0604	−0.1543
		[−5.69]**	[0.57]	[−1.23]	[−3.22]**
	50–59 years old	−0.3673	0.1152	−0.196	−0.312
		[−6.92]**	[2.10]*	[−3.48]**	[−5.69]**
	60 or above	−0.3472	0.1538	−0.2519	−0.4429
		[−5.27]**	[2.26]*	[−3.61]**	[−6.51]**
Marital status	Single	Reference			
	Married	0.0158	0.0844	0.0823	0.0811
		[0.27]	[1.39]	[1.33]	[1.34]
	Divorced	0.0055	0.2545	0.1372	−0.0872
		[0.03]	[1.55]	[0.82]	[−0.53]
	Widowed	−0.1062	0.0695	0.061	0.2436
		[−0.59]	[0.37]	[0.32]	[1.32]
Child	Child dummy	0.3158	−0.0065	0.3183	0.1791
		[6.43]**	[−0.13]	[6.12]**	[3.53]**
House	House (owned) dummy	0.3052	0.1851	0.2188	0.2509
		[8.85]**	[5.18]**	[5.98]**	[7.04]**
Income	Nl of income	0.3664	0.1525	0.1951	0.2312
		[11.32]**	[4.55]**	[5.69]**	[6.92]**
Education	HSC/SSC	Reference			
	Attended college but has not graduated	−0.1141	0.166	−0.0741	−0.2172

(continued)

Table 3.7 (continued)

	Variables	Structural	Particularize (N)	Particularized (RE)	Reciprocity and generalized trust
		[−1.54]	[2.17]*	[−0.94]	[−2.84]**
	College graduate or higher	−0.0705	0.3091	−0.0942	−0.088
		[−1.12]	[4.74]**	[−1.41]	[−1.35]
City size	Large-sized city (population of one million or larger)	Reference			
	Medium-sized city (population of less than one million)	0.0351	−0.101	0.0239	0.0236
		[0.92]	[−2.55]*	[0.59]	[0.60]
	Small-sized city	0.0545	−0.2721	−0.01	−0.0617
		[0.81]	[−3.93]**	[−0.14]	[−0.89]
	Town or village	−0.0593	−0.2672	−0.0666	−0.042
		[−0.93]	[−4.07]**	[−0.99]	[−0.64]
	_cons	−0.6178	−0.5595	−0.4719	−0.3884
		[−7.03]**	[−6.15]**	[−5.06]**	[−4.27]**
	R-squared	0.1267	0.0636	0.0621	0.0736
	Adj-r-squared	0.1225	0.0591	0.0576	0.0692
	N	3566	3566	3566	3566

Note: t statistics in brackets. * < 0.05, ** $p < 0.01$

3.3.1.1 Gender

Women benefited more than men from social capital for PARTICULARIZED(N) but less for PARTICULARIZED(RE). PARTICULARIZED(N) pertains to informal networks, although PARTICULARIZED(RE) pertains to social networks. One interpretation of this result is that women are more likely to gain from participation in informal networks than men, who generally have greater access to social networks (Elgar et al., 2011, p. 1051).

3.3.1.2 Age

Social capital was negatively correlated with age for STRUCTURAL, PARTICULARIZED (RE), and RECIPROCITY AND GENERALIZED TRUST, but positively with PARTICULARIZED (N). Figure 3.3 shows the average level of social capital

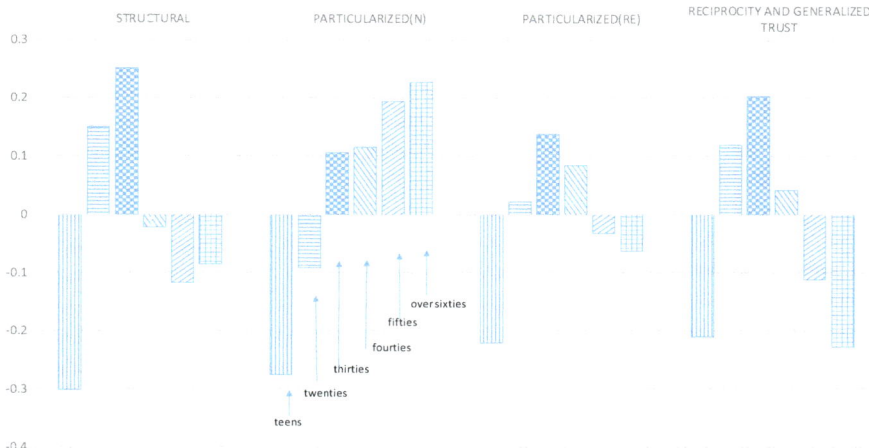

Fig. 3.3 Average of social capital by age (n = 3,565)

by age. Each level of social capital of the teens is minus and large, but the teens do not have a significant effect on social capital according to Table 3.7.

Glaeser et al. (2002) found a strong age effect, where levels of social capital followed an inverted U-shaped curve over the life cycle. However, the same inverted U-shaped curve effect was not found in the present study when the analysis controlled for socio-economic variables.

Social capital declines as age increases except in the case of PARTICULARIZED (N), which contradicts the hypothesis. As PARTICULARIZED (N) includes immediate family members and friends, people as they age are likely to depend on them. If so, this type of social capital might increase for them.

3.3.2 Marriage, Having Children, and Home Ownership: Mobility

The GLS model predicts a negative relationship between mobility and social capital. Variables pertaining to mobility are marriage, having children, and home ownership. Getting married requires time for discussing and deciding about relocation. Furthermore, relocation is expensive because a couple might need to purchase furniture and other household furnishings. In addition to the aforementioned reasons, having children also involves much time and costs such as those related to changing schools. Homeowners are relatively reluctant to move because transaction costs are high in the real estate market. These three variables thus lead to high levels of social capital according to the hypothesis.

Coefficients on each type of social capital for married people were not statistically significant at the 5% level when "singlehood" was the reference variable. Social capital was positively correlated with having children for STRUCTURAL, PARTICULARIZED (RE), and RECIPROCITY AND GENERALIZED TRUST, but not with PARTICULARIZED (N). Coefficients for homeowners were significant at the 1% significance level in each case.

3.3.2.1   Income

The GLS model predicts that social capital investment declines with the opportunity cost of time. The estimation included controls for natural log of income. Coefficients were positively significant in all cases. However, this result contradicted the hypothesis. An interpretation of this result is that because higher income produces higher education, those with higher education invest in social capital when education (human capital) is complementary to social capital.[7]

3.3.2.2   Education

A higher discount factor raises social capital according to the hypothesis. A higher discount rate means more patience, which means higher human capital and a higher education level in human capital theory. Therefore, higher education predicts a higher level of social capital. This relationship emerges in the case of PARTICULARIZED (N).

3.3.2.3   City Size

With increasing urbanization, it has become necessary to assess the effect of urbanization on social capital. The costs of connection are important elements in social connection, and social connection declines as the costs of that connection increase (Glaeser & Sacerdote, 2000, p. 13). In urban areas, people are more likely to form social connections because people are spatially intimate. Figure 3.4 presents the average level of social capital by city size for each type of social capital and shows that the bigger the city size, the greater the social capital. However, this relationship was significant only for PARTICULARIZED (N). The costs of connection had no effect on the other types of social capital.

---

[7] Glaeser et al. (2002), p. F454.

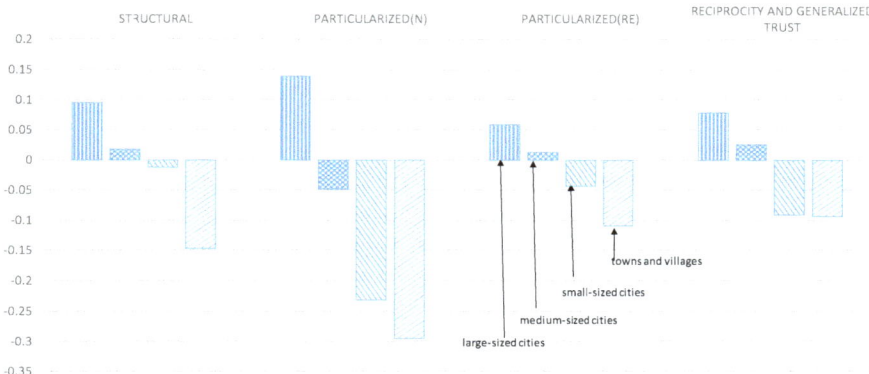

Fig. 3.4 Average of social capital by age (n = 3,565)

3.4 Conclusion

It can now be confirmed that the results of this study fit the usual patterns that are found in the happiness literature. However, there are some specific findings in the case of India. There is no significant education–happiness relationship in the estimation. Happiness had a positive and statistically significant correlation with top-level manager, executive, and self-employed (reference variable is "regular employee"). Being married was not associated with happiness in all cases (whole sample, male and female), whereas being married is likely to have a positive and statistically significant correlation with happiness in the happiness literature. Age was not significant in the whole sample and in men and women, whereas there is a well-defined U-shape between happiness and age in the happiness literature. Only large cities had a statistically significant correlation with happiness. Three dimensions of social capital (i.e., STRUCTURAL, PARTICULARIZED (N), and RECIPROCITY AND GENERALIZED TRUST) had a strong positive correlation with happiness whereas PARTICULARIZED (RE) did not.

The same estimation was attempted using life satisfaction instead of happiness and a marked diversity was found between happiness and life satisfaction. For example, life satisfaction had a positive and statistically significant correlation with being married in the whole sample and in men, whereas happiness did not in all cases. Age had a U-shape over life cycle when life satisfaction was used as the dependent variable. Standard questions about happiness and life satisfaction were used. To date, it is not clear which of the two measures is more suitable for SWB. In fact, many well-being measures have been used in empirical studies (see overview of measures by Bartels (2015). This point will be left for future research.

The results of the research reported here clearly confirmed the presence of a positive relationship between social capital and SWB (for both happiness and life satisfaction). In that sense, social capital was a big predictor of happiness. Finally, the determinants of social capital were estimated. The conclusion was almost hypo-thetical in the case of three types of social capital (i.e., STRUCTURAL, PARTIC-ULARIZED (RE), and RECIPROCITY AND GENERALIZED TRUST) with the exception of PARTICULARIZED (N). SWB plays an important role in the policy-making process in India. Therefore, decisionmakers in India need to explore how public policy contributes to the formation of social capital.

References

Agénor, Richard, P., & Dinh, H. T. (2013). Social capital, product imitation and growth with learning externalities. *Policy research working paper* 6607, World Bank, Washington DC.

Agrawal, J., Murthy, P., Philip, M., Mehrotra, S., Thennarasu, K., John, J. P., Girish, N., Thippeswamy, V., & Isaac M. (2011). Socio-demographic correlates of subjective well-being in urban India, *Social Indicators Research*, 101(3), 419–434.

Albouy, D. (2008). Are big cities really bad places to live? Improving quality-of-life estimates across cities, *NBER Working Paper* 14472.

Andersson, P. (2008). Happiness and health: Well-being among the self-employed. *The Journal of Socio-Economics, 37*, 213–236.

Bartels, M. (2015). Genetics of wellbeing and its components satisfaction with life, happiness, and quality of life: A review and meta-analysis of heritability studies, *Behavior Genetics, 45*(2), 137–156.

Bartolini, S., Bilancini, E., & Sarracino. (2016). Social capital predicts happiness over time. In S. Bartolini, E. L. Bilancini, L.Bruni, & P. L. Porta (Eds.), *Policies for happiness* (pp. 175–198) Oxford University Press.

Benz, M., & Frey, B. S. (2004). Being independent raises happiness at work. *Swedish Economic Policy Review, 12*, 97–138.

Beugelsdijk, S., & Smulders, S. (2009). Bonding and bridging social capital and economic growth, *SSRN working paper*, (2009–27).

Blanchflower, D. G., & Oswald, A. J. (2004). Well-being over time in Britain and the USA. *Journal of Public Economics, 88*(7–8), 1359–1386.

Blanchflower, D. G., & Oswald, A. J. (2008). Is well-being U-shaped over the life cycle? *Social Science and Medicine, 66*, 1733–1749.

Bofota, Y. B., Boucekkine, R., & Bala, A. P. (2012). Social capital as an engine of growth: Multisectoral modelling and implications," unpublished, University of Aix Marseille.

Chou, Y. K. (2006). Three simple models of social capital and economic growth. *The Journal of Socio-Economics, 35*, 889–912.

Clark, A. E., & Oswald, A. J. (1996). Satisfaction and comparison income. *Journal of Public Economics, 61*(3), 359–381.

Dawson, (2017). How persistent is generalised trust? *Sociology, Sociology,* 1–10.

Diener, E., Emmons, R. A., Larsen, R. J. & Griffin, S. (1985). The satisfaction with life scale. *Journal of Personality Assessment, 49*, 71–75.

Elgar, F.J., Davis, C. G., Wohl, M. J., Trites, S. J., Zelenski, J. M., & Martin, M. S. (2011). Social capital, health and life satisfaction in 50 countries, *Health and Place, 17*(5), 1044–1053.

Ghosh, S., Lahiri, S., & Datta, N. (2017). Understanding happiness and psychological well-being among young married women in rural India. *Journal of Comparative Family Studies, 48*(1), 113–131.

Ghosh, A., Millett, C., Subramanian, S. V., & Pramanik, S. (2017). Neighborhood heterogeneity in health and well-being among the elderly in India – Evidence from study on global ageing and adult health, *Health and Place, 47*, 100–107.

Glaeser, E. L., Laibson, D., & Sacerdote, B. (2002). An economic approach to social capital, *The Economic Journal, 112*(483), F437-F458

Glaeser, E., & Sacerdote, B. (2000). The social consequences of housing. *Journal of Housing Economics, 9*(1–2), 1–23.

Growiec, K., & Growiec, J. (2012). Social capital, trust, and multiple equilibria in economic performance," unpublished, Institute for structural research.

Hafen, C. A., Singh, K., & Laursen, B. (2011). The happy personality in India: The role of emotional intelligence. *Happiness Studies, 12*, 807–817. https://doi.org/10.1007/s10902-010-9228-4

Helliwell, J. F., & Putnam, R. D. (1995). Economic growth and social capital in Italy. *Eastern Economic Journal, 21*(3) 295–307.

Helliwell, J. F. (2006). Well-being, social capital and public policy: What's new? *The Economic Journal, 116*(510), C34–C45.

Ichino, A., & Maggi, G. (2000). Work environment and individual background: Explaining regional shirking differentials in a large Italian firm. *The Quarterly Journal of Economics, 115,*1057–1090.

Itaba, Y. (2016). Does city size affect happiness? In T. Tachibanaki (Ed.) *Advances in happiness research: A comparative perspective*, (pp. 245–273). Springer.

Knack, S., & Keefer, P. (1997). Does social capital have an economic payoff? A cross-country investigation, *The Quarterly Journal of Economics, 11*(4), 1251–1288.

Lakshmanasamy, T. (2010). Are you satisfied with your income? The economics of happiness in India, *Journal of Quantitative Economics, 8*(2), 115–141.

Linsen, R., Kempen, V. L., & Kraaykamp, G. (2011). Subjective well-being in rural India: The curse of conspicuous consumption, *Social Indicators Research, 101*(1) 57–72.

OECD. (2013). *OECD guidelines on measuring subjective well-being*, OECD Publishing.

Orlowski, J., & Wicker, P. (2015). The monetary value of social capital, *Journal of Behavioral and Experimental Economics, 57*, 26–36.

Ostrom, E. (2000). Collective action and the evolution of social norms. *Journal of Economic Perspectives, 14*(3), 137–158.

Oztok, M., Zingaro, D., Makos, A., Brett, C., & Hewitt, J. (2015). Capitalizing on social presence: The relationship between social capital and social presence. *The Internet and Higher Education, 26*, 19–24.

Pinquart, M., & Sörensen, S. (2000). Influences of socioeconomic status, social network, and competence on subjective well-being in later life: A meta-analysis, *Psychology and Aging, 15*(2), 187–224.

Polit, K. M. (2005). The effects of inequality and relative marginality on the well-being of low caste people in central Uttaranchal. *Anthropology and Medicine, 12*(3), 225–237.

Van Praag, B., Frijters, P., & Ferrer-i-Carbonell, A. (2003). The anatomy of subjective well-being, *Journal of Economic Behavior and Organization, 51*(1), 29–49.

Putnam, R. D. (1993). *Making democracy work: Civic traditions in modern Italy*. Princeton University Press.

Putnam, R. D. (2000). *Bowling alone: The collapse and revival of American community,* Simon and Schuster, New York.

Roseta-Palma, C., Ferreira-Lopes, A., & Neves Sequeira, T. (2010). Externalities in an endogenous growth model with social and natural capital, *Ecological Economics, 69*, 603–612.

Routledge, B. R., & von Amsberg, J. (2003). Social capital and growth. *Journal of Monetary Economics, 50*, 167–194.

Sato, Y. (2013). Social capital. *Sociopedia.isa*, 1–10, https://doi.org/10.1177/205684601374.

Stutzer, A., & Frey, B. S. (2012). Recent developments in the economics of happiness: Inner wellbeing: concept and validation of a new approach to subjective perceptions of wellbeing—India. A selective overview, *IZA Discussion Paper* No. 7078.

Stutzer, A., & Frey, B. S. (2006). Does marriage make people happy, or do happy people get married? *The Journal of Socio-Economics, 35*, 326–347.

Szreter, S., & Woolcock, M. (2004). Health by association? Social capital, social theory, and the political economy of public health. *International Journal of Epidemiology, 33*, 650–667.

Tavits, M. (2006). Making democracy work more? *Exploring the Linkage between Social Capital and Government Performance, Political Research Quarterly, 59*(2), 211–225.

Veenhoven, R. (2012). Happiness: Also known as "life satisfaction" and "subjective well-being. In K. C. Land, A. C. Michalos, & M. J. Sirgy (Eds.), *Handbook of social indicators and quality of life research*. Springer.

Villalonga-Olives, E., & Kawachi, I. (2015). The measurement of bridging social capital in population health research. *Health Place, 36*, 47–56.

White, S. C., Devine, J., & Jha, S. (2012). The life a person lives: Religion, wellbeing and development in India. *Development in practice, 22*(5–6), 651–662.

White, S. C., Gaines, Jr. O. S., & Jha, S. (2014). Inner wellbeing: concept and validation of a new approach to subjective perceptions of wellbeing-India. *Socio Indicators Research, 119*(2), 723–46.

Chapter 4
Comparison of the Determinants of Well-Being Between India and Japan: Implications for the Future of the Economy and Society of India

Tadashi Yagi

Abstract Future economic changes in India should be predicted with consideration of not only macroeconomic factors such as consumption, investment, and financial situation, but also social factors such as well-being. In this chapter, we start with the premise that changing social factors interactively affect economic behavior. The overview of happiness suggests that the well-being of the Indian people is relatively low and declining, and that the difference between India and Japan is growing. This implies that economic development did not work to improve the well-being of the Indian people on average. It might be that inequality of well-being in India has been expanding, with the people who have benefited from economic growth enjoying increased well-being and low-income groups having decreased well-being. Against this background, we need to analyze the effects of economic factors on well-being in India more rigorously from various aspects, including social value judgements or religious factors, by using micro data. In this chapter, we discuss how the pursuit of happiness affects the society and economy of India by comparison with those of Japan.

4.1 Introduction

Economic development is surging in India, whereas the economy is already mature in Japan. India's economy is expected to grow at a higher rate relative to the world economy by taking advantage of the huge population of the country. However, future economic changes in India should be predicted with consideration of not only macroeconomic factors such as consumption, investment, financial situation, and trade balances, but also social factors such as social relationships, value judgments, and well-being. In this chapter, we start with the premise that changing social factors interactively affect economic behavior.

T. Yagi (✉)
Faulty of Economics, Doshisha University, 601 Genbu-choKarasuma-higashi-iru, ImadegawaKyoto 602-8580, Japan
e-mail: tyagi@mail.doshisha.ac.jp

The ultimate criterion for evaluating economic development in India should be the well-being of its people. In this chapter, we use the well-being of the Japanese people as a reference for comparison. According to the 2018 World Happiness Report by Helliwell et al. (2018), the average degree of happiness in Japan is 5.915, which ranks at 54th out of 156 countries, while that in India is 4.190, which ranks at 133rd. The change in happiness in India from 2008–2010 to 2015–2017 was −0.698, while that in Japan was −0.012. This overview of happiness suggests that the well-being of the Indian people is relatively low and declining, and that the difference between India and Japan is growing.

The overview above suggests that the effect of different stages of economic development on well-being is not straightforward. From 2008–2010 to 2015–2017, India achieved dramatic economic development. According to the World Bank, the country's gross domestic product (GDP) was 1,187 billion USD in 2008 and grew to 2,264 billion USD in 2016.[1] This implies that economic development did not work to improve the well-being of the Indian people on average. However, these facts might tell more than one story. It might be that inequality of well-being in India has been expanding, with the people who have benefited from economic growth enjoying increased well-being and low-income groups ("those getting left behind") having decreased well-being. Moreover, if economic growth breaks down social norms and distorts social value judgments, it might harm the well-being of people in all income classes.

Against this background, we need to analyze the effects of economic factors on well-being in India more rigorously from various aspects, including social value judgments or religious factors, by using microdata. The difference between India and Japan might have arisen from differences in value judgments and the degree of religiousness of the people in both countries. These value judgments affect economic growth and the stability of society. In this chapter, we examine the details in the relation between the formation of well-being and value judgments, and discuss how the pursuit of happiness affects the society and economy of India by comparison with those of Japan.

This chapter is organized as follows. Section 4.2 discusses the macroeconomic situation in India and some related issues. In Sect. 4.3, we examine the differences in well-being and value judgments between India and Japan by using the World Values Survey (WVS). Section 4.4 presents an analysis of differences in social and economic behavior between India and Japan by examining the determinants of well-being.

---

[1] See https://tradingeconomics.com/india/gdp as of March 23, 2018.

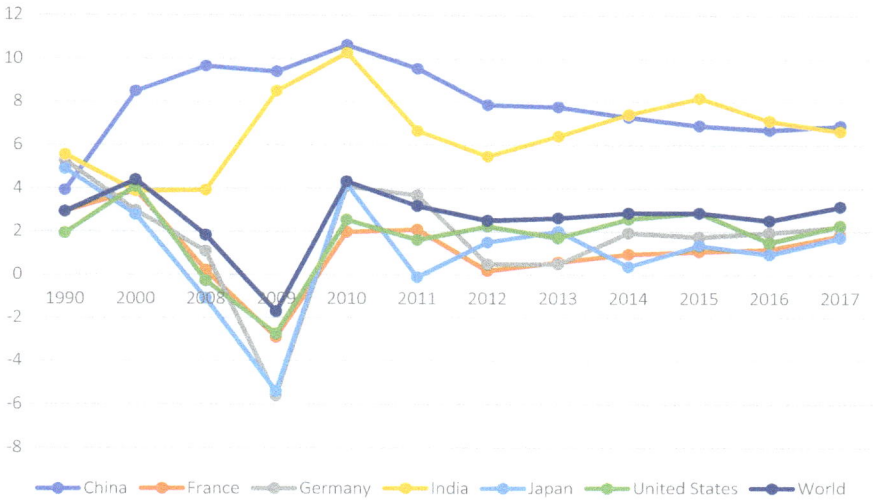

Fig. 4.1 GDP growth rate (%). *Source* World Bank Statistics (2018)

4.2 The Macroeconomic Situation in India and Related Issues

4.2.1 The Macroeconomic Situation

The economic growth rate of India is remarkably high, as shown in Fig. 4.1. Since 2010, the growth rate has been between 6 and 10%, and these rates are considerably higher than those in major developed countries such as the United States, Japan, and European countries. In this section, we discuss the economic situation in India in detail, with consideration of various factors. According to World Bank Statistics (2018),[2] India's gross national product was 450 billion USD in 2000 but increased to 2.5 trillion USD in 2016. In other words, the national income grew fivefold in 16 years. Corresponding to this drastic increase, the labor force participation rate of the working age population (15–64 years) dropped from 61% in 2000 to 56% in 2016. The decline was especially notable in female labor force participation, which dropped from 35.7 to 28.9%. The unemployment rate dropped from 4.31% in 2000 to 3.5% in 2016.

An increase in national income does not necessarily lead to an increase in household consumption expenditure at the same rate as economic growth. The final consumption expenditure of households and non-profit institutions serving households fell from 63.6% in 2000 to 58.9% in 2016 as a percentage of GDP. This implies

---

[2] The data were drawn from DataBank of The World Bank, https://databank.worldbank.org/home.aspx.

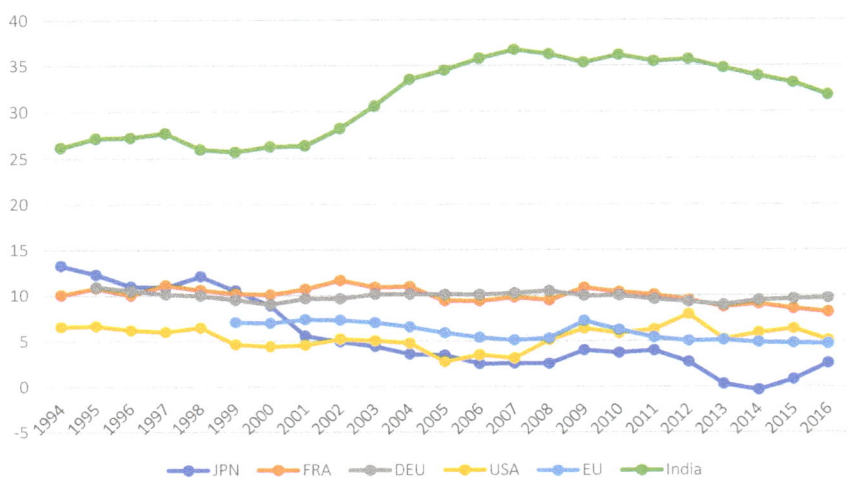

Fig. 4.2 Saving rate (% GDP). *Sources* OECD Statistics (2018),[3] World Bank Statistics (2018)

that the share of the household sector in the economy decreased through the process of economic growth.

As shown in Fig. 4.2, the saving rate as a percentage of GDP is far higher in India than in major developed countries such as the United States, Japan, and European countries. According to the Reserve Bank of India (2018), the interest rate for a 1- to 3-year deposit was high at 8% to 10% during 2010–2015. In addition, because women face various barriers in economic activities such as getting good jobs in the labor market or borrowing money from financial institutions, there are many incentives for them to save money for living (Coad & Tamvada, 2012).

A high saving rate generally has a positive effect on capital formation. Given that the rate of economic growth depends on the rate of capital growth, the high saving rate is expected to contribute to the high economic growth. However, this is not so straightforward in the case of India. Discussing the failure of growth in India at the start of the 1980s, Varshney (1984) noted that the unequal distribution of income hindered development of the domestic consumer market. Because of this obstacle, private investment did not increase as the saving rate increased. Then, once the maturity level of the consumer market had exceeded a threshold for development, the high saving rate became effective for strongly increasing private investment and contributed to economic growth.

Macroeconomic development is closely related to political factors, as discussed by Asher and Novosad (2017). They showed that constituencies represented by the ruling party have significantly better economic outcomes than those represented by opposition candidates, suggesting the importance of political stability, although it couples with political favoritism, in economic development. Given that political

---

[3] The data of OECD Statistics is drawn from OECD.Stat, https://stats.oecd.org/.

stability depends on the well-being of the people in India, the abovementioned decline in the well-being of the Indian people would be an important factor for predicting future economic development in India.

Social and economic structures or systems affect the relation between economic development and well-being in India in various other ways. For example, Mohanty et al. (2014) show that the state of remittance flows within and among the states of India is very distinctive and strongly affects the well-being of the Indian people in connection with diversity in demographics and socioeconomic development. Moreover, Gius and Subramanian (2015) and Hu and Schlosser (2015) focus on the particular circumstances of women in India, and examine the impact of the social status of women on well-being and economic development. These studies suggest that there are some characteristic features of the state of well-being of India. Accordingly, we next examine the state of well-being in India and the value judgments of the Indian people.

4.2.2 Innovation Policy as a Critical Factor for Future Indian Development

Today, India's innovation is increasing influence in the global economy reflecting the rapid growth of Indian economy by integrating technology, financing, human capital, and administration in the global network. It is true that India's innovation started in the information technology (IT) sector but now the new innovation is arising in a much wider range of industries. Especially, process and incremental innovation in the field of transportation and pharmaceutical industries has been effective in improving their competitiveness in the global market (Krishnan, 2010). As Racherla et al. (2016) pointed, India's overall R&D spending is relatively small in the global standard and is around 0.85% of GDP and ranked below that of China. India's gross R&D expenditure was $71.48 billion in 2016.[4]

India's current status in the global economy is not excellent in various indicators. The amount of export of goods from India is ranked around 18th or 19th in the world, India falls much further down the list as an exporter of goods – closer to 18th or 19th place. Internet access, cell phone ownership and labor force participation are less than the global average (see Krishnan & Prashantham, 2019). Despite of these facts, India is deemed as one of the fastest growing country in the global economy, because India is expected to boast the world's fifth largest market economy, and the world's second-largest population size of 1.3 billion.

In this section, we summarize the characteristics of India's innovation, and discuss the potential and limitation of India's R&D strategy. The choices India makes today

---

[4] The comparable data are as follows: U.S. (gross: $514 billion; 2.77% of GDP), China (gross: $396.30 billion; 1.98% of GDP), Japan (gross: $166.6 billion; 3.39% of GDP), and Germany (gross: $109.25 billion; 2.92% of GDP). See https://www.theglobalipcenter.com/incomparable-innovative-india/.

will determine its competitiveness in the global market in the future. The competitiveness of economies has positive relation with the strength of innovation systems. In this sense, it is necessary to design good IP system to attract and keep more foreign direct investment, foster R&D of domestic companies, and to adopt the latest technologies (Liu & Racherla, 2019).

4.2.2.1 The Characteristics of Indian Innovation

The specific characteristics of Indian innovation pattern (see Krishnan & Prashantham, 2019).

(1) Frugal (called as Jugaad) innovation based on ingenuity and adaptation. "Jugaad" innovation have been attractive to MNEs because they brought good profits with lower investments (Radjou et al. 2012).

(2) India-based multinational enterprise (MNE) R&D centers utilizes global innovation efforts of their parent companies. This has been brought scientific technology transfer to India. Through this technology transfer, emerging multinational enterprises (EMNEs) are beginning to develop new original technology (Bhagavatula et al. 2019). MNEs initiates Indian innovation and entrepreneurship ecosystem.

(3) Indian organizations' innovation efforts focus more on adaptation of technologies, process innovation and organizational innovation to meet the local needs of affordability. This is successful especially in areas those matches global needs (software services, generic pharmaceuticals). Those cases are driven by low cost.

(4) Companies start their business by inward innovation for serving the local market, but develop to outward innovation for serving the global market. Frugal innovation is mainly used for inward innovation (Krishnan, 2010), whereas outward innovation is growing by the world-class partnership being ideated at Indian R&D centers (Mudambi et al. 2017).

In this section, we evaluate these characteristics from various points of view.

Question 1: Is it possible to shift from Outward – low /medium tech R&D Outward – to high knowledge R&D.

Conditions for these changes
Obstacle for this change is the tight regulation described as "License Permit Raj". For example, imports of raw materials and components are controlled, and the company which has an industrial license has little incentive to innovate (Forbes, 1999). Economic deregulation is required.

Mismatches in Indian market would be serious point, because advanced technology requires high skills and high costs for maintenance, and not affordable for Indian users.

Contrary to this obstacle, improving technological capabilities has been one of the objectives of the economic reforms as articulated in the Industry Policy Resolution of 1991 (Krishnan, 2003). Some Indian firms such as Tata Steel made substantial investments to change the technology to become globally competitive.

Question 2: What are the successful industri\es in R&D development?

According to Krishnan (2010), pharmaceuticals and transportation industries are evaluated as the most successful industries in R&D development, and the amounts of R&D investment in these industries are close to half of the total industrial R&D investments in India. It is noteworthy that the most R&D-intensive industry in India is the pharmaceutical industry, and especially generic pharmaceutical industry is globally competitive by developing new, low-cost processes for drugs going off patent (NSTMIS, 2013).

It is well known that IT industry in India has a strong competitiveness. Kumar and Puranam (2012) argue, however, that some innovations in the IT industry have been outward oriented. Concerning the transportation vehicle industry, the prominent example is given by the development of the Indica (Tata Motors' entry into the car industry) and the Nano, those were both led by Tata Group Chairman Ratan Tata, and broke through the boundary of Indian innovation represented by the incremental innovation and process improvements, (Krishnan, 2010). Nano revolutionized personal transportation by offering the low price (100,000 Indian rupees which was approximately $2,000 at the time).

Question 3: The expected benefits and risks of outward innovation.

The important benefit for the MNEs of investing into the innovation of Indian company is to exploit India's cost advantages and to tap into the large Indian talent base. India labor costs make foreign companies to save around 30–40% of the total cost Mitra, 2007. It is important to note that the quality of Indian workers' talent is quite high and they are diligent, and they support global research activities. Basant and Mani (2012) observe a significant increase in the number of MNE R&D centers in India from 157 in 2005 to 1,165 in 2015.

Mudambi (2008) points out that MNE research centers has been working for promoting knowledge spillovers. This brought benefits to local firms by making them develop competencies in high value-added activities. In addition, the Indian R&D centers of MNEs is taking the important roles in developing products that can meet the needs of India and other emerging markets in the world. The point is that the products developed in the Indian R&D centers of MNEs incorporate the latest features, but the approach adopted is a frugal approach. This is crucial for MNEs to expand the market not only in India but also other emerging markets.

The risks of MNE R&D centers in India include the sustainability and competitiveness of the developed products in India or emerging market. Basically, the developed products designed for these markets has less original technology and it is easy for other competitive companies to copy the technology. Thus, it is necessary to have a clear strategy to link R&D center and the emerging market business.

4.2.2.2 Indian Innovation System

In general, we need to build up an innovation system by designing education system initially. Especially, STEM education is deemed as the crucial importance for educating engineers and scientists employed in R&D sectors. In the last 25 years, India has been successful in increasing the number of students enrolled in engineering/technology programs. AISHE (2016) reports that 4.2 million students were enrolled in engineering/technology programs in 2014–15.

The most serious problem for this STEM education is the mismatches in labor market. The low employability of the graduates of these engineering colleges is serious, and it is reported that only 18% of engineers graduating are employable in the software services industry according to the National Employability Report-Engineers (Aspiring Minds, 2016). This reflects the polarization of the quality of students in Indian STEM education program. The high-end program by the top university such as Indian Institute of Technology are evaluated highly in the world standard, while the quality of education in a mass of institutions is less evaluated.

In India, the government's role in R&D investment has been increasing, although the size of investment compared to the total economy size is still small. The main target of investment by government funding has been the networks of government-owned and government-operated R&D laboratories (Krishnan, 2010). Basant and Mani (2012) point that about 63% of R&D spending in India was borne by the government spending. This is a quite large portion. In case of the U.S.A., this portion has a declining trend and less than 30% as of 2017 (National Science Foundation, 2019).

It is interesting that the government spending has been directed to support micro, small, and medium enterprises, and used to promote the R&D investment of the firms less than 5 years old by the first Start-up Policy 2016 (Krishnan, et al., 2019). Under this policy, various measures such as funding and tax incentives, supporting industry-academia collaboration, supporting the creation of tinkering laboratories in schools and the formation of incubators in educational institutions are programed.

4.2.2.3 Future Prospect of Indian Innovation

IP (Intellectual Property) system is crucial for promoting innovation in India. IP tools include patents, trademarks, copyrights, and trade secrets, and those are the key factors for guaranteeing return from R&D investment. The current India's IP system is not sufficient for providing both the domestic and foreign companies with incentives for investing much money to R&D.[5] To increase the reliability of India's IP system, it is necessary to decrease exceptions applied to IP legal system. Limiting the patentability of software innovations, or facilitating access to pirated movies and music online are the examples of exceptions.

---

[5] See https://www.theglobalipcenter.com/u-s-and-indian-business-organizations-launch-dialogue-on-ip-collaboration/ as of June 2020.

To solve this problem, the Federation of Indian Chambers of Commerce and Industry (FICCI) started to collaborate with the U.S. Chamber of Commerce's Global Innovation Policy Center (GIPC) at the beginning of 2019.[6] The purpose of this collaboration is to promote IP-led India's innovation. Through this collaboration, the system of patent filing, regulatory landscape, copyright and infringement, technology transfer, and enforcement has been elaborating. The main incentive for the U.S. is the expected return from the development of India's market in which many MNEs from the U.S. have been investing.

4.3 Well-Being of the Indian People

4.3.1 Overview of Indian Society

In this section, we give an overview of Indian society (see Okamitsu & Yamashita, 2016). Two key characteristics of Indian society are the social stratification and numerous social restrictions that arose from the Indian caste system. Despite anti-discrimination laws, various forms of discrimination still exist in Indian society. Family values are deemed to be quite important in the country, and multi-generational patriarchal joint families have been the norm in India. In particular, marriage is crucial for attaining social recognition. The divorce rate is extremely low. The custom of paying a dowry remains widespread, although this custom has been outlawed and causes various kinds of tragedies.

Religious beliefs and practices are diverse in India, and all religions are treated equally by the state. India is the birthplace of Hinduism and home to around 90% of the world's Hindu population. According to the 2011 Indian census, 79.8% of the population of India practice Hinduism, while 14.2% practice Islam. Christianity is the third-largest religion. The percentage of Buddhists in the population is very small, although India is also the birthplace of Buddhism.

4.3.2 Data Used in the Analysis: WVS

Here, we discuss the well-being of the Indian people in order to capture their lifestyle and behavior by using the www.worldvaluessurvey.org (WVS). Using a common questionnaire, this survey is conducted by a global network of social scientists studying changing values and their impact on social and political life. The survey started in 1981 and consists of nationally representative surveys conducted in almost 100 countries containing almost 90% of the world's population. The number of respondents is almost 400,000.

---

[6] https://www.theglobalipcenter.com/india-climbs-eight-places-in-global-ip-rankings/ as of June 2020.

The minimum population sample size of a country is 1,200. Samples must be representative of all people aged 18 years or older. Data collection in the WVS is done primarily through face-to-face interviews at the respondents' homes/places of residence. Respondents' answers are recorded on questionnaire sheets or by computer-assisted personal interviewing.[7] Here, we focus on the Schwartz's value judgment questionnaire.

4.3.3 Changes in the Well-Being of India: Comparative Analysis

According to the WVS data, the happiness felt by people in India is relatively higher than that felt by people in Europe, the United States, Japan, and other parts of Asia. More importantly, the level of happiness has been constant for more than three decades in India but has decreased after 1998 in all other countries and regions. In particular, a sharp decline in happiness has been observed in Japan. In evaluating the drastic economic growth in India, the meaning of the constant level of happiness is considered from various aspects.

Firstly, the decrease in happiness in most countries and regions is attributed to the development of the global economy. Globalization has deepened, especially after the start of the twenty-first century, and has had various negative impacts on economies and societies around the world. Global capital such as major tech companies (Amazon, for instance) has gained competitiveness by expanding the global market and realizing economies of scale. Meanwhile, many local companies have been losing their positions in the local market. In other words, income inequality has been expanding between competitive economic agents and less competitive economic agents due to the development of the global economy.

As is shown in Fig. 4.3, the fact the happiness of the Indian people has remained constant means that Indian companies are, in relative terms, enjoying the benefits of globalization. However, this does not imply that all the people in India are doing so. It is expected that some portion of the Indian people have lost out under globalization while others are certainly enjoying the economic growth achieved under globalization. The percentage of people who enjoy the benefits of globalization seems to be larger in India than in other countries and regions.

4.3.4 Changes in the Value Judgments of Indian People

In this section, we focus on the value judgments in India. As discussed by Sagiv et al. (2017), values are defined as broad desirable goals that motivate people's actions and serve as guiding principles in their lives. Thus, changes in values cause changes in

---

[7] See http://www.worldvaluessurvey.org/wvs.jsp as of February 20, 2018.

Fig. 4.3 Feeling of happiness. *Source* 2014 World Values Survey

people's preferences and behavior. This is why we pay attention to value judgments in predicting changes in human behavior accompanying economic development.

Before examining the data, let us discuss the process of value formation. Sagiv et al. (2017) state that values are formed through a combination of genetic heritage and the impact of exposure to multiple social environments, such as family, the education system, community, and society at large. The dramatic economic development in India has possibly altered multiple social environments and in turn may have changed the values of the Indian people.

The characteristics of Indian value judgments are shown in Fig. 4.4a. Over the long term, religion and work were considered to be the most important and leisure time was considered the least important. Examination of Fig. 4.5b reveals changes in value judgment over a period of about 30 years in India. The importance of religion has been constant, but the importance of work has declined sharply. On the other hand, the importance of leisure time and politics has increased sharply. The importance of work has dropped to the global average, but the importance of leisure time remains the lowest in the world, reflecting the upward shift in the importance of leisure time globally.

The implication of changes in value judgments for economic growth includes the following main two factors. First, the decrease in the importance of work since 2010 suggests that the quality of work has possibly declined in the development process. There are many small companies that use high-quality handcrafting techniques. Before the economy started to develop, many craftspeople worked not only

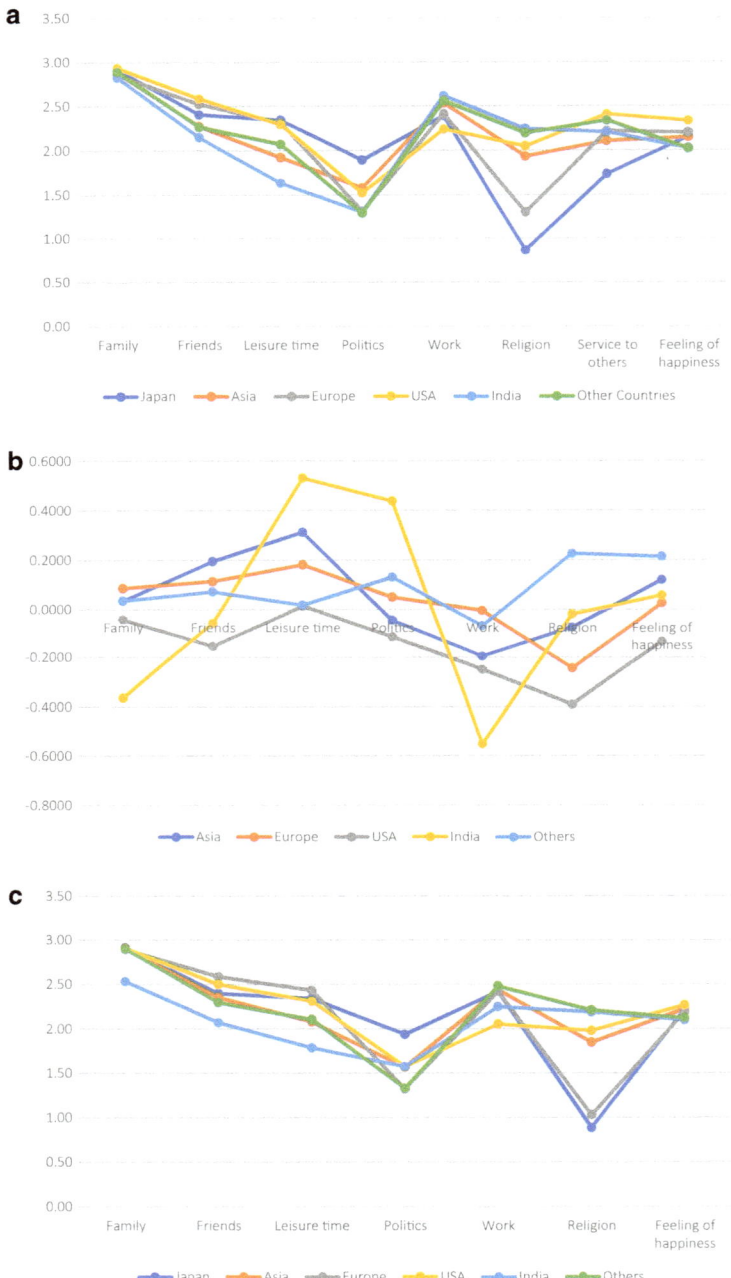

Fig. 4.4 **a** Importance in life: 1993–2010 (whole period: Ascending order). **b** Differences in importance between 1993 and 2010. **c** Importance in life (2010–2013). *Source* 2014 World Values Survey

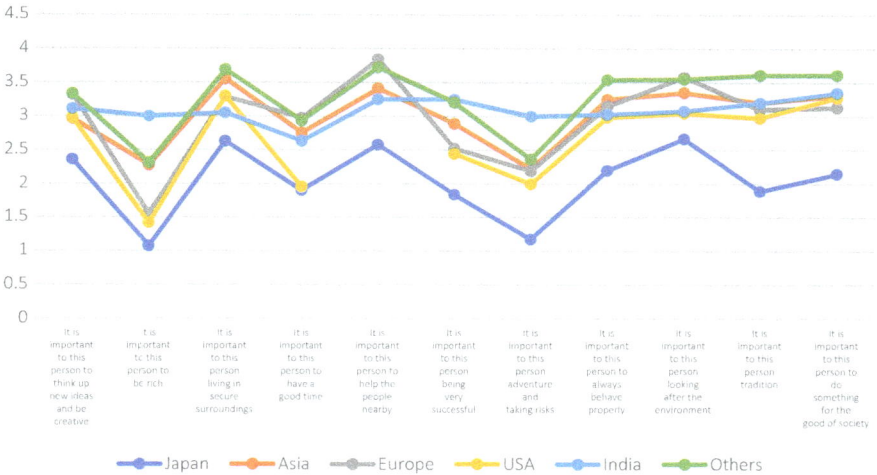

Fig. 4.5 Schwarz value judgments: comparison by country or region (ascending order). *Source* 2014 World Values Survey

to obtain money, but also to achieve a feeling of responsibility for work and self-fulfillment. This is a source of the quality of products. The changes in value judgment suggest that the importance of work has declined and the need for money has increased to enjoy leisure time.

The increase in the importance of leisure time is important for promoting development of the consumer market because most consumption and leisure are complementary. Viewed another way, it can be interpreted that the importance of leisure time has increased because of an increase in consumption due to rising income. These interpretations suggest that the importance of leisure time will increase and the importance of work will decrease as the income level rises in India.

It is worth noting that the importance of happiness and religion has remained almost constant over the whole observation period despite the economic growth in India (Fig. 4.4b). This implies that the happiness of people in India does not depend on income level. As shown in Fig. 4.5c, the importance of religion is relatively high in India compared with the rest of the world, suggesting that the happiness felt by the Indian people might arise from religious factors.

An interesting point is that the importance of politics increased strongly after 2010. This change was the largest in the world (Fig. 4.4b). One possible interpretation is that the impact of public policy on life has increased as the size of the economy expanded. As the economy has expanded, the income gap between the poor and the rich has widened. Income redistribution, for example, has gained more importance as a policy measure, and this leads to an increase of the importance of politics. In addition, the needs for public infrastructure such as transportation and road systems has increased due to economic growth. This also increases the importance of politics reflecting individuals' needs.

Finally, we need to carefully discuss the decrease in importance of family after 2010 (Fig. 4.4c); the income level has increased, and it has become possible for people to secure their life not through family cooperation but through savings. In addition, differences in the interests of family members might have expanded as income level increased, and the time spent together with the family decreased as the variety of leisure opportunities increased. These might have led to the decrease in the importance of family.

4.3.5 Schwarz Value Judgments

In this subsection, we compare value judgments between India and Japan by using the Schwartz theory of basic values in preparation for the analysis in the next section. Schwartz (2015) created cross-cultural indices, and the WVS questionnaires are based on these indices.

As is shown in Fig. 4.5, the values for all items are higher for Japan than for India. The difference between India and Japan is the largest for the item "It is important for this person to be rich." The value for India is 3, while the value for Japan is 1.07. In India, around 21.2% of the population still lives in extreme poverty with income less than 1.90 USD per day (see The World Bank Data Bank).[8] On the other hand, the proportion of the Japanese population living in such poverty was 0.3% in 2008. This suggests that the likelihood of being poor is relatively higher in India, and this led people in India to place greater importance on being rich.

The second largest difference is seen for the item on the importance of "adventure and taking risk." In some sense, these two responses are consistent because people think that it is necessary to take risk or undergo adventure to be rich. Indians think that it is worthwhile to take risk because being rich is important for them.

The third big difference between India and Japan is observed in the importance of "being very successful". In connection to the two previous questions, Japanese do not pursue success in life, because they do not think that being rich is important.

The fourth largest difference is in the importance of "tradition". This poses a kind of paradox because adventure and tradition are largely opposing values. Greater importance was placed on tradition by Indians than by Japanese. The importance of tradition to a person is related to his or her degree of religiousness. Each religion has a specific logic on life and living. For example, a Hindu widow is expected to remove her trinkets and wear a white sari, and is excluded from Hindu ceremonies (see Okamitsu & Yamashita, 2016, p. 229). This kind of custom or tradition is rooted in a religious belief that a widow is a symbol of unhappiness. The dichotomy between "luckiness" and "unluckiness" is similar to the dichotomy between "pure" and "impure", and these dichotomies are regarded as a basis of Hindu culture.

---

[8] See   https://data.worldbank.org/indicator/SI.POV.DDAY?end=2013&locations=1W-IN-JP& start=1981&view=chart, as of February 20, 2018.

Placing strong importance on tradition and custom can be expected to have various kinds of impacts on happiness. In the case of a Hindu widow, she would feel negative emotions for being regarded as a symbol of unluckiness. The question then arises as to whether placing strong importance on custom or tradition has some positive impact on happiness. From ancient times, human society has been faced with various kinds of disasters and tragedies that are beyond our control. Custom and tradition have been relied on as means of avoiding disaster and tragedy through religious teachings or myth. This suggest that the degree of importance of custom and tradition to a person depends on the strength of the belief that religion contributes to safety or luck in life.

The smallest difference between India and Japan is found in the importance of "looking after the environment". The second smallest difference is in the importance of "living in secure surroundings".

4.3.6   Freedom of Choice and Control

Figure 4.6 shows changes in degree of freedom of choice and control before and after 2010. A prominent change can be seen in India. India and Japan are ranked lowest and second-lowest, respectively, in degree of freedom of choice and control. Before 2010, India scored higher than Japan in this measure, but their positions reversed after 2010. The degree of freedom and choice dropped most sharply in India after 2010. This finding holds various implications regarding changes in Indian society.

Fig. 4.6   Belief that there is freedom of choice and control. *Source* 2014 World Values Survey

India has a traditional caste system. This system has worked to reduce the degree of choice and control, especially in freedom of occupational choice. One might expect that as the economy develops, the impact of the caste system would weaken because of need for higher mobility of human resources. The finding shown in Fig. 4.6 is contrary to this expectation. This can be interpreted as follows. As the economy develops, economic organizations become larger, and relationships among economic agents deepen. In addition, the advancement of the monetary economy in India has decreased the degree of freedom of choice and control because people came to feel that the monetary limitations decreased the degree of freedom of choice.

The findings in Fig. 4.6 have various implications for economic development in India. The caste system has various influences on the Indian economy and unites people within the same caste, forming strong social networks. These social networks support various kinds of economic activities such as job referral and mutual insurance. Munshi (2016) focuses on caste networks and argues that caste networks have been active not only in rural areas but also in cities. Particular caste groups have gained some advantages in business and overseas trade, and some new business communities have moved into industry. Figure 4.6 implies that as the economy developed, the importance of caste communities increased because they enhanced economic competitiveness, resulting in exclusive caste communities.

4.3.7 Changes in Incentives for Work and Feelings of Fairness

Incentives for work are crucial for economic development. Incentives influence the quality of work and resulting quality of goods and services. Figure 4.7 show changes in incentives for work as assessed by the question of whether hard work brings success. Worldwide, the decline in incentives for work was largest in India, which had the strongest incentives for work before 2010 and the weakest incentives after. This sharp decline suggests the worsening feeling of fairness in India. Incentives for work are influenced by the sense of achievement or reward from hard work. It can be inferred that India's drastic economic growth has had a detrimental effect on people's sense of fairness as a result of the widening gap between the rich and the poor, and the experiences of seeing some people become rich through good fortune and others become impoverished through bad luck. This has weakened the belief that hard work leads to success.

If people believe that immoral behavior brings good fortune, then the quality of society becomes worse, which would lower economic competitiveness in the world market. Figure 4.7 suggests risks that Indian society faces.

Changes in the sense of fairness can be seen from another aspect in Fig. 4.8. Before 2010, the Indian people viewed competition relatively favorably compared with other countries and regions. After 2010, however, the Indian people tended to view competition as more harmful compared with the rest of the world. The gap

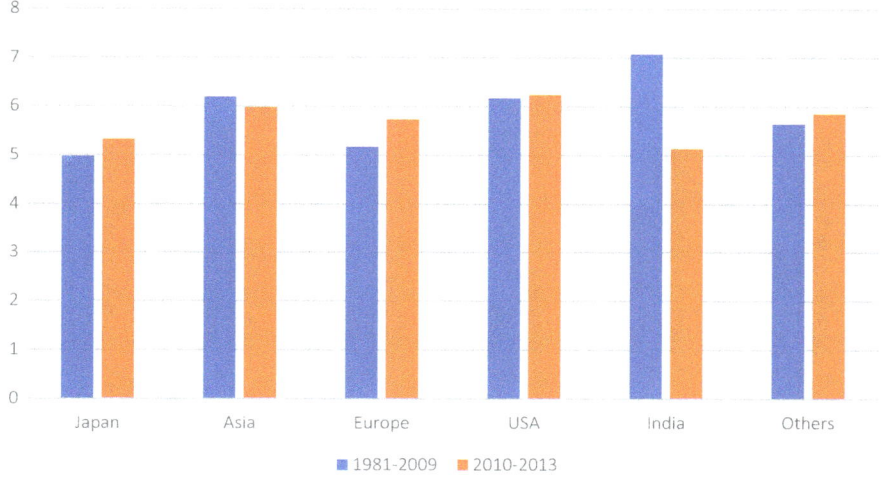

Fig. 4.7 Belief that hard work brings success (10 signifies the belief that "hard work generally brings success"). *Source* 2014 World Values Survey

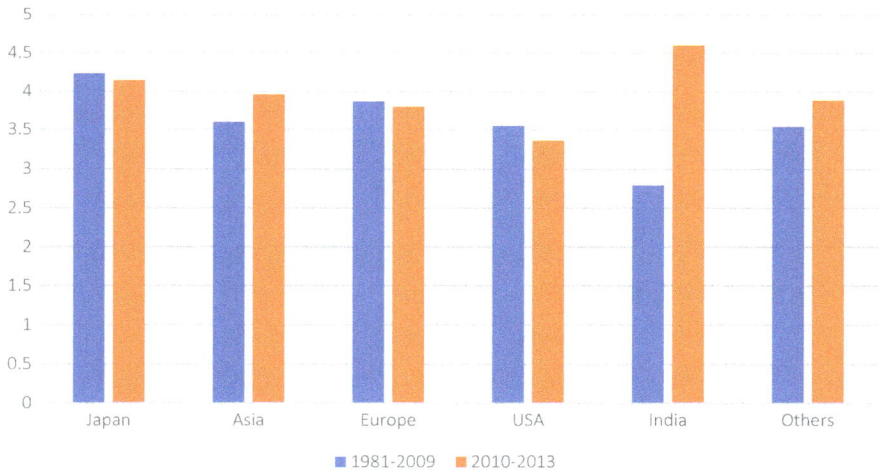

Fig. 4.8 Belief that competition is harmful (5 signifies the belief that competition is harmful). *Source* 2014 World Values Survey

between before and after 2010 is quite prominent in India, and it is worth considering this finding carefully. Figure 4.8 suggests that competition in India is regarded as being unfair. This sense of unfairness seems to be specific to India given the prominent change relative to that in other countries and regions.

The caste system possibly worked to worsen the sense of fairness during the process of economic development. The caste system could serve to strengthen the

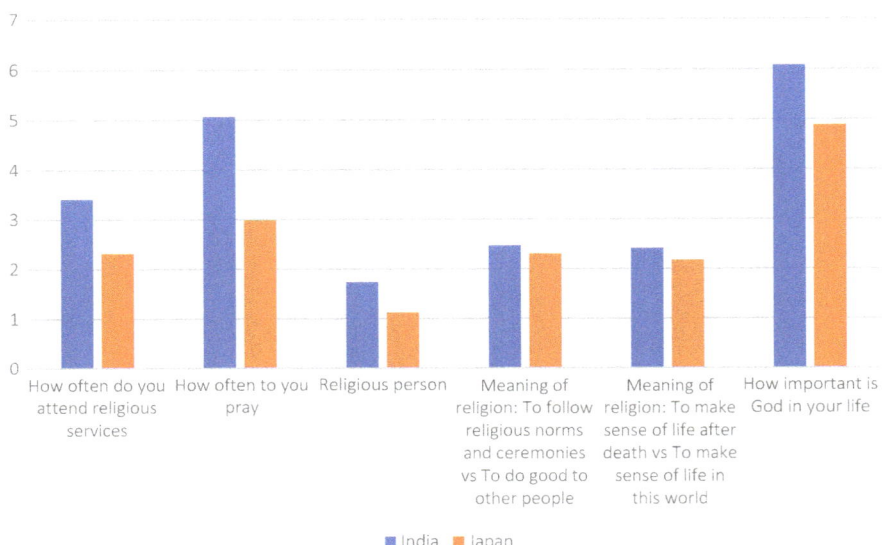

Fig. 4.9 Comparision of degree of religiousness between India and Japan. *Source* 2014 World Values Survey

system of exclusive networks within the castes. Higher castes might have advantageous opportunities in business, and some barriers may exist for lower castes. These differences might have grown larger over the course of economic development.

4.4 Differences in Social and Economic Behavior Between India and Japan

4.4.1 Differences in the Degree of Religiousness Between India and Japan

According to the 2011 Indian Census, the population distribution by religion is as follows: Hindu, 79.8%; Islam, 14.2%; Christian, 2.3%; Sikh, 1.7%; Buddhist, 0.7%; and Jain, 0.4%.[9] The crucial difference between India and Japan is the portion of people who do not believe any religion. It is reported that 51.8% of Japanese believe in no religion, while less than 1% of Indians have no religious belief. The dominant religion in Japan is Buddhism at 34.9%, and Christians account for 2.3%.[10]

---

[9] See http://www.censusindia.gov.in/2011census/Religion_PCA.html, as of March 2018.

[10] See http://www2.ttcn.ne.jp/honkawa/9460.html, as of March 2018.

Nevertheless, Fig. 4.9 shows that the differences in the meaning of religion between India and Japan are not so sharp. To understand this point, it should be noted that many Japanese believe in Shintoism, but this is regarded not as a religion but as a convention because there is no sacred text or teachings in Shintoism. A large proportion of people in Japan pray at Shinto shrines or Buddhist temples for their wishes to be fulfilled—for example, praying for the safety of their family and good health. Moreover, most Japanese have attended various Buddhist ceremonies such as funeral services even though they are not devout followers of Buddhism. This implies that people in Japan recognize the existence of gods unconsciously.

The most important point is that the average value of the degree of religiousness in India is less than 2, which is not very different from the value in Japan. Frequency of praying is the item with the largest difference between India and Japan. A possible interpretation is that Japanese pray on the occasion of certain ceremonies or services, but Indians pray and attend services in daily life.

It is important to note that both Indians and Japanese recognize the importance of gods. The average value in India is around 6, and that in Japan is around 5. For Hindu people, gods include Brahma the Creator, Shiva the Destroyer, Vishnu the Preserver, and Shakti (also called as Devi). For Islam, Allah is the one and only God, an absolute, all-powerful, and all-knowing creator and ruler of the universe. For Buddhists, the Four Truths, which express the basic orientation of Buddhism, are quite important, and there are many gods that have different roles. The fact that most of the people regard God or gods as important in life despite the large differences in their conceptions suggests that people have various kinds of needs that are addressed by these beliefs.

It is interesting that both Indian and Japanese people place greater importance on "doing good for other people" than "following religious norms" and on "making sense of life in this world" than "making sense of life after death". These imply that religion is regarded as a tool for improving life in this world and religion is not the objective of life in either India or Japan.

4.4.2   Differences in Determinants of Well-Being Between India and Japan

In this section, we discuss the determinants of well-being in India and Japan by using microdata compiled through surveys that we conducted in happiness studies. The surveys are summarized below and key details are outlined in Table 4.1. We used microdata collected from a nationwide Internet survey in each country. The survey in Japan was designed and implemented during 2012–2013 for a research project that investigated the socio-economic determinants of subjective well-being.[11] The surveys captured ample information about individuals' subjective assessments of their well-being, personal traits, demographics, socio-economic status, and perceived

---

[11] The survey was funded by JSPS KAKENHI Kiban A no. 22243028.

Table 4.1 Outline of the surveys

	India	Japan
A. Title of survey	Survey of the state of living in India (Survey of Well-being in India)	Survey of the living environment in the region and the sense of happiness
B. Time period of survey	Nov. 6, 2017–Nov. 17, 2017	Oct. 1, 2013–Oct. 31, 2013
C. Survey method	The survey was organized by NTT Com Research by using the Internet. All samples were collected via Internet panels with multiple sources. Each respondent was verified as being unique via IP address	
D. Sample controls	Sampling for the Japanese dataset was controlled so that the age distribution and income distribution of the survey were close to the real distributions	
E. Sample size	4,046	4,927

neighborhood characteristics, all of which are useful for examining the relationship between working conditions and happiness. In the case of Japan, to ensure that the sample was representative of the actual population, we constructed targeted proportions of 15 population groups, which corresponded to a matrix of five age groups (20, 30, 40, 50, and 60 s) and three household income classes (3 million yen or less, 3–6 million yen, and 6 million yen or more) in advance and collected surveys until we obtained the numerical targets.

The survey in India was designed and implemented during 2017 for a research project that investigated the socio-economic determinants of subjective well-being in India.[12]

Figure 4.10a and b show the differences in the relation between overall well-being and educational attainment between India and Japan. A contrast was noted between India and Japan in that well-being was not strongly associated with educational attainment in India, but had a monotonically increasing relationship with educational attainment in Japan. This suggests that job matching in India is not bad in the sense that workers with lower educational attainment have good opportunities to utilize their human capital effectively.

Figure 4.11a and b show a sharper contrast between India and Japan. In India, degree of hope is relatively higher for the people with lower educational attainment. On the other hand, degree of hope increases monotonically with increasing educational attainment in Japan.

Hope is an important source of motivation for work and good deeds. Degree of hope reflects the possibility of achieving one's hopes. These figures suggest that it is possible for people in India to achieve their hopes independently from their educational background. However, this does not mean that the types of hopes are similar between India and Japan. The caste system in India limits people's freedom to choose their occupation, whereas there is almost complete freedom to choose one's

---

[12] The survey was funded by JSPS KAKENHI Kiban B no. 16KT0089.

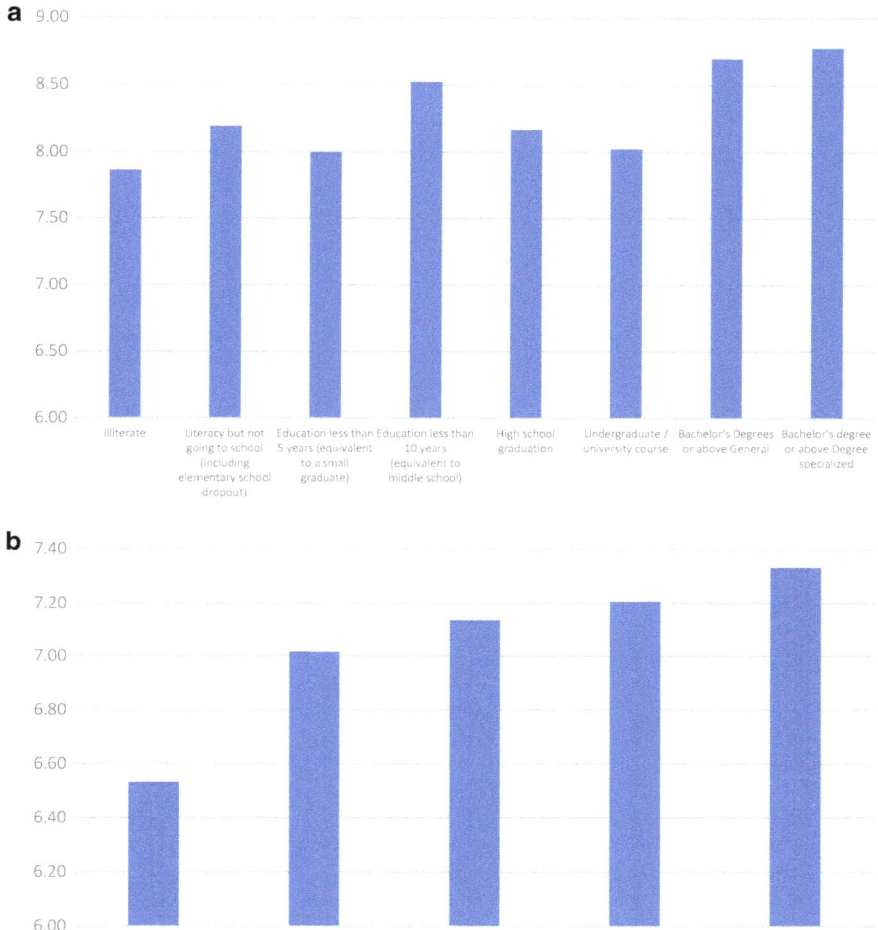

Fig. 4.10 **a** Overall well-being in India. **b** Overall well-being in Japan

occupation in Japan, both legally and traditionally. For this reason, it is inferred that the variety of hopes in India is larger than that in Japan.

The possibility of achieving one's hopes is expected to be related to the quality of human relationships. Figure 4.12a and b show a comparison of differences in degree of trust in others by city size between India and Japan. Two distinct differences can be seen. First, the degree of trust in others is higher in India than in Japan. Second, people trust others more in large cities than in small towns in India, whereas the degree of trust in others is independent from city size in Japan. This suggests that communities in urban areas of India are working well.

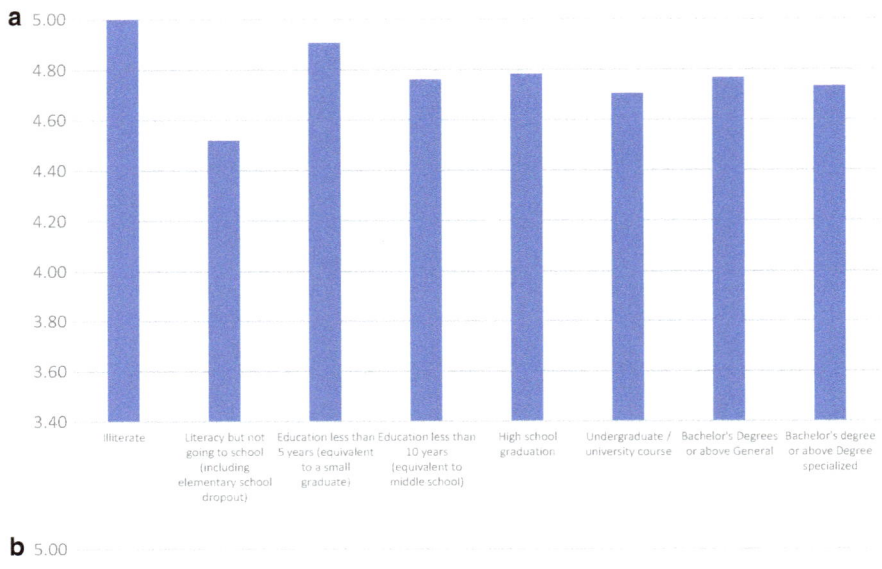

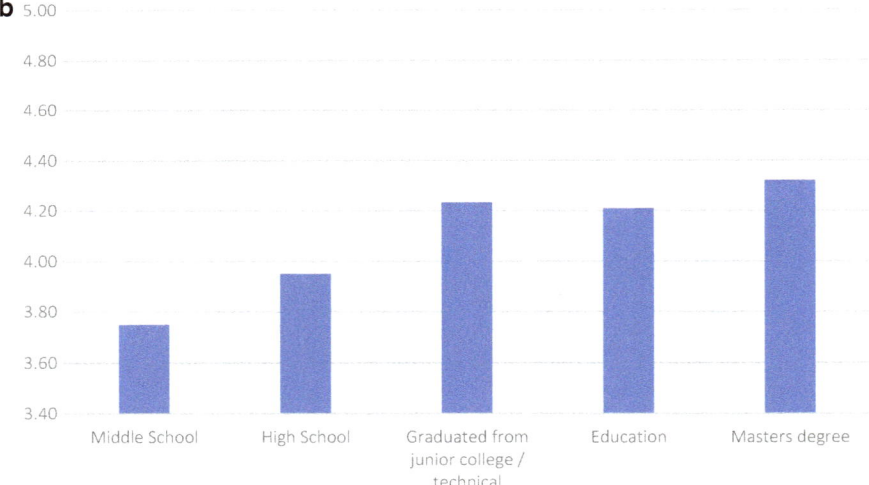

Fig. 4.11 a Hope by educational attainment in India. **b** Hope by educational attainment in Japan

It is evident that human relationships within communities are stronger in India than in Japan, as shown in Fig. 4.13a and b. In India, more than 20% reported having cooperative relationships in daily life within their community, and this ratio was larger for people living in urban areas. Only a small percentage had no social relationships in their community in India. On the other hand, only a small percentage had cooperative relationships in daily living within their community in Japan, and the ratio decreased with increasing city size. These figures show a sharp contrast in social relationships in communities between India and Japan.

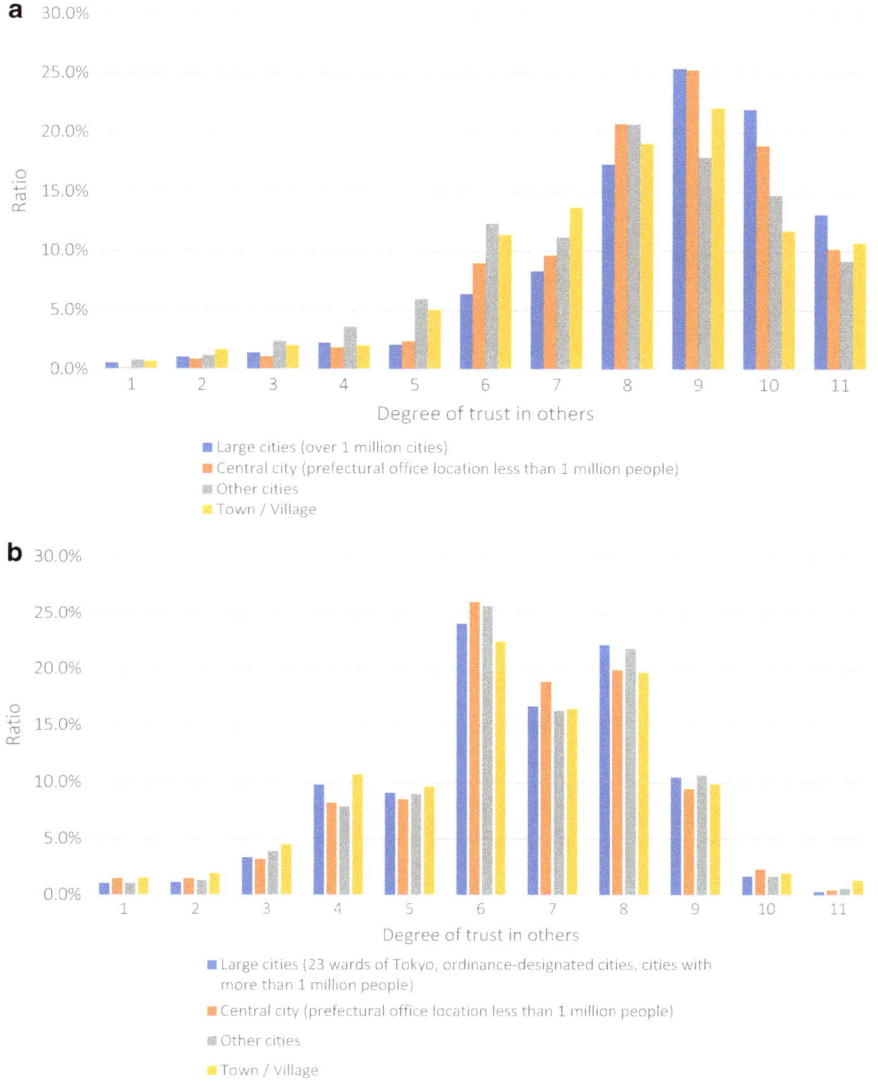

Fig. 4.12 a Degree of trust in others in India. **b** Degree of trust in others in Japan

Khan et al. (2014) explored the relation between social identification in a community and well-being in India. Social identification may provide individuals with meaning from living in their community and social connection with others. Their study shows that social identification in India enables individuals to access social support and escape from stressful situations. Our results here are consistent with those of Khan et al. (2014).

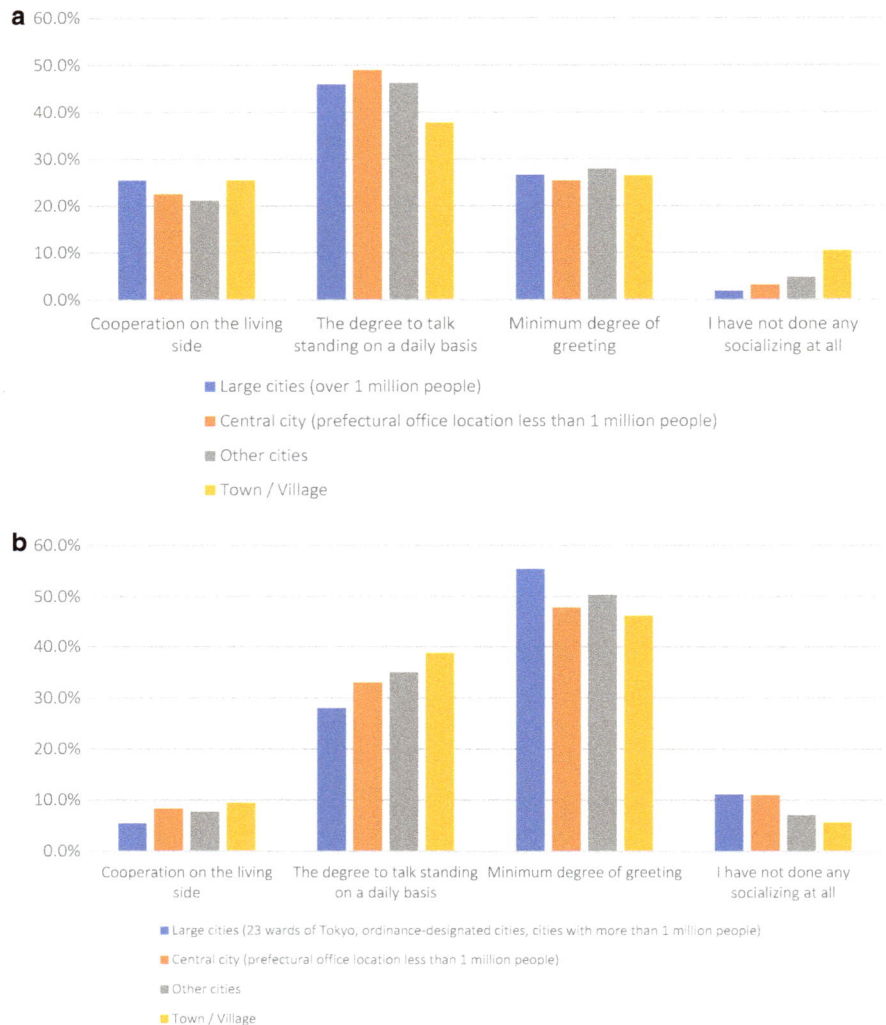

Fig. 4.13 **a** Degree of socialization in communities in India. **b** Degree of socialization in communities in Japan

Figure 4.14a and b show the differences in pro-social behavior such as volunteer activities. In India, around 15% of people participate in volunteer activities, while less than 5% do so in Japan. Only around 15–30% of people do not do volunteer activities in India, while around 70% of people do not do any volunteer activities in Japan.

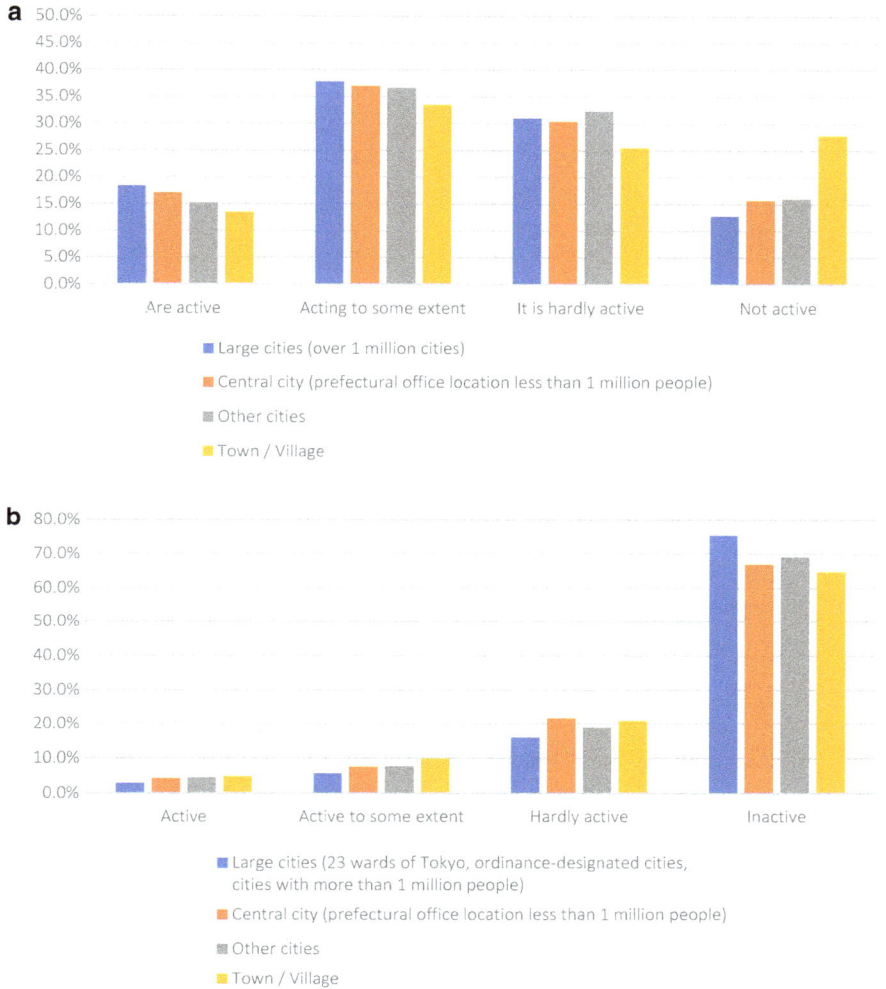

Fig. 4.14 **a** Percentage of people who participate in volunteer activities in India. **b** Percentage of people who participate in volunteer activities in Japan

In this section, we examined differences in social and economic behavior between India and Japan by focusing on religious behavior and social relationships in communities. There are several reasons for focusing on these two factors. The main reason is that these factors affect well-being in various ways and possibly instill in people some non-materialistic values. If non-materialistic values are considered important for generating well-being, economic development would not be so important for the people. Indeed, economic development may hurt well-being in cases where it adversely affects non-materialistic values.

The findings in this section suggest that social interaction and social capital are strong in India. These are considered as the important source of a high degree of well-being in India.

4.4.3 Differences in Determinants of Well-Being Between India and Japan

In this subsection, we examine the determinants of well-being by using a multivariate regression model and compare them between India and Japan. Figure 4.15a and b show the standardized coefficients of the statistically significant determinants of well-being. Standardized coefficients represent the strength of the effect of the explanatory variables on the explained variable, which is well-being in this empirical model. From Fig. 4.15a, it is seen that "physical working conditions", "wages", and "job security" are the strongest factors. How workers are treated is an important factor for well-being in India. In contrast to India, people in Japan are more sensitive to the possibility of designing their own job and utilizing their own skills and knowledge.

Concerning social relationships in communities, people in India regard these factors as important for well-being. "Strength of social relationships in the community", "number of relatives in the community", and "degree of community activities" strongly affect well-being. In addition, the degree of being able to rely on family and relatives also has a positive effect on well-being.

In Japan, no social relationship factors were found to affect well-being, whereas degree of trust in others was found to affect it strongly. The most important factors affecting well-being in Japan were personal and material factors such as satisfaction with leisure, income, and wealth.

It worth noting that "religious activities" significantly contributed to enhancing well-being in India, while this factor was not significant in Japan. In addition, community environment contributed to enhancing well-being in India but not in Japan. These results are consistent with those reported by Zorondo-Rodríguez et al. (2016), who found positive associations between economic and natural capital and subjective well-being.

These results suggest that Indian people feel happiness when they appreciate human relationships in society and when they are treated properly in the workplace. On the other hand, Japanese people tend to feel happiness when they are satisfied with leisure, income, and wealth.

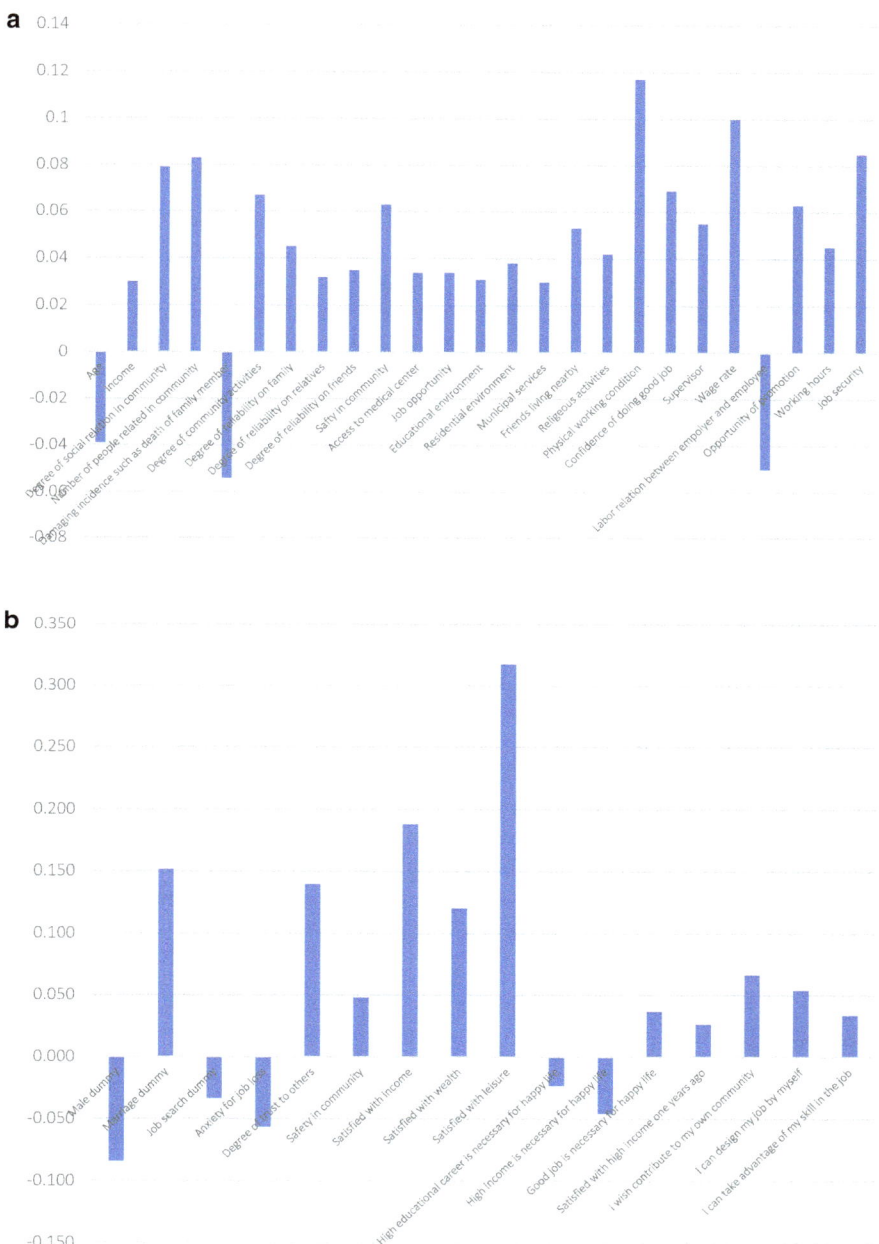

Fig. 4.15 **a** Standardized coefficients of statistically significant determinants of well-being in India. **b** Standardized coefficients of statistically significant determinants of well-being in Japan

4.5 Concluding Remarks

Long-run macroeconomic performance is affected by various factors such as consumption, savings, and labor market structure, and the value judgments of individuals affect behaviors related to consumption, savings, and labor supply. In this way, the value judgments of individuals affect long-run macroeconomic performance. In this section, we discussed the relation between value judgments and economic behaviors.

The most important component of demand at the macroeconomic level is consumption. Determinants of consumption includes income, savings for the future, savings for marriage, religious expenditures, expenditures for communities, education, and leisure preferences. Income is determined by labor supply behavior, which is affected by value judgments on work, competition, and trust. Saving behavior is affected by value judgments such as preference for mutual aid within one's family or community.

Determinants of trust are human relations within the workplace, community, and family. Trust as a means of security affects the efficiency of transactions in the economy. Social rules, conventions, and norms affect trust formation, but the personal and social investment for trust formation incurs some costs. Costs include restrictions on creative activities that usually come from unconventional ways of thinking.

The analysis in this chapter provides some evidence for predicting how economic development in India will bring about the changes in the social structure of the country. As suggested by Gautam and Singh (2010), Indian companies have not adopted a positive stance toward corporate social responsibility and only a few companies have a structured and planned approach. As the economy develops, new social issues will arise from the changes in social structure. In this regard, companies will be expected to play a role in solving these social issues. In conclusion, the way that Indian society changes affects not only macroeconomic performance but also well-being. We need to respond to social changes appropriately by analyzing the essential changes in the economy and society.

References

AISHE. (2016). *All India survey of higher education 2014–15*. Retrieved from http://aishe.nic.in/aishe/viewDocument.action?documentId=206.

Asher, S., & Novosad, P. (2017). Politics and local economic growth: Evidence from India. *American Economic Journal Applied Economics, 9*(1), 229–273.

Aspiring Minds. (2016). *National employability report-engineer*. Retrieved from http://www.aspiringminds.com/research-reports.

Basant, R., & Mani, S. (2012). *Foreign R&D centres in India: An analysis of their size, structure and implications* (Working Paper No. 2012-01-06). Ahmedabad, India: Indian Institute of Management.

Bhagavatula, S., Mudambi, R., & Murmann, J. (2019) The innovation and entrepreneurship ecosystem in India. *Management & Organization Review, 15*(3), 467–493.

Coad, A., & Tamvada, J. P. (2012). Firm growth and barriers to growth among small firms in India. *Small Business Economics, 39*(2), 383–400.

Forbes, N. (1999). Technology and Indian industry: What is liberalization changing? *Technovation, 19*(6–7), 403–412.

Gautam, R., & Singh, A. (2010). Corporate social responsibility practices in India: A study of top 500 companies. *Global Business and Management Research: An International Journal, 2*(1), 41–56.

Gius, M., & Subramanian, R. (2015). The relationship between inadequate sanitation facilities and the economic well-being of women in India. *Journal of Economics and Development Studies, 3*(1), 11–21.

Helliwell, J. F., Huang, H., Huang, H., & Shiplett, H. (2018). International Migration, and World Happiness. In J.F. Helliwell, R. Layard & J.D. Sachs (Eds.), *World happiness report*. New York: Sustainable Development Solutions Network.

Hu, L., & Schlosser, A. (2015). prenatal sex selection and girls' well-being: Evidence from India. *The Economic Journal, 125*(587), 1227–1261.

Khan, S. S., Hopkins, N., Tewari, S., Srinivasan, N., Reicher, S. D., & Ozakinci, G. (2014). Efficacy and well-being in rural north India: The role of social identification with a large-scale community identity. *European Journal of Social Psychology, 44*(7), 787–798.

Krishnan, R. (2003). The evolution of a developing country innovation system during economic liberalization: The case of India. Paper presented at the *First Globelics Conference Innovation Systems & Development Strategies for the Third Millennium*, Rio de Janeiro, Brazil.

Krishnan, R. T. (2010). *From jugaad to systematic innovation: The challenge for India*. Bangalore, India: Utpreraka Foundation. https://www.thehindubusinessline.com/opinion/patents-are-not-just-about-pharma/article64598362.ece.

Krishnan, R. T., & Prashantham, S. (2019). Innovation in and from India: The who, where, what, and when. *Global Strategy Journal 9*(3), 357–377.

Kumar, N., & Puranam, P. (2012). *India inside: The emerging innovation challenge to the West*. Harvard Business Press.

Liu, K. C., & Racherla, U. S. (2019). *Innovation and IPRs in China and India* (Vol. 4, pp. 3–24). Singapore: Springer.

Mitra, R. M. (2007). *India's emergence as a global R&D center* (Working Paper No. 021). Ostersund, Sweden: ITPS, Swedish Institute for Growth Policy Studies.

Mohanty, S. K., Dubey, M., & Parida, J. K. (2014). Economic well-being and spending behaviour of households in India: Does remittances matter? *Migration and Development, 3*(1), 38–53.

Mudambi, R. (2008). Location, control and innovation in knowledge-intensive industries. *Journal of Economic Geography, 8*(5), 699–725.

Mudambi, R., Saranga, H., & Schotter, A. P. (2017). Mastering the make-in-India challenge. *MIT Sloan Management Review, 58*(4), 59–66.

Munshi, K. (2016). Caste networks in the modern Indian economy. In *Development in India*. New Delhi: Springer, 13–37.

National Science Foundation. (2019). National pattern of R&D resources series. *American Association of Advancement of Science*. https://www.aaas.org/programs/r-d-budget-and-policy/historical-trends-federal-rd.

NSTMIS. (2013). *Research and development statistics 2011–12*. Retrieved from http://www.nstmis-dst.org/SnT-Indicators2011-12.

Okamitsu, N., & Yamashita, H. (2016). *Encyclopedia of India*. Tokyodo Press.

Racherla, U. S., Huang, K. G.-L., & Liu, K.-C. (2016). *Introduction: China and India as contrast pair in innovation and IP*. In K. C.

Radjou, N., Prabhu, J., & Ahuja, S. (2012). *Jugaad innovation: Think frugal, be flexible, generate breakthrough growth*. John Wiley & Sons.

Reserve Bank of India (2018) *Handbook of statistics on the Indian economy*. Retrieved January 2019, from https://dbie.rbi.org.in.

Sagiv, L., Roccas, S., Cieciuch, J., & Schwartz, S. H. (2017). Personal values in human life. *Nature Human Behaviour, 1*(9), 630.

Schwartz, S. H. (2015). Basic individual values: Sources and consequences. *Handbook of value*, 63–84.

Varshney, A. (1984). Political economy of slow industrial growth in India. *Economic and Political Weekly*, 1511–1517.

Zorondo-Rodríguez, F., et al. (2016). Contribution of natural and economic capital to subjective well-being: Empirical evidence from a small-scale society in Kodagu (Karnataka) India. *Social Indicators Research, 127*(2), 919–937.

Chapter 5
What Affects Women's Happiness in India?

Kanako Takimoto and Akihiko Kawaura

Abstract This chapter studies the well-being of women in India. Even though Goal 5 of the SDGs is "Gender equality and women's empowerment," India's gender gap widened from 0.601 in 2006 to 0.669 in 2017. This chapter explores the actual situation of women's well-being in India. We analyze the results of two surveys: "AsiaBarometer" in 2005 and "The Survey on Well-being in India" in 2017, using the Ordered Probit Models. The overall results are three points. First, married women are happier than single, divorced, or widowed women. Then, self-employed women are more likely to be happy than employed ones. Finally, being healthy is important for happiness. We draw three implications. India's women need to have the freedom to marry or to remain single and the right to choose their partners in the event of marriage. It is also crucial for India to support the expansion of opportunities for women to start their businesses. Furthermore, providing the correct information and educational opportunity for physical and mental health is beneficial. With the adoption of the 2030 Agenda, the United Nations pledged to ensure "no one will be left behind." Policy measures to assist women would contribute to making this pledge a reality in India.

5.1 Introduction

5.1.1 SDGs in India

Gender equality has emerged as one of the key issues in the process of economic development. This recognition is reflected in the Sustainable Development Goals (SDGs) that the United Nations specified in September 2015. The 2030 Agenda for

K. Takimoto (✉) · A. Kawaura
Faulty of Policy Studies, Doshisha University, 601 Genbu-cho, Karasuma-higashi-iru, Imadegawa-dori, Kamigyo-ku, Kyoto 602-8580, Japan
e-mail: ktakimot@mail.doshisha.ac.jp

A. Kawaura
e-mail: akawaura@mail.doshisha.ac.jp

© Springer Nature Singapore Pte Ltd. 2022
K. Mino and T. Yagi (eds.), *The Cultural Basis of Economic Growth in India*, Creative Economy, https://doi.org/10.1007/978-981-15-9305-5_5

SDGs names the following 17 goals: End poverty in all its forms; Zero hunger; Health; Education; Gender equality and women's empowerment; Water and sanitation; Energy; Economic growth; Infrastructure and industrialization; Inequality; Cities; Sustainable consumption and production; Climate change; Oceans; Biodiversity, forests, and desertification; Peace, justice, and strong institutions; and Partnerships. The gender issue appears as Goal 5.

Goal 5 seeks to achieve gender equality and empower all women and girls as is demonstrated in Fig. 5.1 (The United Nations in India, 2019). The emphasis on women is based on the belief that extending assistance on their behalf has beneficial spillover effects on the whole societies and economies. Figure 5.1 also shows some examples that portray gender issues in India. They represent a glimpse into the whole problems of physical, economic, and social insecurity facing women in India. For instance, the rate of crimes against women in India is over 50%. According to "The United Nations in India," 92% of women in the nation's capital have experienced sexual or physical violence in public spaces.[1] Women's plight in India also has regional consequences in South Asia, as India is the dominant country in the area in terms of population and economy.

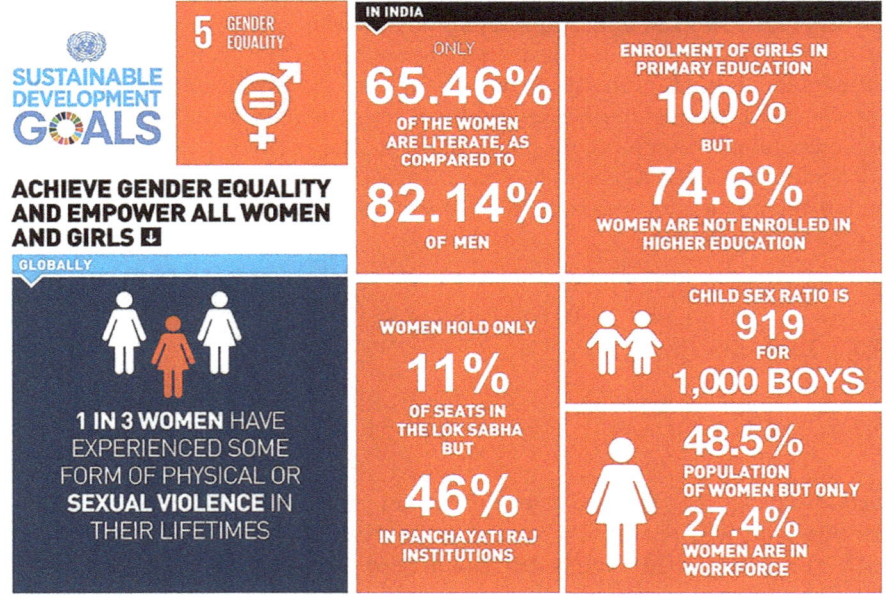

Fig. 5.1 Gender differences for SDGs Goal 5

---

[1] The United Nations India, Gender Equality: Women's Economic Empowerment (https://in.one. un.org/unibf/gender-equality/) last accessed 06/09/2019.

The measurement of the gender gap was pioneered by the World Economic Forum (WEF) and is based on the gap between women and men in four main categories: Economic participation and opportunity; Educational attainment; Health and survival; and Political empowerment.[2] The gender gap takes the value between 0 (or 0%) for total equality and 1 (or 100%) for maximum inequality.

According to the WEF, the gender gap score recorded at the global level was less than 30% in 2017 (World Economic Forum, 2017). Its figure for South Asia stood at 34%, which implies that the region's women had more catching up to do than their peers in the world on the average. This implies, however, that achieving gender equality has great potential to stimulate economic activities. According to IMF estimates, if women could participate in the workforce equally with men, it would increase India's GDP by 27%.[3]

5.1.2   Income, Happiness and Gender

What is the ultimate purpose of gender equality? It is evident that assisting women to attain a higher level of happiness is an important goal, which is closely related to equality in income, educational opportunity, access to jobs and healthcare, and political rights. This chapter focuses on women's happiness, as its understanding should lead to the comprehensive development strategy to embrace a wide spectrum of people including minorities.

The current situation is disappointing. India's gender gap widened from the score of 0.601 in 2006 to 0.669 in 2017. Accordingly, its place in the global gender gap ranking slipped from 98th out of 115 countries in 2006 to 108th out of 144 in 2017. On individual indices, India performs particularly poorly in the sex ratio, as parents still sustain priority for a son instead of a daughter. India's ranking on this index is 141st. Similarly, India lags behind other countries in labor force participation, on which India is ranked at 136th. The country's income imbalance between men and women is also striking, putting it at 137th place in the world. Expressed in actual amounts, this income gap results in $2,424 for women and $10,428 for men in terms of the Estimated Earned Income (PPP, US$) in 2017 (World Economic Forum, 2017). It is thus important to include the impacts of income level on women's happiness in the analysis.

Figure 5.2 presents an example of the relationship between income and happiness for both men and women based on answers from the AsiaBarometer 2005 survey. The survey measures income with the 11-step scale as in Question f8: "What was

---

[2] A total of 14 indices are defined for these four categories combined, which include sex ratio, earned income, and labor force participation.

[3] Speech by Christine Lagarde, Managing Director, IMF "Women's Empowerment: An Economic Game Changer" Los Angeles, November 14, 2016, (transcript available at https://www.imf.org/en/News/Articles/2016/11/14/SP111416-Womens-Empowerment-An-Economic-Game-Changer, last accessed 23/09/2019).

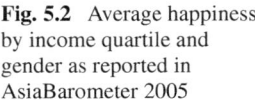

Fig. 5.2 Average happiness by income quartile and gender as reported in AsiaBarometer 2005

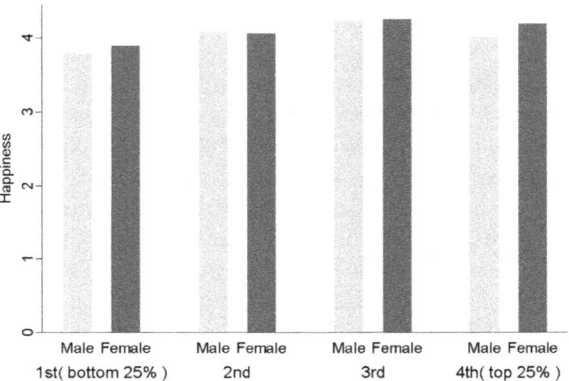

the total gross annual income of your household last year?"[4] Fig. 5.2 shows average happiness by income quartile and gender.[5] In the general trends, women are happier than men, with the exception of the second quartile in which the average happiness for men (4.26 points) exceeds that for women (4.23 points). The happiest group is the third quartile for both sexes.

The observation that those in the third income quartile were the happiest lends support to the "Easterlin Paradox". This paradox is named after Professor Richard Easterlin, who found that increasing income did not necessarily raise average well-being in his 1974 article (Easterlin, 1974). Debate about this paradox continues today (Stevenson & Wolfers, 2013).

On the other hand, we find a different result regarding subjective income. AsiaBarometer 2005 uses a 5-step scale to measure happiness based on subjective income in Question 7: "How would you describe your standard of living?"[6] Fig. 5.3 shows average happiness based on subjective income and gender. In contrast to Figs. 5.2 and 5.3 shows that men are happier than women except in the 3rd and 4th groups. In the 3rd group the men's happiness (3.89 points) is lower than the women's (3.94 points), and in the 4th group the men's happiness (4.27 points) is lower than the women's (4.34 points). Moreover, both the men and the women in the 5th group are the happiest. Figure 5.3 shows that an increase in subjective income yields diminishing marginal gains in happiness.

---

[4] The scale ranges from 1 (Up to 2,500) to 11 (25,001 and above), increasing by 2,500 rupees with each step.

[5] As the survey collects income information as that accruing to individual households, the individual income is calculated for this analysis by dividing the household income by the square root of the number of family members.

[6] The original scale of the AsiaBarometer scale ranges from a high score of 1 to a low score of 5 (1 high, 2 relatively high, 3 average, 4 relatively low, and 5 low). Since most of the indices are designed so that a larger number means greater happiness, we converted to the ordered number scale where 1 is lowest and 5 is highest in our analysis.

Fig. 5.3 Average happiness by subjective income as reported in AsiaBarometer 2005

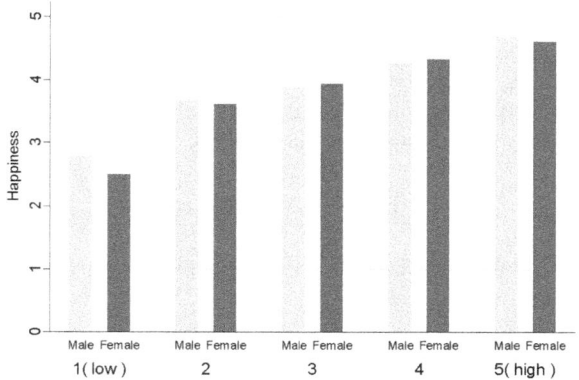

5.2   Basic Analysis

This section examines the factors influencing women's happiness in India. The data and analytical methodology are discussed next, which is followed by the results and interpretations.

5.2.1   Data and Methodology

This analysis combines information from two surveys: "AsiaBarometer" in 2005 and Doshisha University's "The Survey on Well-being in India" in 2017. The sample size of AsiaBarometer was 2,039, with the men's share of 53.0% (1,080). The survey targeted people who lived as the middle class in seven cities: Delhi, Mumbai, Bangalore, Hyderabad, Ahmedabad, Chennai, and Kolkata. The sample size of the Survey on Well-being in India was 4,046. The sex composition was 59.7% men (2,415) and 40.3% women (1,631). This survey took place in 26 cities.

The questions on happiness and scales used in the two surveys are as follows. First, Question 5 in AsiaBarometer 2005 asked: "All things considered, would you say that you are happy these days?" Possible answers spanned a 5-step scale: (1) Very happy—(2) Quite happy—(3) Neither happy nor unhappy—(4) Not too happy—(5) Very unhappy (a small "Don't know" category is not studied here). Second, Question f44 in the Well-being 2017 survey measured happiness: "On a scale from 0 to 10, please rate your overall level of happiness." The question used an 11-step scale ranging from (0) very unhappy to (10) very happy. In order to make these indices comparable, we reversed the AsiaBarometer 2005 answer order so that (5) represents the highest happiness.

By comparing the responses to the two surveys, we tried to arrive at a clear picture of women's happiness. More specifically, we were interested in the potential shifts underlying women's happiness. Our question therefore was: "Have there been any changes in the factors that influence women's happiness?" Explanatory variables we included in the regressions were: income, age, education level, marital status, occupation, health condition, residence type, and religious devotion. The basic regression for this analysis was based on Di Tella and MacCulloch's happiness model (2008) with minor changes, which takes the following form:

$$HAPPINESS_{i,s,t} = \alpha MICRO_{i,s,t} + \eta_s + \mu_{i,s,t}$$

[$HAPPINESS$: individual happiness, $MICRO$: individual factors, $\mu_{i,s,t}$: error term].

where $HAPPINESS_{i,s,t}$ represents the happiness of the individual i, who lives in country s ($s =$ India), in the year t ($t = 2005$ or 2017).

Individual characteristics were converted to dummy variables. Because the answer to the happiness question used an ordinal ranking, we used the ordered probit model. In addition, we estimated their marginal effects for the purpose of comparing the effect of individual variables.

5.2.2 Results by Ordered Probit Models

Table 5.1 shows the results of the ordered probit estimations for (1) AsiaBarometer and (2) The Survey on Well-being in India. Since all explanatory variables enter the analysis as dummy variables, it was necessary to determine the baseline group for each category. For example, we chose the first quartile as the baseline in the income quartile group category. Hence the estimated coefficients for other income quartiles represent effects that arise by belonging to the category. The coefficient for the third income quartile takes a positive sign, which is statistically significant at the 10% level. Its marginal effects of scale 5 were + 9.9% points. The marginal effects of AsiaBarometer were scale 5 and those of the Well-being Survey in India were scale 10. Some variables are different between these two surveys. Examples are subject income that is only available in AsiaBarometer and the teenage group, which is available exclusively in the Well-being Survey. The baseline variables are: Income quartiles (first quartile), Subjective income (average), Age (twenties in 2005 and teenage in 2017), Education (average), Marital status (married), Employment status (employed), Health (unhealthy), House (did not own) and Religious devotion (did not believe any religions). Estimated coefficients that satisfy the statistical significance test with at least 10% level are marked by asterisks in Table 5.1.

The variables that passed the significance test (i.e., variables that had actual impacts on the happiness level) in 2005 include: Income quartile (third quartile), Subjective income (low, relatively high, and high), Age (thirties and forties), Education level (lower), Marital status (divorced/separated/widowed), and Health (healthy). Among the variables that were found to affect happiness in 2017 are: Income quartile

Table 5.1   Results by ordered probit models from 2005 and 2017

Variables		(1) AsiaBarometer, 2005			(2) The Survey on Well-being in India, 2017		
		Coefficient	Std. Error	Marginal effects (5)	Coefficient	Std. Error	Marginal effects (10)
Income quartile							
	Second	0.059	(0.132)	2.0%	0.110	(0.076)	1.5%
	Third	0.284*	(0.148)	9.9%	0.229**	(0.089)	3.1%
	Fourth	0.105	(0.177)	3.6%	0.155*	(0.089)	2.1%
Subjective income							
	Low	−1 187***	(0.416)	−28.6%			
	Relatively low	−0.290	(0.256)	−9.3%			
	Relatively high	0.417***	(0.129)	14.7%			
	High	1.067***	(0.185)	38.6%			
Age							
	20–29	(omitted)			0.153	(0.135)	2.1%
	30–39	−0.306**	(0.129)	−10.2%	−0.001	(0.148)	0.0%
	40–49	−0.262*	(0.148)	−8.6%	−0.046	(0.153)	−0.6%
	50–59	−0.169	(0.221)	−5.6%	0.040	(0.163)	0.6%
	60 or above	−0.339	(0.357)	−10.7%	−0.191	(0.216)	−2.8%
Education							
	Lower	−0.244*	(0.136)	−8.1%	−0.151	(0.213)	−2.2%
	Higher	−0.105	(0.122)	−3.5%	0.021	(0.098)	0.3%
Marital status							
	Single	−0.250	(0.175)	−8.2%	−0.263***	(0.082)	−3.9%
	Divorced/ Separated/ Widowed	−1.646**	(0.774)	−32.8%	0.154	(0.162)	2.1%
Employment status							
	Self-employed	0.238	(0.317)	8.3%	0.335***	(0.066)	4.8%
	Not Employed	0.233	(0.156)	7.7%	−0.066	(0.080)	−0.9%
Health	Healthy	0.526**	(0.259)	16.0%	0.747***	(0.093)	11.3%
House	Owned	0.001	(0.104)	0.0%	0.189***	(0.062)	2.7%
Religious devotion	Have	0.174	(0.247)	5.7%	0.213***	(0.056)	3.0%
Observations		532			1,458		

Standard errors in parentheses
***p < 0.01, **p < 0.05, *p < 0.1

(third quartile), Marital status (single), Employment state (self-employed), Health (healthy), House (owned), and Religious devotion (have religious devotion). The details of the results with respect to individual variables are discussed in Sect. 5.3.

5.2.3 Marginal Effects

Table 5.1 also shows the marginal effects (scale 5) for the AsiaBarometer survey for income quartile; the group of the third income quartile has positive effects (Third: + 9.9% points). On the other hand, the marginal effects (scale 5) for the AsiaBarometer survey for the subjective income show that the biggest positive factor is observed for the highest subjective income group; (High: + 38.6% points) and that the relatively high subjective income group shows less than half the positive effect when compared with the highest group; (Relatively high: + 14.7% points). On the contrary, the lower subject income group displays a big negative effect (Low: –28.6%). The subjective income variable is characterized by bigger effects than the actual income quartile, and the group who felt their income was lower than average reported that their happiness was lower. One interpretation is that the happiness was predisposed to be determined by comparison to that of other people.

There was also a negative effect for the ages of thirties and forties; the marginal effects (scale 5) for women in their thirties are bigger than for those in their forties (30–39: –10.2% points, and 40–49: –8.6% points). The lower education group has a negative effect (Lower: –8.1% points). In marital status those who were divorced, separated, or widowed had a large negative effect (Divorced/Separated/Widowed: –32.8% points). Being in good health positively affected women's happiness (Healthy: + 16.0% points).

In Table 5.1, the marginal effect (scale 10) for the 2017 survey shows the group of the third income quartile had a positive effect (Third: + 3.1% points). There was only one statistically significant negative factor, which is the single group for marital status (Single: –3.9% points). In employment status, the self-employed group had a positive effect (Self-employed: 4.8% points). Finally, the biggest positive factor in 2017 was health status (Healthy: +11.3% points), while the variables for housing and religious devotion were of similar, smaller impacts (Owned housing: +2.7% points), and (Have religion: +3.0% points).

There are three differences between the 2005 and 2017 findings. First, the negative effect of aging seems to be disappearing. Second, the situations of women who are divorced, separated, or widowed may be improving. The situation of single women might not have changed, and they may therefore be distressed by the conflict with the traditional value of marriage. Finally, women who are self-employed or who are top-level managers or executives have become happier. To support women's social advancement might lead to more happiness for women. On the similarity side is the importance of health. Being healthy makes women happier by more than +10% points. To stay healthy is the most crucial factor in women's happiness.

The limitation of this analysis is that we used two different surveys to compare respective results. Since the 2017 survey did not follow the same set of respondents of the 2005 survey, a comparison in the strict sense is not possible. In order to minimize the potential bias arising from this non-uniformity of sample designs, however, we converted the survey's numerical results to dummy variables by category. While it would be desirable if a continuous survey with a fixed set of respondents were implemented in the future, the chapter's findings would contribute to formulation of policies based on SDGs.

5.3 Women's Happiness

This section will illustrate regression results in Table 5.1 in the context of the graphical presentation of the data from two surveys. The detailed account of variable treatment is also provided when necessary. They will facilitate the understanding of survey findings.

5.3.1 Age

Figure 5.4 shows average happiness by age, where the dotted line is the survey result from AsiaBarometer 2005 and the solid line is the survey result of Well-being in India 2017. In 2005, the effect of age on happiness followed a U-shaped trend, with women in their thirties at the bottom. This is consistent with the findings of previous studies, such as Frijiters et al. (2001), Senik (2002), Blanchflower and Oswald (2004), and

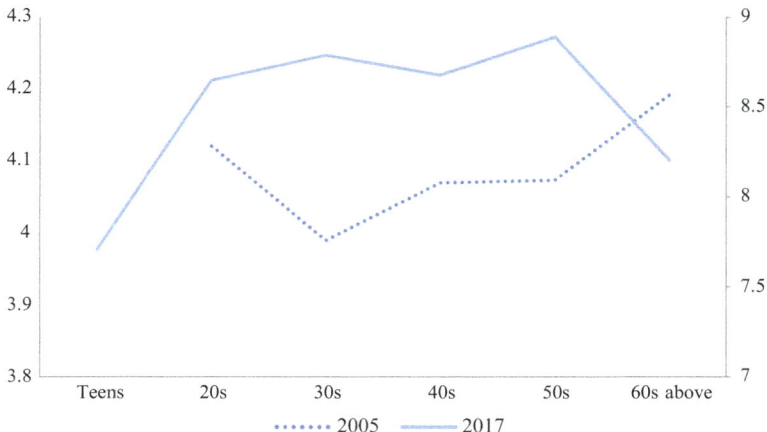

Fig. 5.4 Average happiness by age

Becchetti et al. (2014). Specification (1) in Table 5.1, the ordered probit model for AsiaBarometer, shows that women in their twenties are happier than those in their thirties and forties; these differences are statistically significant for women in their twenties ($p = 0.018$) and thirties ($p = 0.076$). This is consistent with the graphical presentation.

In contrast to the graph for 2005, the one for 2017 has data that displays a reversed U-shaped trend for the age effect, with women in their fifties at the top. A few studies have reported this type of reversed U-shape with women in their twenties and thirties at the top (Otake et al. 2010). According to the results for (2) in Table 5.1, however, age has no statistically significant effect on the happiness level.

The shift in the effect of age observed in Table 5.1 between 2005 and 2017 suggests that Indian women have experienced some changes with respect to the age–happiness link. Figure 5.4 reveals that their relationship shifted from the U-shape to the reversed U-shape, which may suggest that working-age women have acquired various opportunities. In traditional society, the opportunities for self-realization must have been severely restricted for women. One could easily presume that the kinds of jobs they could get after their marriage were limited. As society has embraced more diversity, they might have gained access to more opportunities, which must have led to the absence of negative age effects in the thirties and forties in the more recent survey.

5.3.2 Education

In the ordered probit analysis, we classified education level into three: Lower, Average, and Higher. This was done to make different questions that were asked in the two surveys more comparable. The AsiaBarometer survey used the 6-category scale for education level in Question f3, which asked: "What is the highest level of education you have completed?" We compressed these six categories into three as follows: Lower (No formal education; Elementary school; Junior high school; or Middle school), Average (High school), and Higher (Professional school; Technical school; University; or Graduate school).

The question in the Well-being in India survey Question f10_1 on education level was: "Please indicate the highest level of education (or equivalent) completed by you...." We adopted three categories in the following manner: Lower (Illiterate; Literate but no formal schooling; School: Up to 4 years or Up to 5–9 years), Average (HSC/SSC; or Some college but did not graduate), and Higher (Graduate or Post-Graduate-General; Graduate or Post-Graduate-Professional).

The AsiaBarometer results in Table 5.1 indicate that the lower education level is characterized by a negative effect on happiness. Figure 5.5 indicates, on the other hand, that the average happiness for the group with an average education level declined relative to people in other education categories. How can one reconcile these findings? One interpretation is that the education level composition has undergone a dramatic change, which negatively affected those with average education.

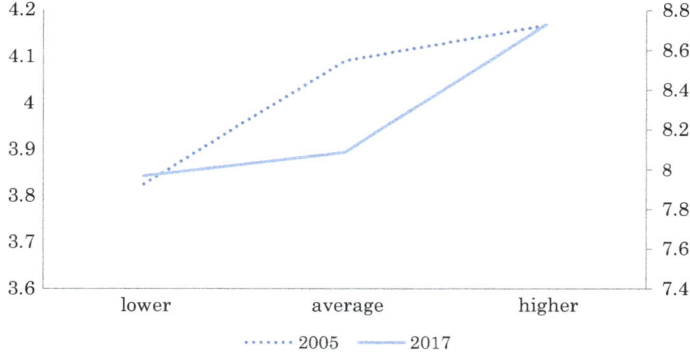

Fig. 5.5 Average happiness by education

The hypothesis is that the comparative education level may have larger effects than the actual education level. For instance, if the majority of society belonged to the higher education group, those in the average education group would find it difficult to find a job. To assess whether this line of reasoning has any relevance, we present the composition of the education level in Fig. 5.6.

The figure shows that the percentage composed of women in the lower group, who had no formal education or schooling only up to 9 years, shrank substantially from 22.92% to a meager 1.9% of the total from 2005 to 2017. The higher education group, however, expanded from 39.23 to 84.16%. As those with average education have been squeezed by the growing number of women in the higher education group with college degrees, their happiness level declined. This has diminished the happiness level difference between the lower and average groups, resulting in the loss of statistical significance for the negative impacts for the former group. One should note, however, that this interpretation should not eclipse the educational advancement enjoyed by many Indian women.

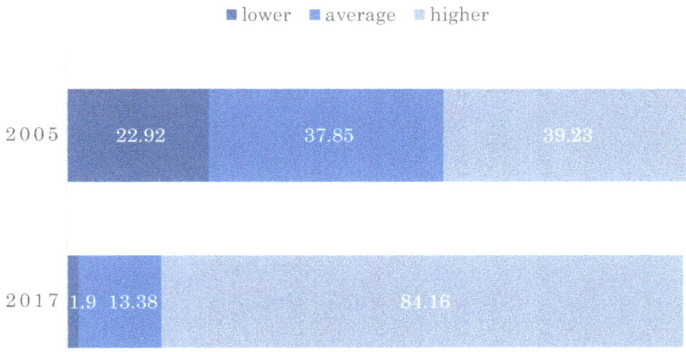

Fig. 5.6 The composition of education level for women

5.3.3 Marital Status

Table 5.1 indicates that there was no difference in happiness between single and married women in terms of statistical significance in 2005. On the other hand, women who were divorced, separated, or widowed were less happy than married women, as reflected in the negative coefficient estimate ($p = 0.033$). This confirms the Indian traditions that are popularly reported in the media. Widowed women are faced with the historical weight of the Hindu funeral practice of "sati" or "suttee", in which they are expected to burn themselves on their husband's funeral pyre. Although the government of Rajasthan formally banned "sati" in 1987, many widows are still shunned by their communities and abandoned by their families in India.

The analysis for the 2017 survey data in Table 5.1, however, indicates that the divorced, separated, or widowed group no longer reported different happiness levels relative to married women. The unfortunate group in this 2017 survey were the single women, who were less happy than married women.

Where do the differences come from? Fig. 5.7 shows average happiness by marital status. As the Divorced, Separated, and Widowed groups were too small to include in the equation respectively as independent categories; we combined them in the regression analysis. Data in Fig. 5.7 for "Divorced/Separated" and "Widowed" are before they were aggregated. Members of the Widowed group were happier on average than were members of the Divorced/Separated group both in 2005 and 2017. This gives the impression that the plight of the widowed women may be exaggerated. An alternative explanation can be offered based on the location of the surveys. The surveys took place in cities, and widowed women there may not face as much harassment from the families of their diseased husband compared with their counterparts in the rural areas.

It is disappointing that, in spite of the SDG's goal of achieving gender equality and empowering all women, single women's happiness declined compared to married

Note: The 2005 happiness score is measured on the left vertical axis, and the 2017 score on the right axis.

Fig. 5.7 Average happiness by marital status

women's in 2017. One explanation is possible in the context of the information revolution through the Internet and SNS. Those in the "single" category constitute the youngest generation in the marital groups.[7] They must be more prepared to adopt new technologies to gain knowledge about the world through such media as the Internet and SNS. They must also be the ones who recognize and appreciate changes in value in their society. For example, Indian women traditionally did not have the right to choose their partner by themselves, and the option of inter-caste marriage was almost non-existent. Most women married to the partner whom their parents selected for them among the same caste. As young, single women are exposed to the cultural and value system of the outside world, they may experience the gap and frustration between their expectations and reality, which has led to the decline of their happiness relative to that of married women.

5.3.4 Employment Status

The WEF reported a serious gender gap in economic opportunity and participation. India's ranking in terms of women's economic participation declined from 110th place in 2006 to 139th place in 2017. The labor force participation ratio (female/male) is about half the average: while the world average is 0.667, its value in India is 0.347. In addition, the ratio of legislators, senior officials, and managers is also low (0.148), which is less than two women out of ten men.

Figure 5.8 indicates that women who are self-employed are generally happier than those who are employed; this finding was significant at the 1% level in 2017. The employment status did not affect the happiness level in 2005, however. One possible reason for this difference may have to do with the composition shift in the employment status among women. According to AsiaBarometer, 85.4% of women did not work, 11.8% were employed, and only 2.8% were self-employed in 2005. In 2017, on the other hand, 28.6% of women did not work, 38.6% were employed, and 32.8% were self-employed. The share of self-employed women increased over ten times between 2005 and 2017.

Self-employment in 2017 was classified into two sub-categories: Top-level manager or executive (19.6%) and self-employed (13.2%). According to Fig. 5.8, the average happiness score for the "Top-level manager, executive" category is the highest of all the occupations (9.23 points). Those who are "Self-employed" report the second-highest happiness level (9.09 points).

In spite of the WEF report's low score for legislators, senior officials, and managers, the happiest women in India are top-level managers or executives. Gender equality in the job market is a very important condition for improving women's happiness.

---

[7] The average ages in 2017 for each category were: Single, 24.8 years; Married, 43.1 years; Divorced, 47.9 years; Widowed, 52.5 years.

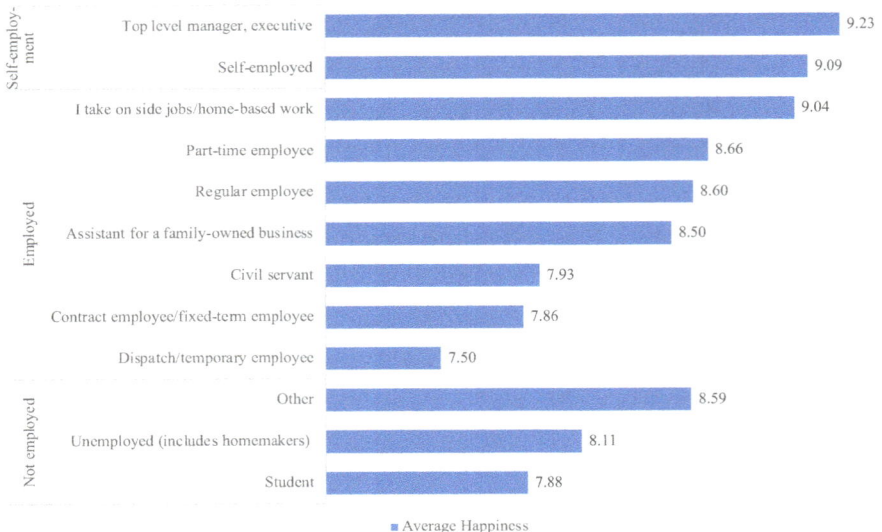

Fig. 5.8 Average happiness by employment status in Survey, 2017

5.3.5 Health

Health is a basic factor for women's (and presumably for men's) happiness, since it is hard to live and work daily without physical and mental health. Table 5.1 shows that good health has a positive effect on happiness in both surveys, and their significance levels were at the 5% level in 2005 and 1% level in 2017. In 2017, women who chose the answer "Unhealthy" or "If pressed to say, I would say 'unhealthy'", (about 10% of the total) reported the average happiness of 7.15 points. And women who identified themselves as with "Normal level of health", "If pressed to say, I would say 'healthy'", or "Healthy" (about 90%) showed that their average happiness was 8.78 points.

To illustrate the relationship between health and happiness, Fig. 5.9 shows average happiness by health status and indicates that the healthier group was happier in both years. In 2017, the happiness gap between the unhealthy group and the healthy group was over 1.5 points; the average score for unhealthy was 7.61 points when it was 9.40 points for the group of healthy women.

According to World Development Indicators (WDI), health conditions in India improved from 2005 to 2017, one example of which is the life expectancy at birth. It increased from 64.6 years in 2005 to 68.8 years in 2017. In the context of the gender gap, the life expectancy for women was 65.4 years, which was only 1.7 years longer than it was for men in 2005. In 2017, this gap expanded and Indian women were expected to live longer by 3.1 years than men (70.4 years for women and 67.3 years for men). As income rises, the gap usually becomes greater, reaching 5.2 years in high-income countries (women's 83.4 years relative to men's 78.1 years). Indian women are fast closing this gap.

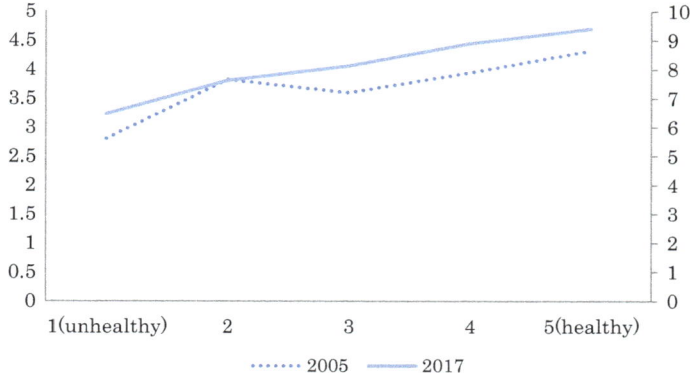

Note: The 2005 happiness score is measured on the left vertical axis, and the 2017 score on the right axis.

Fig. 5.9 Average happiness by health status

5.3.6 Housing

Table 5.1 shows that, according to the 2017 survey, women who live in houses that they own are happier than those who do not. This observation, however, does not hold for 2005, as this variable does not have a coefficient that is significant even at the 10% level in AsiaBarometer.

In the 2017 survey, over 70% of women owned their house or condominium, and the detailed breakdown is as follows. A total of 66.7% of women lived in their own house and 5.5% of them lived in their own condominium. Figure 5.10 shows that women who own their house have the highest happiness score (8.82). Living in one's own house is an important factor for happiness.

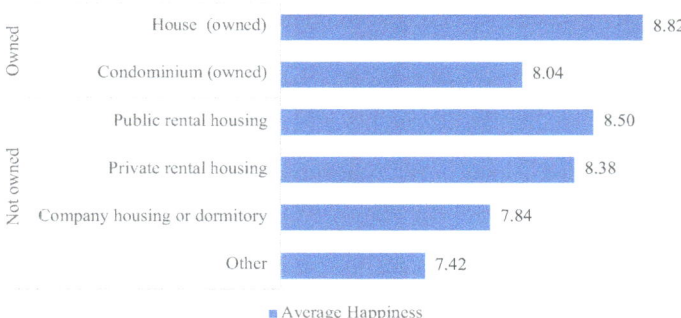

Fig. 5.10 Average happiness by residence on the Well-being survey in India 2017

5.3.7 Religious Devotion

Religion is a major factor in women's happiness. Religion not only affects the level of happiness, but also gives value to happiness. Religion also defines women's daily lives, including the food they eat, the clothes they wear, and the things they think about. To measure the conduct of religious practice, we used a surrogate variable to indicate strength of religion or faith. We would expect happiness to rise in relation to whatever they believe.

Table 5.1 shows that women who "normally conduct religious practices, such as attending worship, scripture readings, religious training, and missionary work" experience a positive effect on happiness. The estimated coefficient was statistically significant at the 1% level in 2017. In 2005, however, the corresponding coefficient did not pass the significance test. Did religion's impact change between the surveys?

This change in the regression result may be due to the increased share of non-believers in the 2017 survey. In 2005, 90.8% of women were Hindu, 3.1% were Muslim, 2.3% were Catholic, and 0.9% were Buddhist. The small size of the comparison group, i.e., those who did not belong to any religion, might not have allowed isolating the effects of religion in 2005. In 2017, 7.4% of women in the survey did not believe anything related to religion or faith. The average happiness of women who did not belong to any religion was lower than that of religious women: the former was 8.42 points and the latter was 8.78 points. One interpretation is that to have religious devotion is good for women's psychological health, whatever they believe.

5.4 Conclusion

This chapter opened with the focus on Goal 5 of SDGs "Gender equality and women's empowerment" and conducted quantitative analyses of two survey results as an effort to seek determinants of women's happiness in India. The investigation produced several observations that have implications for SDGs. They are in the area of marriage, labor conditions, and healthcare.

First, the SDGs have the target for marriage as 5.3, which is to "[E]liminate all harmful practices, such as child, early, and forced marriage, and female genital mutilation." The relevant finding of the chapter's analysis is that single women were not as happy as married women in 2017, and this difference is statistically significant. Target 5.3 is important to protect women's human rights and dignity. It may be equally meaningful to make sure that women be given the right to decide whether to marry and (in the event they choose marriage) the right to choose their partner by themselves.

The SDGs has a specific work-related proposal in Target 5.a, "[U]ndertake reforms to give women equal rights to economic resources, as well as access to ownership and control over land and other forms of property, financial services, inheritance, and natural resources, in accordance with national laws." The chapter's finding that self-employed women are happier than those who are employees underscores the importance of this target. There is a scope for greater happiness among women if the share of businesses run by women in India (only 14% in 2018) can be expanded (The United Nations in India, 2018).

One example of women's entry into self-employment is Unilever's Shakti program that is supported by microfinance (The United Nations in India, 2018). In this program, women in remote areas can work as "Shakti entrepreneurs" who distribute Unilever's products. There are as many as 70,000 "Shakti entrepreneurs", and they earn twice or three times compared before. To offer job opportunities of this kind would raise women's happiness in the future.

Finally, good health is the only non-income factor that was found to contribute to an increase in happiness in both the 2005 and 2017 surveys. Goal 3 of the SDGs is Health, and, although they do not offer any targets for health education, we believe that education and community building for healthcare are the key elements for women's happiness. It is crucial for women to obtain the right physical and psychological health information through education. Sharing the information with others, including families and communities, would facilitate the dissemination of useful health knowledge.

With the adoption of the 2030 Agenda, member states of the United Nations pledged to ensure "no one will be left behind." Policy measures to assist women would surely contribute to making this pledge a reality.

References

Becchetti, L., Massari, R., & Naticchioni, P. (2014). The drivers of happiness inequality: Suggestions for promoting social cohesion. *Oxford Economic Papers, 66*(2), 419–442.

Blanchflower, D. G., & Oswald, A. J. (2004). Well-being over time in Britain and the USA. *Journal of Public Economics, 88*, 1359–1386.

Di Tella, R., & MacCuloch, R. J. (2008). Gross national happiness as an answer to the Easterlin Paradox? *Journal of Development Economics, 86*, 22–42.

Easterlin, R. A. (1974). does economic growth improve the human lot? Some empirical evidence. *Nations and Households in Economic Growth, 89*(2), 89–125.

Frijiters, P., Haisken-DeNew, J. P., & Shields, M. A. (2001). The value of reunification in Germany: An analysis of changes in life satisfaction. *Tinbergen Institute*, mimeo.

Otake, F., Shiraishi, S., & Tsutsui, Y. (2010). *Nihon no Kouhukudo* (Well-being in Japan), (pp. 33–73). Tokyo: Nihon Hyo-ron Sha. (In Japanese).

Senik, C. (2002). When information dominates comparison: A panel data analysis using Russian subjective data. *DELTA, Discussion Paper* No. 2002-02.

Stevenson, B., & Wolfers, J. (2013). Subjective well-being and income: Is there any evidence of satiation? *American Economic Review, 103*(3), 598–604.

The United Nations in India. (2018). *The Fact Sheet 2018*. Retrieved September 13, 2019, form https://in.one.un.org/wp-content/uploads/2018/07/Gender_Thematic-Business-Case_5Jun 2018.pdf.

The United Nations in India. (2019). Retrieved August 29, 2019, form https://in.one.un.org/page/sustainable-development-goals/sdg-5/.

World Economic Forum. (2017). *The Global Gender Gap Report 2017* (pp. 176–177). Geneva.

Chapter 6
Socio-Economic Implications of the Rajasthani Traditional Folk Drama *Gavari*: A Poverty Trap or a Revival of Social Capital in the Indian Tribal Community?

Sayaka Sakoda, Ryuichi Fukuhara, and Pramod Tiwari

Abstract This chapter examines the economic rationality of the poor's individual religious behaviours who belong to a non-organized religion in India. The poor's expenditure on religious events is likely to be treated as a "poverty trap," not as an investment for economic growth in mainstream development economics. We conducted the economic survey on participants and host communities of the traditional folk dance-drama "Gavari" performed collectively by the Bhil males, Schedule Tribe in Rajasthan. Gavari performers from the same community need to be absent from their work for 40 days while touring around neighbouring communities. Our survey in 2016 reveals that participation in Gavari reduces their income because rewards from hosting communities could not compensate for the 40-day income loss. Nevertheless, participating performers show their willingness to join the next Gavari occasion. It suggests performing Gavari would not be motivated by the temporary economic gain. We then clarified the long-term investment effect in Gavari by the treatment effect of performers and found out that investing their time and cost for performing Gavari is not for the short-term economic incentive but presumably the long-term investment for the social capital, bonding within the Bhil community and bridging over with other communities, in the region.

S. Sakoda (✉)
Faculty of Economics, Doshisha University, Karasuma-higashi-iru, Imadegawa-dori, Kamigyo-ku, Kyoto 602-8580, Japan
e-mail: ssakoda@mail.doshisha.ac.jp

R. Fukuhara
Center for Southeast Asian Studies, Kyoto University, 46 Yoshida Shimo Adachi-chi-cho, Sakyo-ku, Kyoto 606-8304, Japan
e-mail: fukuhara@cseas.kyoto-u.ac.jp

P. Tiwari
Institute for Financial Management and Research, Krea University, No: 196, T.T.K. Road, Alwarpet, Chennai 600-018, India
e-mail: pramod.tiwari@ifmr.ac.in

© Springer Nature Singapore Pte Ltd. 2022
K. Mino and T. Yagi (eds.), *The Cultural Basis of Economic Growth in India*, Creative Economy, https://doi.org/10.1007/978-981-15-9305-5_6

6.1   Economic Growth, Poverty Reduction, and Religion

It is a classic socio-economic question whether secularization or the loss of religiosity has been caused by economic development. A century ago, Durkheim (1912–1995) proposed that technological and socio-economic advances would come to displace the functions of religion; this was the origin of the so-called "secularization hypothesis".In contrast, Weber (1905–2001) contended that monotheistic religion—the so-called Protestant work ethic of diligence—plays a vital role at the early stage of modern capitalism.

A correlation between economic development and secularization is evident, and highly religious countries tend to be the poorest (Deaton, 2008; Inglehart & Welzel, 2005). However, it is not clear how economic development and secularization interact. Nor is it apparent which change precedes which, that is, whether development causes secularization (Paldam & Gundlach, 2013) or vice versa (Campante & Yanagizawa-Drott, 2015), or whether both changes are co-driven, with different time lags, by factors such as advances in education or technology (Hungerman, 2014; McCleary & Barro, 2006). Secularization, which Kuznets (1973) identified as one of six characteristics of modern economic growth, leads to structural, social, and ideological changes of the society affected by religion. On the other hand, Iyer et al. (2011) suggest that religion's resilience in both developed and developing countries has been observed by scholars investigating the economics and sociology of religion in the twenty-first century. The new approaches to empirical analysis that use microdata rather than macro-empirical studies have found more results that do not support the secularization hypothesis (Iannaccone & Berman, 2008; Iyer, 2008). Buser (2015) uses data from Ecuador to demonstrate that higher-income individuals are more involved in religious activities. Ruck, Bentley, and Lawson (2018) find evidence that a rise in secularization has generally preceded economic growth over the twentieth century by comparing a 100-year time series of secularization factors in different nations, derived from historical gross domestic product figures in the recent World Value Survey. Will this tendency of the twentieth century continue in the twenty-first century?

Alternative approaches from new institutional economics and anthropology relate to religion as "institutional structure" or "social capital". Ensminger (1994, 1997), Gramajo (2007), Landa (1994), and Wood (2007) contribute to this discussion of the "Economics of Religion". Seele (2011) argues for the translation of Williamson's (1975) and Coleman's (1988) concept of institutional trust into religion to explain motivations influenced by trust-based relations and by beliefs and faith. However, there is a criticism that the rational choice basis of the "Economics of Religion" means that it does not entirely capture the influence of religion on individual decision-making (Seele, 2011).

To date, most studies of the relationship between economics and religion have targeted developed countries and Christianity. Only a few studies focus on the rest of the world, with such exceptions mainly focusing on Hinduism and Islam, including Yang (2012) and Yang and Hu (2012) on Asia, Iyer (2016) on the Middle East, and Iyer (2018) on India. Even in the case of these studies, the main target is orga-nized religions. Thus, the relationship between poor economies and "non-organized" religion has not been studied or has been ignored in past socio-economic research, despite the fact that there are many cases in which economically poorer and socially more vulnerable minorities belong to non-organized religions.

6.2 Religious Vulnerable Groups in India's Modern Economic Development

India is officially a secular state with no state religion, but it is characterized by economic inequality, ethnic groups, an implicit social class structure, and, conse-quently, cultural diversity of religious beliefs, behaviours, and practices. Religion has remained influential in society, despite India's experiencing economic growth in the last decades. By 2018, India's per capita gross domestic product was 26 times that of 1958, yet more than 90% of respondents still rated religion as "very important" or "rather important" in the latest round of the World Values Survey from 2010–2014. India is one of only two nations in which the number of people who consider religion an essential part of their lives grew by over 10 percentage points in the decade to 2014 (the second nation being Kyrgyzstan). According to the World Values Survey, India experienced a 12.1% growth, from 79.2 to 91.3%, in this factor, although it should be noted that the increase could be caused by the promotion of so-called Hindu Nationalism, the political slogan of the Prime Minister Narendra Modi.

It is well known among economists that puzzling trends have characterized India's economic growth in recent decades (Corbridge et al., 2018). One of the puzzles is why, despite India's economic success, poor people have remained mired in extreme poverty compared with those in China and some countries in east and south-east Asia.

Topalova (2008) finds a convincing answer to this puzzle, i.e., that Scheduled Caste (SC) and Scheduled Tribe (ST) households failed to keep pace with the growth rates in average per capita consumption recorded by members of non-SC/ST households after 1993–1994. The bottom line is that significant sections of Indian society—in particular, the scheduled communities—have not significantly benefited from the years of economic growth.

India adopted a market-oriented model of development from 1991, resulting in a marked shift in how the benefits of growth were distributed across income groups. In the 1980s, the growth rate of consumption for those at the bottom of the income distribution was substantially higher than for those at the top. In contrast, in the 1990s, the top income groups enjoyed a substantially larger share of the gains from economic growth driven by the manufacturing and service sectors. This uneven distribution of the gains from economic growth significantly increased income inequality within and across states, and between rural and urban areas (Topalova, 2008).

Unlike their counterparts in China and East Asia, the SCs and STs continue to be locked out of growth areas in the Indian economy, both on account of their low levels of human capital formation (poor healthcare and education provision) and because of their continuing exclusion from asset pools and physical capital (Corbridge et al., 2018).

Among the socially vulnerable groups in India, the proportion of the rural absolute poor is much larger than for other parts of society; 45% of STs fall into this category and 40% of SCs (Government of India, Planning Commission, 2012). Some studies suggest that the low human capital levels of the scheduled communities are the result of their accumulated lack of investment in human capital. They argue that the poor spend more of their income on religious events and obligations rather than on education or investment for economic growth. In principle, mainstream development economics regards expenditures on cultural and traditional events, such as weddings, funerals, and religious festivals, as stopgap remedies that distract from poverty but are detrimental to efforts to eradicate it. Based on their poverty research in Rajasthan, India, Banerjee and Duflo (2007) highlight this tendency, noting that "[i]n Udaipur … more than 99% of extremely poor households spend money on a wedding, a funeral, or a religious festival. The median household spent 10% of its annual budget on festivals". Based on a survey of the economic trajectories of 35 Indian villages, Krishna (2003) is critical of the "[h]igh expenses on death feasts and marriages [which] constituted the second principal reason for the decline into poverty".

In some analyses of the spending of the poor, expenditure on traditional cultural and religious activities and those for commercialized entertainments are categorized as the same type of expenditure. This perspective in which these expenditures are mixed appears to remain trapped with the secularization hypothesis and conventional development paradigm, as both expenditures could hardly be considered investment for human capital and social capital of the poor, but, rather spending money on a kind of barrier toward secularization. Although the development concept is often used to solve the poverty problem in tribal areas, displacement due to development destroys the traditional livelihoods of the tribal people, which results in their being denied access to resources and makes them more vulnerable to poverty (Pal, 2015).

Many studies of India on religions from a demographic perspective and ones on poverty from a development perspective are disconnected. There is little micro-empirical analysis of the relationship among individual income and consumption, collective religious behaviour, and economic growth. To analyse the socio-economic implications of the religious behaviour of poor individuals in terms of economic growth, we focus on a unique religious festival called *Gavari*, a traditional folk dance–drama performed by the Bhil, the largest Scheduled Tribe in Rajasthan. Performing the *Gavari* festival requires the performers to sacrifice their work and incomes because they must undertake a pilgrimage in a group from the same community for 40 days from mid-August to late September except the first and last days of the 40-day period, when they initiate and close the pilgrimage in their village. Their primary destinations are those villages with which the tour group has a kinship to reassure their clans of their ties. The dance drama, however, is hosted widely by communities of other social classes, even in the urban areas, in the Mewar region. Our limited

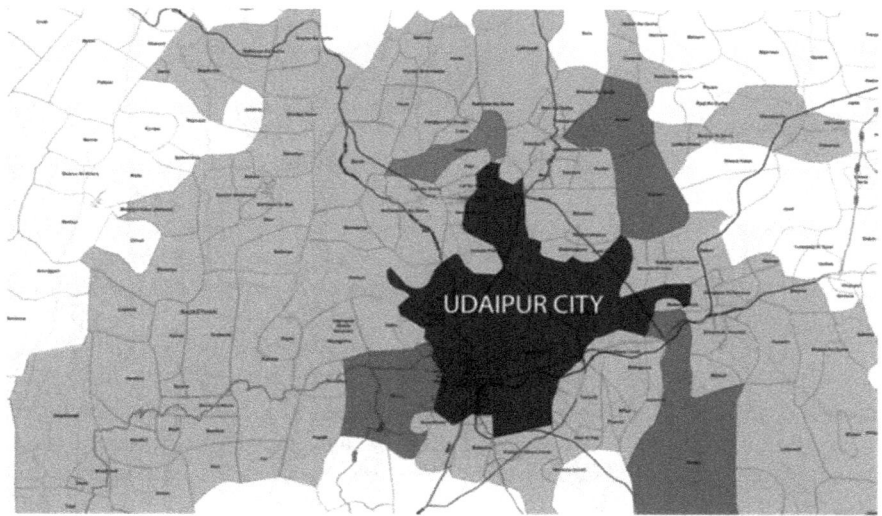

Fig. 6.1 Geographical coverage of the *Gavari* performance. (*Note Black* shows Udaipur city borough. *Light grey* (The village surrounding Udaipur) shows places they performed *Gavari*. *Deep grey* shows the origin of Performers)

trace of several *Gavari* performance groups presumes that all the communities in the whole region engage with and celebrate *Gavari* (Fig. 6.1).

Thus, we can find critical elements in *Gavari* that make it suitable for our research question: whether or not motivations for (ir)rational economic choices in individual religious behaviour are for social bonding capital within a community and social bridging capital to other groups. Although there are some anthropological and ethnographic studies (e.g., Mio, 1994; Vyas et al., 1978) on the Bhil's festivals and *Gavari*, those studies have not investigated the socio-economic implications at a local society level. Is there any economic or social rationality in deciding to give up 40-days' income to perform *Gavari*? Or is it simply a temporary escape from the daily quagmire of poverty?

Our research objectives are (1) to examine whether the performers' participation in *Gavari* is economically rational; (2) if it is not rational, to determine what the motivations are for individuals to join and the implications for the Bhil communities; and (3) to understand what the social implications of *Gavari* are for the communities in the Mewar region. Objectives (2) and (3) correspond to Varshney's (2001) argument on the existence of intra- and interethnic engagements for social stability in a multi-ethnic society. To answer our research questions, we conducted an original survey questionnaire from March to May 2017, supported by the Institute for Financial Management and Research (IFMR), the Indian think-tank with extensive experience in field surveys in the rural areas of Rajasthan. We questioned *Gavari* performers, hosts, and audiences in the 2016 season about their economic status, socio-economic situation, cultural and religious behaviour and preferences, and the financial condition of their hometowns.

6.3   Overview of the Bhil Tribe in the Mewar Region
of Rajasthan

Until Independence, the Mewar region, which stretches across the south-eastern part of the state of Rajasthan, was the territory of the Mewar clan, ruled by the Maharaja, the oldest family in India. The region is located on the eastern side of the Aravalli Range, which runs through the central part of Rajasthan and has a rather complex topography with plains, hills, and mountains. The annual precipitation is about 500 mm and, except for the rainy season from July to September, the weather is mostly dry in the plains and mountains.

The largest tribal group in the Mewar region, who are the main inhabitants of this mountainous region, is the Bhil tribe. The Bhil is one of the largest tribal groups in India, living across the three states of Rajasthan, Gujarat, and Madhya Pradesh.

According to the 2011 Census, the Bhil is the largest tribal group listed as an indigenous group of Gujarat, Madhya Pradesh, Chhattisgarh, Maharashtra, and Rajasthan, and is classified as an ST under Indian national law. STs account for approximately 8% of India's total population but 25% of its poorest populations. In 2018, India's National Data found that STs in India were the poorest populace. According to The National Family Health Survey 2015–2016, 45.9% of ST members lived in the lowest wealth bracket, a shocking finding, particularly given that there are even more STs in the lowest wealth bracket than there are SCs, who were previously known as the untouchable castes.

The Bhil tribe in the Mewar region were primarily Adivasi people from north-western India before founding the Hindu Mewar Kingdom in Rajasthan. The relationship between the Bhil tribe and Hinduism in this region can be traced back at least to the time of Akbar the Great in the sixteenth century.

The Kingdom of Mewar was one of the Rajput Kingdoms that most stubbornly resisted the Muslim invasion of India but ultimately could not prevent it. After Chittorgarh, the former capital of Mewar, fell to the Mughals, Pratap Singh, the King of Mewar, fled from the capital to the west and continued his resistance, rebuilding the royal capital in the area that the Bhil almost wholly inhabit in the present day, Udaipur. The Kingdom of Mewar was a Hindu kingdom with the Rajputs as its ruling power. The westward expansion of the Rajputs was likely a result of the Hindu influx, leading to driving the Bhil to more remote areas. Legends tell of alliances between several kings and the Bhil against invasions. However, they were not always allied. Rebellions by the Bhil against the Kingdom of Mewar were often documented up until the early twentieth century, suggesting that the actual course of events may have been complicated. In general, SCs and STs have different positions in Indian society. Whereas SCs are at the bottom of mainstream Hindu society, they are an integral part of it, whereas the STs have been outsiders. However, the Bhil tribe in the Mewar region share a common history with other social classes because of the above-mentioned historical events.

After independence in 1947, owing to the Indian Government's programme of positive discrimination for scheduled communities and classification of the Bhil as an ST, the Bhil have successfully preserved their many traditions, especially that of *Gavari*, which is unique to the Mewar region.

Gavari: Religious and Traditional Folk Dance–Drama.

As noted above, *Gavari*, the traditional folk dance–drama, is a 40-day long celebration that runs from mid-August to late September and is performed by a group of 30–60 Bhil men from the same hamlet, who visit 20–30 communities. Historically, the period during which *Gavari* occurs was an interval in the schedule of premodern maize cultivation. After the maize plants began to grow in the fields, they required little attention until they were ready for harvest in October, allowing the Bhil men to leave their fields to perform the *Gavari*.

The *Bhopas*, the shamans of the Bhil community, petition the goddess of fertility, Gauri (the alias of the Hindu goddess Parvati), to permit the villagers to perform the *Gavari* ritual and to accompany them on their pilgrimage. Not every village undertakes the exacting task of performing *Gavari* every year. The average wait time for Gauri's consent is three to five years. However, the authors were informed that the village that performed the *Gavari* in 2016 did so after a gap of almost 20 years. From the viewpoint of the participants, such a rotation is reasonable given the extraordinary character of *Gavari* and the fact that the participating villages devote all their time and resources to the performance. It is also reasonable in terms of mutual reciprocity of visiting and hosting.

Gavari expresses a passion for health and happiness on their own and gratitude to the goddess of fertility while strengthening intercommunity ties. The men do this by touring 20–30 villages during their pilgrimage. The destinations of the pilgrimage are traditionally classified into three categories.

One category of destinations is the villages where their married sisters and daughters live, to remember their kinship. As summer ends, *Bhopa* from each hamlet petition the goddess for permission to perform the *Gavari* ritual. In addition to *Bhopa*, those who perform *Gavari* are farmers or non-farm labourers; thus, they are not professional actors, singers, or dancers. Men portray all the female characters. Picture 6.1 shows two Bhil men disguised as females playing goddesses.

During the 40-day pilgrimage, all performers stop working, and drinking alcohol and sexual intercourse are taboo, as they need to show their dedication to the goddess of fertility.

A *Gavari* performance group has a stock of 10–15 classic traditional and new dance-dramas. The overarching themes are worship of the supernatural being, the sacredness of the natural world, radical human equality, the feminine nature of the divine, and the historical events of the Bhil community and the Mewar region. These reflect the key ethics in traditional Bhil society. The selected stories include the following.

Bhilurana: Bhilurana is the King of the Bhil, a composite leader representing five centuries of Bhil resistance to oppression and intrusions of all kinds. The play compresses and conflates the armed might of Turkic, Mughal, and British invaders and depicts goddess-inspired Bhil warriors finally driving all the invaders away.

Picture 6.1 Bhil men disguised as females for *Gavari*. (Photo by Ryuichi FUKUHARA)

Lakha Banjara: Lakha Banjara is an adventurous trader from the Banjara tribe who travels with his caravan. While he is travelling, he often has to confront corrupt officials or thieves. Inspired by Gauri, he is energized to defeat the villains.

Goma the plunderer: Goma, a poor boy from the Bhil community, plunders a temple and robs the community during a devastating drought in the region. The goddess punishes his behaviour to show that the community needs to obey the rules for its solidarity even at the worst times.

Gurulia the blacksmith: Gurulia asks all the gods and goddesses to support him in a difficult task. Nevertheless, in the end, only Gauri can solve his problem.

Thus, the *Gavari* ritual hypostatizes faith in the goddess Gauri, showing that negatives are always defeated by positive energies as rightn triumphs over wrong. It also informs other communities about the Bhil culture through the performance.

Members of the Bhil community from one village visit other villages in performing *Gavari*. The villages that they visit are within their neighbourhood, roughly 20–25 km away. Traditionally, the villages visited were classified into three categories: (a) villages with which the performers have kinship through marriages, (b) villages with economic connections, and (c) villages connected through ritual exchanges. More recently, due to the urbanization of the Udaipur district, a fourth category, (d) the urban communities, comes up, including both Hindu and Muslim communities where the *Gavari* festival is enjoyed as a theatrical entertainment. These four types of destinations, with different types of relationships, provide some clues to the socio-economic implications of the *Gavari* ritual for the whole society in the Mewar region.

6.4 Survey Description and Model

As noted earlier, *Gavari* is held before the harvest season, from mid-August to late September, which was traditionally a short break for farming communities. However, the number of Bhil engaging in migrant work in urban areas has increased in recent years and the *Gavari* season does not correspond with the off-period for migrant labour. Consequently, migrant workers need to give up working if they decide to participate in the *Gavari* festival. A few studies have examined seasonal labour migration in India—for example, Breman (1996), Mosse et al. (2002), Haberfeld et al. (1999), and Rogaly et al. (2002)—but much remains unknown. One reason for this is the absence of seasonal migration data in the official data sources, such as the National Sample Survey or local labour records. The existing economic research does not incorporate seasonal labour migration or attempt to understand the precise household income of such labourers. As we observed that many migrant workers performed in the *Gavari* festival, household income data for migrant workers are essential to examine the relationship between religious behaviour and economic conditions at an individual level.

This section describes the details of the data collected by our survey. As noted earlier, in co-operation with IFMR, the survey was conducted from March to May 2017. We collected 1,028 responses and after data cleaning, had a sample of 1,015. Among the sample, 1,005 respondents belonged to the ST or SC communities, one was from Kadia Kumbhar (another disadvantaged caste), and the remaining nine were Rajput, the dominant Hindu military caste. Table 6.1 shows the sub-caste distribution of the collected sample.

Table 6.1 Sub-caste distribution

Caste	Observation	Percent	Cum	Caste	Observation	Percent	Cum
Gameti	332	32.71	32.71	Meena	101	9.95	60.2
Aahari	9	0.89	33.6	Meghwal	6	0.59	60.79
Chohan	1	0.10	33.69	Patela	2	0.20	60.99
Dama	2	0.20	33.89	Beel	292	28.77	89.75
Damor	8	0.79	34.68	Loor	2	0.20	89.95
Dana	2	0.20	34.88	Tavad	16	1.58	91.53
Paragi	41	4.04	40	Lakhubara	17	1.67	93.2
Bargat	2	0.20	40.2	Vadera	26	2.56	95.76
Kalasuva	5	0.49	40.69	Gameti-Pargi	1	0.10	98.62
Gorna	2	0.20	40.89	Dana-Bhil	2	0.20	98.82
Rajput	7	0.69	41.58	Dana-Lakhubara	1	0.10	98.92
Rawat	2	0.20	41.77	Vadera-Bhil Bhil	1	0.10	99.01
Kalava	16	1.58	43.35	Rawat-Meena	6	0.59	99.61
Kher	15	1.48	44.83	Kharadi-Bhil Bhil	2	0.20	99.8
Kharadi	47	4.63	49.46	Katara-Bhil Bhil	2	0.20	100
Katara	3	0.30	49.75	Place name	11	1.08	35.96
Mansa	5	0.49	50.25	Unknown	28	2.76	98.52
				Total	1,015	100	

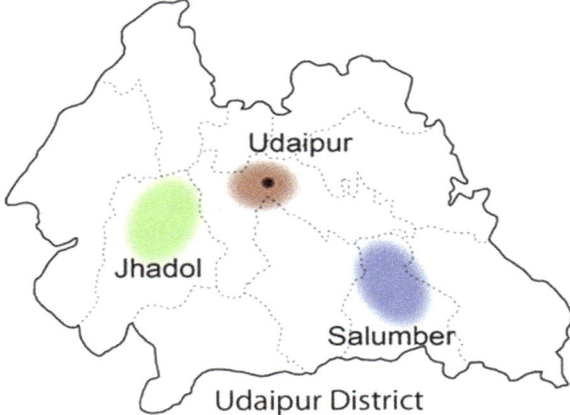

Fig. 6.2 Areas in Udaipur District

Because the *Gavari* festival aims not only to sanctify the goddess but also to entertain audiences, we divided survey respondents into the following three subgroups: Performers, who are the individuals who performed *Gavari* in 2016; Hosts, those who invited Performers to their hamlets in 2016; and Audiences, who did not directly invite the Performers in 2016 but experienced *Gavari* in the hosting hamlets. To understand the behaviour of the Performers, we collected a sample size of 493. For Hosts and Audiences, we have samples of 281 and 241, respectively. This survey seized on the following three areas with different characteristics in social composition. One is Udaipur city and its urban environs (Red) and the second is mountainous Jhadol, where the Bhil dominates (Green), and the last is plain farmland areas in Salumber, where Bhil and other social classes live together (Blue) (Fig. 6.2).

There are many cultural anthropological studies on the *Gavari*, but few socio-economic studies, with one exception being Mio (1994). According to Mio (1994), in *Gavari*, audiences pay between Rs. 1 and Rs. 5 at most if they like the songs and dance of the performers. This remuneration is voluntary and referred to as *Inam*, while gifts in kind, such as food and small amounts of money and clothes given to the performers are referred to as *Perauni*, and these are obligatory (Mio, 1994).

Although it is said that revelation decides whether a person plays the *Gavari* in the community, our survey indicated that a key person inside the community also tends to decide to play out the *Gavari*. The next questions that we ask are: What are the socio-economic determinants of performance? Does it bring socio-economic benefits to performers? Suppose the choice of a given household is binary such that individuals choose to either perform *Gavari* or not, the adoption decision-making process and impact of performing *Gavari* on household welfare can be modelled in an optimization framework.

To assess the effect of *Gavari* participation on welfare, it is necessary to consider the problem of self-selection bias. For this reason, we use an endogenous treatment effect model.

Given that households are risk neutral and tend to optimize their utility by maximizing socio-economic output, we can evaluate the net welfare (S^*) associated with participating in *Gavari* or not participating, denoted by (U_{Ai}) and (U_{Ni}), respectively. To the extent that the participation status is known to the researcher, but household preferences, such as net welfare, are known only to households, the net welfare of participant i, which is unobserved, is represented by ($S^* = U_{Ai} - U_{Ni} > 0$).

We define S = 1 as the state where the participant joined *Gavari* as a performer and S = 0 as the state where the participant did not join *Gavari* as a performer.

The net welfare from participation can be expressed with respect to a vector of household explanatory variables in a latent variable framework as:

$$S_i^* = \beta X_i + u_i \tag{6.1}$$

$$S_i^* = 1 \text{ if } S_i^* > 0 \text{ otherwise, } S_i = 0 \tag{6.2}$$

If the Bhopa had informed the whole village about *Gavari* and everyone had participated, there would be no need for analysis. However, about 29 of 493 respondents said that they had not participated in the last *Gavari*. To analyse the determinants of performance, we present the descriptive statistics on reasons respondents gave for not attending the last *Gavari* in Table 6.2.

Most of our respondents did not participate because they did not know that *Gavari* was celebrated. The second most common reason was lack of availability due to work commitments. Thus, some endogenous socio-economic reason for participating is hidden.

In general, experiments are difficult in the field of social sciences. However, in recent years, methods have been developed that attempt to predict social phenomena by assuming hypothetical values. One such method is the treatment effects model, which we will utilize to delve into the above issues.

In our analysis, S is the index of treatment, the Performers are the treatment group, and the non-Performers (i.e., the Hosts and Audiences) are the control group. The wage income of the treatment and control groups is denoted by w_1 and w_0, respectively. The average gap between the two wage incomes is defined as the average treatment effect (ATE):

Table 6.2 Reasons for not participating in *Gavari*

	Freq.	Percent
Could not take time off work	8	27.59
Doing migrant work	5	17.24
Could not raise money	1	3.45
Not interested	3	10.34
Did not know that *Gavari* was held	13	44.83
Total	29	100.00

$$ATE = E(w_1 - w_0) \tag{6.3}$$

The average treatment effect on the treated (ATET) of the Performers' treatment group is defined as:

$$ATET = E(w_1 - w_0|S = 1) = E(w_1|S = 1) - E(w_0|S = 1) \tag{6.4}$$

The ATET is the effect of the Performer on the non-Performer which are Hosts and Audiences. Under various assumptions, we estimate $E(w_0|S = 1)$ using information from the control group, who did not participate as Performers. This endogenous treatment effect model estimates the ATE and the other parameters of a linear regression model augmented with an endogenous binary treatment variable, which is based on the Heckman (1979) selection model. To obtain the ATE, stronger assumptions are required:

$$ATE = P(S = 1)E(w_1 - w_0|S = 1) + P(S = 0)E(w_1 - w_0|S = 0) \tag{6.5}$$

Both $E(w_0|S = 1)$ and $E(w_1|S = 0)$ are unobservable and, given that the expected values of w_1 and S are independent, the same approximation can be used for ATE and ATET:

$$ATE = E(w_1|S = 1) - E(w_0|S = 0) \approx ATET \tag{6.6}$$

For this equation to be valid, it is assumed that the selection of the treatment and control groups is completely random. If this choice is not random, then selection bias should be considered. We consider the following estimation model to account for the bias in the endogenous determination of the Performers. We use the equivalence of labour income earned by households in 2016. The following latent variables are assumed y_i^*

$$\ln(y_i) = \alpha + \beta X_i + \beta InMills + \beta G + u_i, \tag{6.7}$$

$$S^* = \chi + \tau V_i + \varepsilon_i \tag{6.8}$$

$$u_i \sim N(0, \sigma)$$

$$\varepsilon_i \sim N(0, 1)$$

$$\rho = corr(u_i, \varepsilon_i).$$

When the dependent variable is labour income, some samples do not earn labour income or do not provide any answer to the labour income question in the survey. The dependent variable is not always seen; we can describe it as follows,

$$\ln(y_i) = \delta + \gamma Z_i + v_{1i} \tag{6.9}$$

$$\theta N_i + v_{2i} > 0 \tag{6.10}$$

$$v_{1i} \sim N(0, \sigma)$$

$$v_{2i} \sim N(0, 1)$$

$$\rho = corr(v_1, v_2)$$

To control for these issues, we use a selection bias model developed by Heckman (1979) to estimate the inverse Mills ratio, which is measured by the probit function in the first stage, and we add these equations to Eq. (6.7). The determination of working is as follows.

N_i: the amount of savings, area dummy, husband's educational level, wife's educational level, age, and its square.

The results of accounting for bias in the endogenous decision to select a treatment group are attached in the Appendix. The independent variable, $X_i X_i$ is composed as follows:

X_i: husband's educational level, wife's educational level, primary occupation, sub-caste, age, its square, the inverse Mills' ratio obtained from Eqs. (6.9) and (6.10), and dummy variable S, which is an endogenous variable that indicates the choice of statement.

The dummy variable S is marked with an asterisk in Eq. (6.8) because selection by statement is an unobserved outcome. V_i, which determines S, is defined as follows:

V_i: the frequency of communication inside the tribe, husband's educational level, wife's educational level, a dummy for the National Rural Employment Guarantee Act (NREGA), which we explain in the following section, the amount of saving, the area dummy, age, and its square.

In the next section, we explain the variables used, including the NREGA dummy. The subscript i denotes individual i; u and ε are random error terms; and τ, γ, and θ denote the estimated coefficient of each factor.

Before showing the results, we show the descriptive statistics for the dependent variables used in Table 6.3.

Table 6.3 shows the results of the t test, examining the differences in labour income by group. We can see significant differences in equivalent labour income

Table 6.3 Descriptive statistics for dependent variables used

Variable	Observation	Average	SD.	Min.	Max.
Number of household members	1,015	5.63	2.16	1.00	21.00
Equivalence income	888	26,795.17	13,271.04	756.19	96,598.13

Table 6.4 Descriptive statistics and test for equivalence of income by group

Group	Observation	Mean	Std. Err.	Std. Dev.
S = 0 Control	455	25,634.58	523.81	11,173.20
S = 1 Treated	433	28,014.72	724.86	15,083.44
Combined	888	26,795.17	445.35	13,271.04
t = −2.68				

between the control and treatment groups because we obtain t = −2.68. This result presents the mean difference in certain indicators between the control group and the treated Performers group. It shows that there is a significant difference in household characteristics and variables of interest between the control and treatment groups in the study area (Table 6.4).

Table 6.5 shows the descriptive statistics of the independent variables used.

Now, we explain the dependent variables. We sort the educational levels of husbands and wives, which indicates that the educational level is lower for women than for men. The occupational variable, consistent with the Census, indicates that non-farm casual labour is the dominant occupation.

We used two types of NREGA dummies, one for the individual, male NREGA, and one for the household, household NREGA. NREGA was publicly announced on 7 September 2005. This Act guarantees a minimum of 100 days of employment per year to all rural households with adult household members who intend to engage in unskilled manual labour. The main objective of NREGA is to create employment opportunities in rural areas. It is estimated to have created more than 12 billion person-days of employment at a cost of 1,668 billion rupees (Rs) in the first six years of implementation (Government of India, Planning Commission, 2012). The beneficiaries of NREGA are the rural poor, including casual labourers engaged in unskilled manual wage work and farmers with small landholdings. According to the Planning Commission (2012), such workers receive 90 Rs (US$1.50) per _____ on average. In this chapter, we used the household variable: "Is the household employed in the NREGA (100-days work) programme?" and individual variables: "Has your household ever participated in the NREGA programme?" and "Do you participate in the NREGA programme?" We construct a dummy variable if the respondent is male and replied yes, which means he participated in NREGA.

6.5   Results

The major factors that significantly affect performing decisions are reported in column 2 (selection equation) of Table 6.6.

We found that the husband's educational level, wife's educational level, primary occupation, area, age, the communication variable, and financial status were all statistically significant.

Table 6.5   Descriptive statistics for independent variables used

Variable	Option	Observation	Percent
Husband's educational level			
	Illiterate	296	29.16
	Literate	290	28.57
	Educated	392	38.62
	No answer	37	3.65
Wife's educational level			
	Illiterate	684	67.39
	Literate	183	18.03
	Educated	102	10.05
	No answer	46	4.53
Primary occupation			
	Agriculture/ Animal husbandry/ Farm labourer	134	13.20
	Non-farm casual labourer	766	75.47
	Petty trade/Own business/ Trade/Manufacturing	25	2.46
	Salaried private job/ Salaried government job	70	6.90
	None/Other	20	1.97
Male NREGA			
	None	552	54.38
	Received	463	45.62
Area			
	Rural = 1	321	31.63
	Urban/Peri-Urban = 0	694	68.37
Communication			
	Every day	39	3.84
	Once every few days	216	21.28
	Once a month	164	16.16
	Rarely	305	30.05
	Never	291	28.67
Bhil			
	No	335	33.00
	Yes	680	67.00

Variable	Observation	Mean	Std. Dev.	Min.	Max.
Age	1,015	43.23	13.32	2.00	90.00
Age squared	1,015	2046.36	1219.44	4.00	8100.00
The length of months worked	1,015	9.22	2.30	0.00	12.00
Number of household members	1,015	5.63	2.16	1.00	21.00

Table 6.6 Endogenous treatment effect estimation result

Variables	Outcome equation		Selection equation	
	Y_i		S	
Husband's educational level				
Illiterate	0.178	(0.190)	−0.205*	(0.118)
Literate	0.0476	(0.189)	−0.227**	(0.110)
No answer	0.440	(0.409)	−0.509**	(0.247)
Wife's educational level				
Literate	−0.124	(0.193)	−0.210*	(0.118)
Educated	−0.276	(0.238)	−0.319**	(0.149)
No answer	−0.0498	(0.267)	0.0164	(0.201)
Primary occupation				
Agriculture/ Animal husbandry/Farm labourer	−2.491***	(0.298)		
Petty trade/Own business/ Trade/Manufacturing	−4.057***	(0.716)		
Salaried private job/ Salaried government job	−5.583***	(0.407)		
None/Other	−5.121***	(0.757)		
Inverse mills ratio	0.504	(1.727)		
Area	−0.205	(0.201)	−0.574***	(0.0893)
Age	0.0281	(0.0389)	0.0348*	(0.0194)
Age squared	−0.000504	(0.000436)	−0.000335	(0.000210)
Bhil	0.0384	(0.151)		
S	1.424**	(0.669)		
Communication				
Every day			0.495**	(0.246)
Once every few days			−0.0154	(0.114)
Once a month			−0.376**	(0.157)
Never			−0.735***	(0.113)
NREGA			0.244***	(0.0832)
Amount of saving			0.0966**	(0.0485)
Constant	9.190***	(0.851)	−0.267	(0.428)
Atanh ρ	−0.487**	(0.248)		
Ln σ	0.708***	(0.0653)		
Observations	1,015		1,015	

Standard errors are shown in parentheses

The symbols ***, ** and * indicate $p < 0.01$, $p < 0.05$, and $p < 0.1$, respectively

LR denotes the likelihood ratio test of independent equations. ($\rho = 0$): $\chi^2 = 432.46$; prob > $\chi^2 = 0.0000$

NREGA, _____

Except "No Answer" of Wife's educational level, all educational level variables showed significant results. We cannot solve the puzzle of the impact of the educational level. However, we can observe that those who communicate "every day" inside the tribe are more dynamic with regard to participating in *Gavari*, whereas negative results are shown for those who communicate only "once a month" or "never". Concerning the financial variables, both NREGA and the amount of household savings show positive results. According to the Planning Commission (2012), about 100 million bank/postal savings accounts have been opened since NREGA went into effect, and about 80% of NREGA-related payments are made through these saving accounts. Siddhartha (2008) finds that casual labourers are not familiar with basic procedures and documents in banks and post offices, and Sato (2015) notes that NREGA resulted in "unintentional savings" or "forced savings", despite increases in wage rates and wage income.

Given the estimated coefficients, in column 1 in Table 6.6 we show the treatment effect model estimation results for both our regression/outcome equation and the selection equation.

The likelihood ratio (LR) tests if $\rho = 0$. This ratio test is a comparison of the joint likelihood of the independent probit model for the selection equation and a regression model on the observed data against the treatment effect model likelihood. In this case, $\chi^2 = 432.46$ ($p < 0.01$) and, therefore, we can reject the null hypothesis and conclude that ρ is not equal to zero.

The result in column 1 shows that attending a *Gavari* performance positively affects the welfare of households. Hereafter, we explain the estimated results. First, the variable Inverse Mills ratio, which was introduced to exclude the effect of the sample without wage incomes, is insignificant. There is no financial bias influencing performing in *Gavari*. See the Appendix for an estimation restricted to the sample who earned wage incomes.

Second, we examine the coefficient of the treatment variable (S) in column 1. This positive and statistically significant result indicates that the estimated ATE of the impact of performing *Gavari* is 1.424.

Below, we calculate the ATET. We estimate the counterfactual wage income and treatment effects among Performers (ATET) and obtain the same coefficient as in the case of the ATE because there is no sample bias. That is, the ATET is the same as the ATE in this case because the treatment indicator variable has not interacted with any of the outcome covariates, and the correlation and variance parameters are identical across the control and treatment groups. When the estimated ATET and ATE are the same, it indicates that the average predicted outcome for the treatment group is equal to the average predicted outcome for the whole population. Hence, all things being equal, the households that choose to perform in *Gavari* will have a 314% ($e^{1.42}$) higher wage income in comparison with households that do not perform (Table 6.7).

Table 6.8 summarizes the natural log of wage income when resolving the selection bias, the natural logs of wage income with and without treatment, and their difference. This is a linear prediction.

Table 6.7 The result of ATET

Unconditional

	Contrast	Std. Err	95% Conf. interval	
S	1.424	0.669	0.113	2.735

Table 6.8 Summary of the natural log of wage income

Variable	Observations	Mean	Std. Dev.	Min.	Max.
ln (wage income)	1,015	9.087	2.625	2.297	11.478
ln (wage income with treatment) $E(w_1\|S = 1)$	1,015	9.046	1.811	2.730	10.896
ln (wage income without treatment) $E(w_0\|S = 1)$	1,015	9.129	1.810	2.911	11.203
Difference between wages with and without treatment $ATE = E(w_1\|S = 1) - E(w_0\|S = 1)$	1,015	−0.083	0.055	−0.440	−0.040

According to Table 6.8, the results for the ATE are negative, indicating that, on average, participating in the *Gavari* as a Performer leads to a financial loss.

From an economic perspective, the *Gavari*, to which Performers are required to devote themselves for 40 days, reduces their income and job opportunities. Given that there are meaningful differences in certain indicators between the control group and the treated Performers group in Table 6.8 and that the ATET has positive effects, because the coefficient of the treatment variable (S) equals 1.42, the *Gavari* is a puzzle from an economic perspective. It may be controversial that we find opposing results; whereas we find negative results for the ATE, we find positive results for S. Further explanation is provided in the next section; however, we hypothesize that the *Gavari* has both "bonding" and "bridging" functions.

6.6   Discussion

Taking *Gavari* as an example, we have attempted to examine the socio-economic implications of religious festivities. We combined quantitative studies with econometric analysis and qualitative studies with a cultural anthropological approach. We found that participation in *Gavari* as a Performer has a detrimental effect on household income, for households that already have relatively low annual incomes. Our survey revealed that the offerings received for performing the *Gavari* cannot compensate for the loss of 40 days' worth of income and, therefore, participation in the *Gavari* certainly reduces Performers' incomes. Thus, the reason households choose to perform is not for short-term, rational economic reasons. In addition, our survey showed that more than 80% of performers responded that they would participate in the next *Gavari* even if they received no economic gains.

Our results suggest that the *Gavari* has "bonding'" features that may have contributed to long-term intercommunal well-being and to maintaining a sense of belonging within the community. Moreover, we mapped the geographical coverage of the *Gavari* performance in the 2016 season, which indicated that the *Gavari* is welcomed by both the Bhil community and by non-tribal groups all around the Mewar region. In our field survey, we witnessed that even Islamic communities hosted the *Gavari* performers. This pervasiveness of *Gavari*'s welcome indicates that it has a unique "bridging" feature with other communities, which many other religious festivals and behaviours do not possess. In addition, performing *Gavari* contributes to co-existence and mutual understanding in the multi-layered and diverse society in the Udaipur district.

Moreover, the informal form of the *Gavari*'s intra-ethnic and interethnic engagements mean the festivals are conceived, as Varshney (2001) puts it, as "everyday forms of engagement", which also need to be complementary with the formal and institutional type of engagement in modern society. We need to reconsider criticizing the poor for spending their money and time on rituals and festivals, and carefully review how the religious activities to which they devote themselves function in terms of the local community and society, and in the socio-economic context. Even if the Bhil performers are unconscious of investing their time and money in maintaining social bonding and bridging capital in the multi-ethnic society in Udaipur, supporting their tradition and by keeping intact its informal intra- and interethnic and engagements through the *Gavari* performance, could be considered a policy option for sustaining multi-ethnic society.

Our survey in 2016 was limited to the area where the *Gavari* is performed. We have shed light on the economic aspects of *Gavari* as an example of the non-organized religious behaviour of economically vulnerable communities. To analyse further *Gavari*'s function as possible bonding and bridging social capital in the Mewar region, we had planned to conduct comparative research on the social relationship between the Bhils and other social classes in the neighbouring region where the *Gavari* is not a tradition. Unfortunately, our plans for such a survey were postponed due to the commencement of the COVID-19 pandemic in early 2020, and it has proved difficult to reschedule at present. We have been informed that the Bhil communities have suffered from the pandemic and that the performance of the *Gavari* has been disrupted. We hope to resume our research in future when the COVID-19 situation has improved, and to examine the effect of the pandemic on religious behaviour, the Bhil's socio-economic life, and the local communities.

Acknowledgements we would like to acknowledge and thank W. David Kubiak Research Services. Without their generous sponsorship, the workshop and this volume of collected papers would have been possible. We would like to express our sincere thanks to Mr. Amit Kumar and Mr. Jagdish Dana. Our deepest condolences to Jagdish passed on 18th May 2021.Our deepest condolences to his family upon his passing.This research is funded by The Murata Science Foundation and The Resona Foundation for Asia and Oceania.

Appendix

See Table 6.9.

Table 6.10 shows the endogenous treatment effect estimation result for wage-earning households. In contrast to the results in Table 6.6, this model excludes the inverse Mills ratio to correct bias. However, λ shows the estimate of the standard error of the estimate and the confidence interval. We find that S is positive and statistically significant. Thus, the estimated ATE of the impact of performing *Gavari* on welfare is 0.27. The ATET is the same as the ATE in this case because the treatment indicator variable has not interacted with any of the outcome covariates, and the correlation and variance parameters are identical across the control and treatment groups.

Table 6.9 The probit function of a sample selection model

Variables	2nd		1st	
The amount of savings			−0.356***	(0.118)
Area			−0.156	(0.244)
Age	0.000567	(0.0119)	0.0964***	(0.0328)
Age squared	−1.96e-05	(0.000132)	−0.00103***	(0.000345)
Husband's educational level	−0.00742	(0.0164)	0.0343	(0.0781)
Wife's educational level	0.00463	(0.0145)	0.151	(0.118)
Primary occupation	0.0423	(0.0467)		
Constant	9.981***	(0.282)	0.762	(0.774)
Ln σ	−0.451***	(0.0282)	−0.451***	(0.0282)
Atanh ρ	0.257**	(0.112)	0.257**	(0.112)
Observations	1,015		1,015	

Standard errors are shown in parentheses

The symbols ***, ** and * indicate that $p < 0.01$, $p < 0.05$, and $p < 0.1$, respectively

Table 6.10 Endogenous treatment effect estimation result for wage-earning households

Variables	Outcome equation		Selection equation	
	Y_i		S	
Husband's educational level				
Illiterate	0.0357	(0.0583)	−0.288**	(0.127)
Literate	0.107*	(0.0544)	−0.279**	(0.119)
No answer	0.0446	(0.115)	−0.551**	(0.255)
Wife's educational level				
Literate	0.111**	(0.0559)	−0.282**	(0.127)
Educated	0.137*	(0.0745)	−0.304*	(0.169)
No answer	−0.0739	(0.0954)	0.178	(0.214)

(continued)

Table 6.10 (continued)

Variables	Outcome equation		Selection equation	
Primary occupation				
Agriculture/ Animal husbandry/Farm labourer	−0.453***	(0.0629)		
Petty trade/Own business/ Trade/Manufacturing	−0.644***	(0.158)		
Salaried private job/ Salaried government job	−0.530***	(0.126)		
None/Other	−0.582***	(0.212)		
Area	−0.213***	(0.0525)	−0.576***	(0.0959)
Age	0.000919	(0.00962)	0.0385*	(0.0218)
Age squared	−1.53e-05	(0.000105)	−0.000370	(0.000238)
Bhil Bhil	−0.0842*	(0.0455)		
S	0.269*	(0.153)		
Communication				
Every day			0.577*	(0.294)
Once every few days			−0.0253	(0.123)
Once a month			−0.412***	(0.132)
Never			−0.695***	(0.118)
NREGA			0.223**	(0.0934)
The amount of saving			0.127**	(0.0554)
Constant	10.12***	(0.219)	−0.354	(0.476)
λ			−0.159*	(0.0961)
Observations	888		888	
Standard errors are shown in parentheses				
The symbols ***, ** and * indicate that p < 0.01, p < 0.05, and p < 0.1, respectively				
Likelihood Ratio (LR) test of independent equations. (rho = 0): chi^2 = 197.27; Prob > chi^2 = 0.0000				

Hence, all things being equal, the households that choose to perform will have a 30.8% ($e^{0.269}$) higher consumption expenditure than households who do not perform *Gavari*. This result is lower than the result given in the main text, and it implies that financial returns become low when restricted to wage-earning households.

References

Banerjee, A. V., & Duflo, E. (2007). The economic lives of the poor. *Journal of Economic Perspectives, 21*(1), 141–168. https://doi.org/10.1257/jep.21.1.141

Breman, J. (1996). *Footloose Labour: Working in India's Informal Economy (Vol. 2)* Cambridge, Cambridge University Press.

Buser, T. (2015). The effect of income on religiousness. *American Economic Journal: Applied Economics, 7*(3), 178–195. https://doi.org/10.1257/app.20140162

Campante, F., & Yanagizawa-Drott, D. (2015). Does religion affect economic growth and happiness? Evidence from Ramadan. *The Quarterly Journal of Economics, 130*(2), 615–658. https://doi.org/10.1093/qje/qjv002

Coleman, J. S. (1988). Social capital in the creation of human capital. *American Journal of Sociology, 94*, S95–S120. https://doi.org/10.1086/228943

Corbridge, S., Harriss, J., & Jeffrey, C. (2018). The Political Economy of Growth and Development in India. In *The Oxford Handbook of the Politics of Development Edited by Carol Lancaster and Nicolas van de Walle.* https://doi.org/10.1093/oxfordhb/9780199845156.013.18

Deaton, A. (2008). Income, health, and well-being around the world: Evidence from the gallup world poll. *Journal of Economic Perspectives, 22*(2), 53–72. https://doi.org/10.1257/jep.22.2.53

Durkheim, E. (1995). *The elementary forms of the religious life.* Fields, The Free Press.

Ensminger, J. (1994). The political economy of religion: An economic anthropologist's perspective. *Journal of Institutional and Theoretical Economics, 150*(4), 745–754. https://www.jstor.org/stable/i40034122

Ensminger, J. (1997). Transaction costs and islam: Explaining conversion in Africa. *Journal of Institutional and Theoretical Economics, 153*(1), 4–29. https://www.jstor.org/stable/40752982

Government of India, Planning Commission, Planning Commission. (2012). Twelfth Five Year Plan (2012–2017). Economic Sectors. Vol. II. https://mofpi.nic.in/sites/default/files/vol_2.pdf.pdf. Accessed 15 Aug 2021.

Gramajo, A. M. (2007). Wayuu crafts: A dilemma of culture and development. *Research in Economic Anthropology, 25*, 217–238. https://doi.org/10.1016/S0190-1281(06)25010-8

Haberfeld, Y., Menaria, R. K., Sahoo, B. B., & Vyas, R. N. (1999). Seasonal migration of rural labour in India. *Population Research and Policy Review, 18*(5), 471–487. https://www.jstor.org/stable/40230244

Heckman, J. J. (1979). Sample selection bias as a specification error. *Econometrica: Journal of the Econometric Society, 47*(1), pp. 153–161. https://doi.org/10.2307/1912352

Hungerman, D. M. (2014). The effect of education on religion: Evidence from compulsory schooling laws. *Journal of Economic Behaviour & Organization, 104*, 52–63. https://doi.org/10.1016/j.jebo.2013.09.004

Iannaccone, L. R., & Berman, E. (2008). Economics of religion. In S. Durlauf & L. Blume (Eds.), *The new Palgrave dictionary of economics.* Basingstoke and New York: Palgrave Macmillan.

Inglehart, R., & Welzel, C. (2005). *Modernization, Cultural Change, and Democracy: The Human Development Sequence.* Cambridge University Press.

Iyer, S. (2008). Religion and economic development. In S. N. Durlauf & L. E. Blume (Eds.), *The new Palgrave dictionary of economics.* Basingstoke and New York: Palgrave Macmillan. https://doi.org/10.1057/978-1-349-95121-5_2598-1

Iyer, S. (2016). The new economics of religion. *Journal of Economic Literature, 54*(2), 395–441. https://doi.org/10.1257/jel.54.2.395

Iyer, S. (2018). *The Economics of Religion in India.* Harvard University Press.

Iyer, S., Velu, C., Xue, J., & Chakravarty, T. (2011). Divine innovation: Religion and service provision by religious organizations in India. *Cambridge Working Papers in Economics* CWPE 1135. https://doi.org/10.17863/CAM.5565

Krishna, A. (2003). Falling into poverty: Other side of poverty reduction. *Economic and Political Weekly, 38*(6), 533–542. https://www.jstor.org/stable/4413189

Kuznets, S., S. (1973). Modern economic growth: Findings and reflections. *American Economic Review, 63*(3), 247–258. https://www.jstor.org/stable/1914358

Landa, J. T. (1994). *Trust, Ethnicity, and Identity: Beyond the New Institutional Economics of Ethnic Trading Networks, Contract Law, and Gift-Exchange.* University of Michigan Press.

McCleary, R. M., & Barro, R. J. (2006). Religion and economy. *Journal of Economic Perspectives, 20*(2), 49–72. https://doi.org/10.1257/jep.20.2.49

Mio, M. (1994). A Contemporary historical festival consideration on the transformation of the goddess festival in Rajasthan, India. *Japanese Journal of Ethnology, 58*(4), 334–355 (in Japanese). https://doi.org/10.14890/minkennewseries.58.4_334

Mosse, D., Gupta, S., Mehta, M., Shah, V., Rees, J. F., & Team, K. P. (2002). Brokered livelihoods: Debt, labour migration and development in Tribal Western India. *Journal of Development Studies, 38*(5), 59–88.https://doi.org/10.1080/00220380412331322511

Pal, G. C. (2015). Poverty among tribals in India: Variations and vulnerabilities. *Journal of Social Inclusion Studies, 1*(2), 91–107. https://doi.org/10.1177/2394481120150205

Paldam, M., & Gundlach, E. (2013). The religious transition. A long-run perspective. *Public Choice, 156*(1–2), 105–123. https://doi.org/10.1007/s11127-012-9934-z

Rogaly, B., Coppard, D., Safique, A., Rana, K., Sengupta, A., & Biswas, J. (2002). Seasonal migration and welfare/illfare in eastern India: A social analysis. *Journal of Development Studies, 38*(5), 89–114. https://doi.org/10.1080/00220380412331322521

Ruck, D. J., Bentley, R. A., & Lawson, D. J. (2018). Religious change preceded economic change in the 20th Century. *Science Advances, 4*(7), eaar8680. https://doi.org/10.1126/sciadv.aar8680

Sato, T. (2015). The economic impacts of India's national rural employment guarantee act (NREGA), Special issue frontiers of development studies on Africa and India. *Journal of Economics & Business Administration, 211*(1), 73–90. https://doi.org/10.24546/81009235

Seele, P. (2011). Trust, faith and calculativeness: A theoretical extension of O. Williamson's 'Institutional Trust.' *The Economics of Religion: Anthropological Approaches, 31*, 3–21. https://doi.org/10.1108/S0190-1281(2011)0000031004

Siddhartha, A. V. (2008). CAG report on NREGA: Fact and Fiction. *Economic & Political Weekly, 43*(25), 39–45. https://www.jstor.org/stable/40277587

Topalova, P. B. (2008). India: Is the Rising Tide Lifting All Boats? (SSRN Scholarly Paper No. ID 1112156). Rochester, NY: Social Science Research Network. https://papers.ssrn.com/abstract=1112156

Varshney, A. (2001). Ethnic conflict and civil society: India and beyond. *World Politics, 53*(3), 362–398. https://doi.org/10.1353/wp.2001.0012

Vyas, N. N., Mann, R. S., & Chaudhary, N. D. (Eds.). (1978). *Rajasthan Bhils* (Vol. 10). Manikyalal Verma Tribal Research and Training Institute, Social Welfare Department, Government of Rajasthan. http://www.new.dli.ernet.in/handle/2015/117493

Williamson, O. E. (1975). *Markets and Hierarchies.* Free Press.

Wood, E. J. (2007). Field research during war: Ethical dilemmas. In L. Joseph, M. Mahler, & J. Auyero (Eds.), *new perspectives in political ethnography*, pp. 205–23. New York, NY: Springer New York.

Weber, M. (2001) The Protestant Ethic and the Spirit of Capitalism. T. Parsons, Transl. Routledge.

Yang, F. (2012). *Religion in China: Survival and Revival under Communist Rule.* Oxford University Press.

Yang, F., & Hu, A. (2012). Mapping Chinese Folk religion in Mainland China and Taiwan. *Journal for the Scientific Study of Religion, 51*(3), 505–521. https://doi.org/10.1111/j.1468-5906.2012.01660.x.